Database	Telecommunications	Networks and Data Communications	Society
AN END USER'S GUIDE TO DATABASE	TELECOMMUNICATIONS AND THE COMPUTER (third edition)	PRINCIPLES OF DATA COMMUNICATION	THE COMPUTERIZED SOCIETY
PRINCIPLES OF DATABASE MANAGEMENT (second edition)	FUTURE DEVELOPMENTS IN TELECOMMUNICATIONS (third edition)	TELEPROCESSING NETWORK ORGANIZATION	TELEMATIC SOCIETY: A CHALLENGE FOR TOMORROW
COMPUTER DATABASE ORGANIZATION (third edition)	COMMUNICATIONS SATELLITE SYSTEMS	SYSTEMS ANALYSIS FOR DATA TRANSMISSION	TECHNOLOGY'S CRUCIBLE
MANAGING THE DATABASE ENVIRONMENT (second edition)	ISDN	DATA COMMUNICATION TECHNOLOGY	VIEWDATA AND THE INFORMATION SOCIETY
DATABASE ANALYSIS AND DESIGN	**Distributed Processing**	DATA COMMUNICATION DESIGN TECHNIQUES	TELEVISION AND THE COMPUTER
VSAM: ACCESS METHOD SERVICES AND PROGRAMMING TECHNIQUES	COMPUTER NETWORKS AND DISTRIBUTED PROCESSING	SNA: IBM's NETWORKING SOLUTION	THE WORLD INFORMATION ECONOMY
DB2: CONCEPTS, DESIGN, AND PROGRAMMING	DESIGN AND STRATEGY FOR DISTRIBUTED DATA PROCESSING	ISDN	**Systems In General**
IDMS/R: CONCEPTS, DESIGN, AND PROGRAMMING	**Office Automation**	LOCAL AREA NETWORKS: ARCHITECTURES AND IMPLEMENTATIONS	A BREAKTHROUGH IN MAKING COMPUTERS FRIENDLY: THE MACINTOSH COMPUTER
SQL	IBM's OFFICE AUTOMATION ARCHITECTURE	OFFICE AUTOMATION STANDARDS	SAA: IBM's SYSTEMS APPLICATION ARCHITECTURE
Security	OFFICE AUTOMATION STANDARDS	DATA COMMUNICATION STANDARDS	
SECURITY, ACCURACY, AND PRIVACY IN COMPUTER SYSTEMS		CORPORATE COMMUNICATIONS STRATEGY	
SECURITY AND PRIVACY IN COMPUTER SYSTEMS		COMPUTER NETWORKS AND DISTRIBUTED PROCESSING: SOFTWARE, TECHNIQUES, AND ARCHITECTURE	

LOCAL AREA NETWORKS

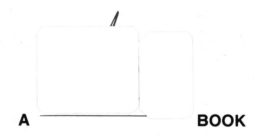

A ———————— BOOK

THE JAMES MARTIN BOOKS

currently available from Prentice Hall

- Application Development Without Programmers
- Communications Satellite Systems
- Computer Data-Base Organization, Second Edition
- Computer Networks and Distributed Processing: Software, Techniques, and Architecture
- Design and Strategy of Distributed Data Processing
- Design of Man-Computer Dialogues
- Design of Real-Time Computer Systems
- An End User's Guide to Data Base
- Fourth-Generation Languages, Volume I: Principles
- Future Developments in Telecommunications, Second Edition
- Information Engineering, Volume I: Introduction and Principles
- An Information Systems Manifesto
- Introduction to Teleprocessing
- Managing the Data-Base Environment
- Principles of Data-Base Management
- Recommended Diagramming Standards for Analysts and Programmers
- Security, Accuracy, and Privacy in Computer Systems
- Strategic Data-Planning Methodologies
- Systems Analysis for Data Transmission
- System Design from Provably Correct Constructs
- Technology's Crucible
- Telecommunications and the Computer, Second Edition
- Telematic Society: A Challenge for Tomorrow
- Teleprocessing Network Organization

with Carma McClure

- Action Diagrams: Clearly Structured Specifications, Programs, and Procedures, Second Edition
- Diagramming Techniques for Analysts and Programmers
- Software Maintenance: The Problem and Its Solutions
- Structured Techniques: The Basis for CASE, Revised Edition

with The ARBEN Group, Inc.

- A Breakthrough in Making Computers Friendly: The Macintosh Computer
- Data Communication Technology
- DB2: Concepts, Design, and Programming
- Fourth-Generation Languages, Volume II: Representative 4GLs
- Fourth-Generation Languages, Volume III: 4GLs from IBM
- Local Area Networks: Architectures and Implementations
- Principles of Data Communication
- SNA: IBM's Networking Solution
- VSAM: Access Method Services and Programming Techniques

with Adrian Norman

- The Computerized Society

with Steven Oxman

- Building Expert Systems

LOCAL AREA NETWORKS
Architectures and Implementations

JAMES MARTIN

with
Kathleen Kavanagh Chapman
The **ARBEN** Group, Inc.

PRENTICE HALL, Englewood Cliffs, New Jersey 07632

Library of Congress Cataloging-in-Publication Data
MARTIN, JAMES.
  Local area networks: architectures and implementations/James Martin with Kathleen Kavanagh Chapman.
    p.   cm.
  "A James Martin book"—1st prelim. p.
  Includes index.
  ISBN 0-13-539644-1:
1. Local area networks (Computer networks) I. Chapman, Kathleen Kavanagh. II. Title.
TK5105.7.M37 1989
004.6'8—dc19   88-28641
                                                                                        CIP

Editorial/production supervision: *Kathryn Gollin Marshak*
Jacket design: *Bruce Kenselaar*
Manufacturing buyer: *Mary Ann Gloriande*
Jacket photo: *Richard Wahlstrom Photo Inc*. © 1984

Printed in the United States of America

10 9 8 7 6 5 4 3 2 1

ISBN 0-13-539644-1

PRENTICE-HALL INTERNATIONAL (UK) LIMITED, *London*
PRENTICE-HALL OF AUSTRALIA PTY. LIMITED, *Sydney*
PRENTICE-HALL CANADA INC., *Toronto*
PRENTICE-HALL HISPANOAMERICANA, S.A., *Mexico*
PRENTICE-HALL OF INDIA PRIVATE LIMITED, *New Delhi*
PRENTICE-HALL OF JAPAN, INC., *Tokyo*
SIMON & SCHUSTER ASIA PTE. LTD, *Singapore*
EDITORA PRENTICE-HALL DO BRASIL, LTDA, *Rio de Janeiro*

TO CORINTHIA
—*JM*

TO JOHN AND MY PARENTS
—*KKC*

CONTENTS

Preface *xv*

PART **I** **CONCEPTS**

1 **Local Area Network Concepts** *3*

Wide Area Networks 3; Local Area Networks 3;
Metropolitan Area Networks 4; Local Area Network Defined 4;
LAN Applications 5; LAN Requirements 7; LAN Components 8;
LAN Characteristics 10; Summary 10

2 **Physical Transmission Characteristics** *11*

Transmission Medium 11; Twisted-Wire Pairs 11;
Coaxial Cable 12; Fiber-optic Links 13;
Wiring for Local Area Networks 13; Cabling Systems 14;
IBM Cabling System 14;
DECconnect Communication System 16;
Transmission Techniques 19; Baseband Transmission 19;
Broadband Transmission 20;
Digital Transmission over an Analog Channel 25;
Encoding Schemes 26; Synchronization 26; Summary 30

3 **Access Control Methods** *31*

Network Topologies 31; Transmission Control 33;
Random Transmission Control 37;
Distributed Transmission Control 40;
Centralized Transmission Control 43; Summary 45

4   Network Architectures   47

Goals of a Network Architecture 47;
The Nature of Architecture 48; Developers of Architectures 48;
Characteristics of Network Architectures 50; The OSI Model 52;
IBM's SNA 54; IEEE Project 802 55;
A Family of Standards 57; Summary 59

PART **II**   **IEEE PROJECT 802 ARCHITECTURE**

5   IEEE 802.2: Logical Link Control   63

Service Interface Specifications 63; Peer-to-Peer Protocols 64;
Service Access Points 64; LLC Data Unit 65;
Commands and Responses 65;
Service Access Point Addresses 66; Station Addresses 66;
Network/LLC Interface Service Specification 67;
Service Primitives 68; Primitives for Type 1 Operation 69;
Primitives for Type 2 Operation 70;
Service Primitive Parameters 70;
LLC/MAC Interface Service Specification 71;
LLC Peer-to-Peer Protocol Procedures 72;
Protocols for Type 1 Operation 73; Unnumbered Commands 73;
Protocols for Type 2 Operation 74;
Establishing and Terminating Connections 75;
Information Transfer Commands 75; Supervisory Commands 76;
Sending Acknowledgments 78; Flow Control 79; Summary 80

6   IEEE 802.3: CSMA/CD   81

CSMA/CD Operation 81; CSMA/CD Functions 81;
The LLC/MAC Interface 83; CSMA/CD Transmission Frame 84;
CSMA/CD Media Access Management 86;
Collision Detection 86; Backoff after Collision 88;
CSMA/CD Physical Layer Standards 89;
Physical Signaling Functions 90;
Physical Signaling Interfaces 91;
The MAC/PLS Interface 91; The PLS/PMA Interface 92;
Attachment Unit Interface 92;
Baseband Medium Attachment Unit 94;
Broadband Media Access Unit 95; Summary 96

7   IEEE 802.4: Token Bus   *97*

Token Bus Operation 97; Token Bus Functions 97;
Token Handling 98; Service Classes and Access Classes 99;
Optional Priority Scheme 100; Ring Maintenance 101;
Fault Management 103; Sending and Receiving Frames 104;
LLC/MAC Interface Service Specification 106;
Station Management/MAC Interface 107;
Physical Layer Specification 108;
MAC/Physical Layer Interface 108;
Physical Layer/Station Management Interface 109;
Transmission Types 109; Summary 111

8   IEEE 802.5: Token Ring   *113*

Token Ring Access Protocol 113; Fault Management 116;
Optional Priority Scheme 118; Frame Format 118;
Service Specifications 120; Token Ring Physical Layer 122;
Summary 123

PART III   OTHER LAN ARCHITECTURES

9   Fiber Distributed Data Interface (FDDI)   *127*

FDDI Access Protocol 128; Capacity Allocation 128;
Fault Management 131; Frame Format 132;
MAC Service Specifications 132;
Physical Layer Specifications 134; Data Encoding 134;
Physical Specifications 135; Reliability 135;
Future of FDDI 138; Summary 139

10   MAP and TOP Specifications   *141*

Layer Protocols 141; MAP and TOP Network Structure 144;
MAP and TOP Protocols 144;
The Physical and Data Link Layers 145;
Access Control Methods 145; Network Layer 145;
Transport Layer 147; Session Layer 148;
Presentation Layer 148; Application Layer 148; Summary 150

11   PBX Networks   *151*

Private Branch Exchanges 151;
Telephone Network Topology 153;
Data Communication Using the Telephone System 155;
Digital PBXs 155; PBX Networks 157; Network Reliability 157;
Switching Techniques 158; Digital Switching 158;
Distributed Network Structures 159;
Packet Switching on PBX Networks 160;
Future of PBX Local Area Networks 161; Summary 161

12   Inter-LAN Connections   *163*

Interconnected Network Configurations 163; Repeaters 167;
Bridges 168; Routers 170; Gateways 175;
Inter-LAN Networks 176;
Digital Equipment Corporation: An Example of Connectivity 180;
DEC Intervendor Connectivity 180;
DEC Inter-LAN Connectivity 182; Summary 182

PART **IV**
LAN IMPLEMENTATIONS BY IBM

13   Local Area Network Implementations   *187*

Basic LAN Functions 187; Physical Components 188;
Common Implementations of IEEE Architectures 188;
Network Operating Systems 189;
Relationship to Higher Layers 191; Standardization 193;
Summary 193

14   IBM LAN Architectures and Products   *195*

IBM LAN Products 195; Connectivity 197; Gateways 199;
Summary 207

15   IBM Token Ring Network   *209*

Network Components 209; Media Access Management 211;
Priority Scheme 211; Error Conditions 213;

Media Access Control Services 213; Frame Format 214;
Addressing 216; Routing 216; Source Routing 217;
Routing Information 218; Direct Interface 219;
Physical Layer 221; Summary 222

16   IBM PC Network   223

Network Interfaces 223; Media Access Management 223;
Collision Detection 224; Backoff after Collision 225;
IBM PC Network—Broadband 226;
IBM PC Network—Baseband 229; Summary 229

17   IBM LLC, NETBIOS, and APPC Interfaces   *231*

Logical Link Control 232; SAPS and Link Stations 232;
LLC Data Unit 234; LLC Interface 234;
Type 1 Operation 236; Type 2 Operation 236;
Acknowledgment and Sequence Checking 237;
S-Format Frames 238; Sending Acknowledgments 239;
Pacing 240; U-Format Frames 240; NETBIOS 241;
NETBIOS Interface 242; NETBIOS Functions 242;
NETBIOS Name Service 242; NETBIOS Routing 243;
NETBIOS Session Service 243;
NETBIOS Datagram Service 244;
General NETBIOS Commands 245;
NETBIOS as a De Facto Standard 245; APPC/PC 245;
APPC and PU 2.1 246; APPC and LU 6.2 248;
APPC Conversation Verbs 248;
APPC Synchronization 249; Change of Direction 251;
APPC Control Verbs 251; APPC/PC Interface 252;
APPC Network Protocols 252; Summary 253

18   The IBM Redirector/SMB Interface   255

IBM PC LAN Program Functions 255;
Station Configurations 256; Naming 256;
Disk and Directory Sharing 257;
Menu and Command Interface 257;
Redirector/SMB Interface 257; DOS Function Calls 260;
Server Message Blocks 262;
IBM PC LAN Program as a De Facto Standard 264;
Summary 267

PART V   LAN IMPLEMENTATIONS BY OTHER VENDORS

19   Routing Protocol Alternatives   *271*

NETBIOS Protocols 272; APPC/PC 272; XNS 273;
XNS Courier Protocol 273;
XNS Internet Transport Protocols 273;
XNS Internet Routing Services 277;
TCP/IP 278; TCP Packet Format 278;
TCP Reliable Data Transfer 279; TCP Flow Control 279;
TCP User Datagram Protocol 279;
Internet Protocol Services 280; IP Addressing 280;
IP Routing 281; MAP/OSI Protocols 282;
MAP Session and Transport Layer Functions 283;
MAP Network Layer Functions 284; MAP Addressing 284;
MAP Routing 284; Routing Standardization Issues 285;
Summary 286

20   Ethernet   *287*

Ethernet Goals 287; Ethernet Definitions 287;
Ethernet Functional Model 288; Layer-to-Layer Services 290;
Ethernet Frame Format 290; Network Addresses 292;
Data Encapsulation/Decapsulation 292;
Link Management 293; Ethernet Physical Model 293;
Data Encoding/Decoding 294; Channel Access 295;
Physical Specifications 295; Summary 296

21   3Com: 3+   *297*

3 + Share 298; 3 + Share File Sharing 298;
3 + Share Printer Sharing 299; 3 + Share Name Service 299;
3 + Mail 300; 3 + Network Connectivity Products 300;
3 + Network Protocols and Interfaces 300;
Ethernet and Token Ring 301; Microcom Network Protocol 301;
MS-DOS Internal Network Drive Scheme 302;
Internet Datagram Protocol 302;
Sequenced Packet Protocol 302; Packet Exchange Protocol 304;
MINDS Programming Interface 305;
Redirector/SMB Protocol 305; Name Service 307; Summary 307

22 Novelle: Advanced NetWare 309

File Sharing 309; Printer Sharing 310;
Electronic Mail 310; Remote Access 310;
LAN-to-LAN Connection 310;
Asynchronous Communication 310;
SNA Gateway 311; Naming and User Access 311;
Utility Programs and Commands 311; IBM Compatibility 315;
Advanced NetWare System Architecture 315;
Redirector/SMB Emulation 315;
Advanced NetWare File Server Protocol 317;
Internet Packet Exchange 319; Summary 320

23 Apple Computer: AppleTalk 321

Basic AppleTalk Characteristics 322;
Physical Specifications 322;
AppleTalk Link Access Protocol 322;
Datagram Delivery Protocol 325;
Routing Table Maintenance Protocol 328;
Name Binding Protocol 330;
AppleTalk Transaction Protocol 331;
Other Protocols 333; Summary 333

24 AT&T: STARLAN 335

STARLAN Protocols and Interfaces 336; Network Topology 338;
The LLC and MAC Sublayers 338;
Network and Transport Protocols 339; Name Service 339;
Datagram and Virtual Circuit Services 340;
Call Control Component 340; Data Transfer Component 340;
Flow Control 342; Error Detection and Correction 342;
MS-DOS Program Interface 343;
UNIX Program Interfaces 343;
UNIX Listener Library 343;
UNIX Transport Library 344;
UNIX Server Program Support Features 346; Summary 346

25 Allen-Bradley: VistaLAN/1 349

Functional Capabilities 349;
Network Names and Addresses 350;
Media Access Control Protocols 351;
Token Retransmission 351; Reconfiguration Timeout 352;
Error Processing 352; Physical Specifications 353;
Summary 353

Index 355

PREFACE

Until early in the 1980s the mainframe was the centerpiece of computing. Terminals and distributed processors were regarded as minor adjuncts to large corporate computing systems. By the end of the 1980s a radical change in perception had occurred. Individual knowledge workers could have powerful personal computers on their desks, each with a large personal database. To them, these personal computers were the center of their computing world. They needed many servers to support their computing activities—central databases, departmental databases, printers, perhaps plotters or slide makers, electronic mail facilities, access to large machines for numeric-intensive computing, perhaps access to a supercomputer. The connection to these facilities needed high-bandwidth cabling. The local area network changed the desktop computer from an isolated machine into a rich environment with a wealth of information and resources that the knowledge worker could access.

The need to communicate—to send messages, to share data, to access computing resources, to share expensive peripheral devices—has contributed to the development and spread of local area networks. A local area network is a network that connects users in a moderately sized geographic area. Typically, a local area network connects users located in the same office, on the same floor, or in the same building. The challenge for local area networks has been to provide facilities that meet users' communication needs at a reasonable cost. Compatibility is a key issue in keeping costs reasonable. Local area networks must be able to connect a wide variety of hardware and software products in a single network, without having to build complex and costly interfaces for different products. To facilitate this compatibility, various national and international standards organizations and computer and network vendors have developed network architectures that allow a variety of equipment to be connected together in a network.

In this book we present an explanation of the concepts that underlie local area network technology. We then examine in detail key local area network standards being developed by standards organizations. Finally, we discuss several local area network implementations, examining how their architectures reflect both formally published standards and the development of de facto standards and in what ways and to what levels compatibility is achieved.

ACKNOWLEDGMENTS   The authors would like to thank the many representatives of the companies whose local area network products we describe in this book for providing us with information about their products. We also express our appreciation to Joe Leben for his valuable help in the writing of this book. Joe helped to refine the content, did the final editing of the manuscript, and prepared the final versions of the illustrations.

James Martin
Kathleen K. Chapman

PART I CONCEPTS

1 LOCAL AREA NETWORK CONCEPTS

The design, installation, and operation of computer networks is vital to the functioning of modern computerized organizations. Over the past decade, complex and diverse networks have been established, tying together mainframes, minicomputers, personal computers, terminals, and other devices, such as communications controllers and cluster controllers.

WIDE AREA NETWORKS

Many of today's networks use public telecommunications facilities to provide users with access to the processing capabilities and data storage facilities associated with the mainframes and to permit fast interchange of information among the users of the network. As the cost of microelectronic devices has dropped, the intelligence in the various devices that are attached to the network has increased. Intelligent terminals, minicomputers, personal computers, and other programmable devices are all part of these large networks. Networks such as these that tie together users who are widely separated geographically are called *wide area networks* (WANs).

LOCAL AREA NETWORKS

In parallel with the growth of wide area networks, there has been another area of expansion in the use of computing facilities. Personal computers have spread rapidly and widely throughout organizations. Various types of small computers are routinely used for word processing, financial analysis, sales reporting, order processing, and many other business functions. As the use of personal computers has grown, so has grown a need for these personal computers to communicate—with each other and with the larger, centralized data processing facilities of the organization. Personal computers may initially be used for local applications that can be processed in a stand-alone manner. But typically, additional requirements soon arise, for example:

- To access data that is stored in some other area
- To allow a group of personal computers to share devices that are too expensive to be used by a single person only
- To give users a way of communicating electronically, using the personal computers that are already in place

A type of networking technology, known as *local area networks* (LANs), has developed as a way of meeting the requirements for relatively short distance communication among intelligent devices. The range of distances supported by typical local area networks range from a few feet to about 5 km.

METROPOLITAN AREA NETWORKS

In some cases, it is desirable to distinguish between wide area networks and *metropolitan area networks* (MANs). Metropolitan area networks sometimes link an organization's buildings within a city; sometimes they link a cluster of factories and offices that are within about 50 km of one another. Metropolitan area networks are used to fill the gap between local area networks and wide area networks and cover the range of from, say, 1 km to 50 km.

LOCAL AREA NETWORK DEFINED

Many definitions for the term *local area network* have been proposed. Instead of inventing a new one, we will examine the definition that has been published by the Institute of Electrical and Electronics Engineers (IEEE). The IEEE is an organization in the United States that has developed an important set of standards regarding architectures for local area networks. The IEEE defines a LAN as follows:

A datacomm system allowing a number of independent devices to communicate directly with each other, within a moderately sized geographic area over a physical communications channel of moderate data rates.

Let us look at each element in this definition and examine its significance.

First, a local area network *allows a number of independent devices to communicate directly with each other*. A local area network, then, supports *peer-to-peer communication,* where all communicating devices have similar status in the system. This is in contrast with *hierarchical* or *centrally controlled* communication, where one communicating entity is assumed to be more intelligent than the others and has the primary responsibility for controlling the network. The idea of all stations on a LAN being peers holds true even when there are many different types of devices attached to the network.

Second, the communication *takes place within a moderately sized geographic area*. This is an important distinction between wide area networks and local area networks. Local area networks are typically confined to a single building or to a group of buildings that are relatively close together. A local area network does not ordinarily span a distance greater than about 10 km.

Third, communication *takes place over a physical communications channel*. In a local area network, devices are hooked together directly via a dedicated cable or other communication medium. This is in contrast to wide area networks, which often use public, switched telecommunications facilities or packet-switched data networks for communication.

Last, the communication channel of a local area network *supports a moderate data rate*. This distinguishes local area networks from the very high speed connections used within the computer room to connect peripheral devices to mainframe computers and also from the slower speeds typically supported by the telecommunications channels used to construct wide area networks. Direct computer room connections typically operate at speeds of 20 million bits per second (Mbps) and greater. Many wide area networks use dial-up or leased telephone lines, where maximum data rates are in the area of 9600 or 19,200 bps, with some circuit-switched and packet-switched systems supporting 56,000 or 64,000 bps. The moderate data rates supported by typical local area networks have fallen between those two speed categories, in the 1 Mbps to 10 Mbps range. Optical fiber cables are coming into use for local area networks, and these can support bit rates of 100 Mbps—faster than traditional machine-room channels. So the phrase "moderate data rates" in the definition may soon have to be replaced with the phrase "moderate to high data rates."

LAN APPLICATIONS

A local area network can be used for many different applications. In an office environment, local area networks are commonly used for shared access to data. A local area network allows a person using one computer on the network to access a file that is stored on another computer's disks or to use the other computer's disks for storing files created on the first computer. Depending on how the local area network is implemented, it may be possible for several users to access the same file at the same time. Local area networks also allow many network users to share the same printer. Print jobs created on one computer can be sent to another computer and printed using a printer attached to that computer. Typically, print queues are provided so that multiple print jobs from different computers can be sent to the printer and stored there until it is their turn to be printed. In this way, all the users on the network can take advantage of the capabilities of a more expensive printer than an individual user would be able to justify. Local area networks can also be used to send messages from one computer to another and may provide electronic mail facilities, including editing and formatting aids, group addressing capabilities, and message notification and storing. Local area networks may also support alarm and security systems and are sometimes extended to the factory environment to provide process monitoring and control.

Local area networks are used in two ways. First, they are used for transmission that *could* take place at low speeds. The desktop machines are used in the same way that they would be used if the local area network did not exist and telephone lines were used as they have been for many years. Second, and more interestingly, they are used for applications that *require* their high bandwidth. Portions of a large database can be loaded into a desktop machine at reasonable speed. A user can transfer a spreadsheet to another user while the two talk on the phone. Displays that use bit-mapped graphics can be sent over the network and still painted with a subsecond response time. A megapixel screen could take 100 seconds to paint if transmitted over a telephone network and a fraction of a second with a LAN.

In one decade, the transmission speed available to the desktop computer went from a maximum of 9600 bps to 10 Mbps and then to 100 Mbps in some cases. Nowhere else in computing have performance numbers changed so dramatically as this. The capability of LANs combines with the increasing power and ease of use of personal computers and workstations to bring a revolution in computer usage.

For years, telecommunications transmission speeds have represented a constraining bottleneck in the way we use computers. User interfaces have been designed with the assumption that transmission is no faster than 9600 bps and response times are several seconds. Unfortunately, much software is still being designed today that fails to take advantage of LAN speeds. Designers need to think in megabits per second, not kilobits per second. To adopt this way of thinking is a major paradigm shift for designers who have grown up with the speeds of voice-grade lines.

A particularly important application of high-speed LANs is *cooperative processing,* in which an application runs partly on a desktop computer and partly on a mainframe, taking advantage of the best features of each. The desktop machine provides good human factoring, bit-mapped graphics, a mouse, windows, and almost instantaneous response; the mainframe provides a database shared with many users and a high level of computing power. Much software is now being produced for cooperative processing and needs the high-bandwidth transmission of local area networks.

The range of applications for local area networks can be extended by *interconnecting* networks. Network interconnection allows for multiple local area networks to be interlinked, sometimes using common carrier telecommunications facilities, thus allowing information to be passed between widely separated locations. Network interconnection can extend the communications capabilities of local area networks far beyond the geographic limits of a single local area network, yet still retain the ease of use and interconnection on a local level that is characteristic of local area networks. The use of high-bandwidth LANs has led to a demand for high-bandwidth bridges between LANs. Microwave and optical fiber circuits between buildings are used and long-distance lines are leased that transmit at more than 1 million bps (the T1 and T3 tariffs in North America, for example).

LAN REQUIREMENTS

When organizations employ local area networks, the networks are generally expected to achieve a number of objectives, for example:

- Improving employee productivity through automation of routine job functions
- Improving manageability of information through reduced duplication and improved accessibility

BOX 1.1   Local area network requirements as originally stated by the developers of Ethernet.

- Data rates of 1 to 10 megabits per second (Today the requirements extend up to speeds of 100 megabits per second or higher.)
- Geographic distances spanning at most 1 kilometer (Today longer distances are sometimes spanned by one LAN, and often by inter-LAN connections.)
- Ability to support several hundred independent devices
- Simplicity, or use of the simplest possible mechanisms that have the required functionality and performance
- Reliability and good error characteristics
- Minimal dependence on any centralized components or control
- Efficient use of shared resources, particularly the communication network itself
- Stability under high load
- Fair access to the system by all devices
- Easy installation of a small system, with graceful growth as the system evolves
- Ease of reconfiguration and maintenance
- Low cost

- Improving employee interaction through the sharing of information
- Reducing or controlling costs through the use of cost-effective communication methods
- Cooperative processing with high-speed links between personal computers and mainframes
- Providing for standardization of computer and communication usage

These objectives, combined with the basic definition of a local area network, have helped define the requirements that a particular local area network implementation must meet to be commercially successful. Although there is no single formal definition of the requirements for a local area network, agreement on a local area network's general characteristics is widespread. Box 1.1 lists the requirements for a local area network as articulated by the developers of Ethernet, a widely used architecture for local area networks initially developed by Xerox.

LAN COMPONENTS   Figure 1.1 shows that the physical components that make up a typical local area network fall into two categories: *computing devices* and a *cabling system*. A local area network interconnects computing devices, such as personal computers, which may be of the

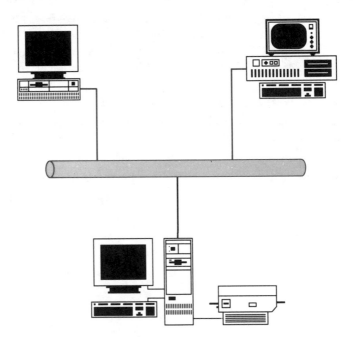

Figure 1.1   The main components of a local area network are network stations and a cabling system that links them together.

same or different types. Devices attached to a network are commonly referred to as *stations*. Each station attached to the network must be sufficiently intelligent to handle the communications control functions that are required for attachment to the network. Peripheral devices, such as hard disks and printers, are not typically stations on the network. Instead, each peripheral device is attached to one of the computers that is a station on the network. Peripheral devices can, however, be made accessible to other stations on the network and can be shared by all network users. Other types of peripherals and devices that can be part of the network include terminals, modems, television transmitters and receivers, facsimile devices, and sensors. These devices must either be attached through one of the network stations or have sufficient intelligence to provide the communications control necessary to be connected directly to the network as a separate station.

All stations on the local area network are interconnected via a cabling system, which includes the wire or cable that interconnects the devices and any attachment units needed to attach the device to the cable. Communication takes place when the stations send and receive signals over the cable.

As these signals travel along the cable, they gradually lose strength. If communicating stations are widely separated from one another, *repeaters* may be needed at key points along the cable to regenerate the signal periodically (see Fig. 1.2). In some implementations, network stations themselves may act as repeaters, receiving signals and then retransmitting them at their original strength.

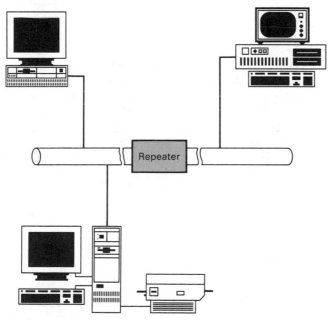

Figure 1.2   The use of repeaters allows cable lengths to be longer.

LAN CHARACTERISTICS

Four characteristics have become important in describing the architecture of a particular local area network implementation. These characteristics allow us to compare one type of local area network with another. We will introduce these four characteristics now and examine them in detail in later chapters.

- **Transmission Medium.** The *transmission medium* is the type of cable that is used. Typical LAN transmission media, which we examine in Chapter 2, are twisted-wire-pair telephone wire, various types of coaxial cable, and optical fibers.

- **Transmission Technique.** The *transmission technique* determines how the physical medium is used for communication. The most common techniques used with local area networks, which we also examine in Chapter 2, are called *baseband* and *broadband* transmission.

- **Network Topology.** The *network topology* identifies the shape the cabling takes when it is used to interconnect the network devices. Common network topologies, which we discuss in Chapter 3, are the *bus,* the *ring,* and the *star.*

- **Access Control Method.** The *access control method* describes the method by which communicating stations control their access to the transmission medium. Devices on a local area network share the cabling system that connects them and the transmission facilities it provides. However, a local area network generally allows only one station to transmit at a time. Some method must be used to control when each station can use the transmission facilities. Commonly used LAN access control methods, which we discuss in Chapter 3, are *contention, token passing,* and *circuit switching.*

SUMMARY

A local area network provides peer-to-peer communication among independent devices located within a moderately sized geographic area. Communication takes place over a physical communication channel, with data rates in the range of 1 Mbps to 10 Mbps. Network components can be divided into two categories: communicating stations and the cabling system that connects them. Network stations must be intelligent enough to handle the communication control functions required by the network. Key local area network characteristics are transmission medium, transmission technique, network topology, and access control method.

2 PHYSICAL TRANSMISSION CHARACTERISTICS

The physical characteristics of a local area network deal with the transmission of bits across a physical medium. These physical characteristics can be divided into two main categories: the *physical medium* used for transmission and the *transmission technique* that is used to transmit data over the physical medium. We will begin our discussion of physical transmission characteristics by examining the three types of physical media that are used most often in constructing local area networks.

TRANSMISSION MEDIUM

The telecommunications industry has employed a wide variety of physical media for the transmission of information. These media range from the open-wire pairs that were carried on poles in the early days of telecommunications to the high-speed satellite links that are today used to connect distant points on the globe. Although most of the media employed in conventional telecommunications could be employed in the construction of local area networks, three media are used most often in today's LAN implementations: *twisted-wire pairs, coaxial cable,* and *fiber optics links*. Each has different transmission characteristics and different costs.

TWISTED-WIRE PAIRS

A twisted-wire pair consists of two insulated strands of copper wire that have been braided. A number of twisted-wire pairs are often grouped together and enclosed within a protective sheath or jacket to form a cable. Figure 2.1 illustrates a cable made of twisted-wire pairs.

The wiring used in buildings for telephone systems consists of twisted-wire-pair cable. One of the main reasons that this type of cable is being used to

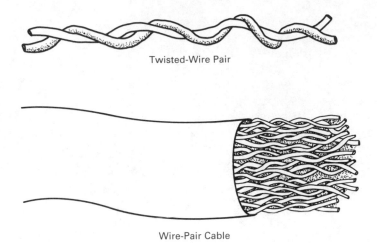

Figure 2.1   Twisted-wire pairs

implement local area networks is that it is already installed in many locations. Some local area network products are now available that use ordinary telephone wire to support transmission speeds of up to about 10 Mbps, although many implementations that use twisted-wire pairs support data rates much lower than this. Most high-performance local area network implementations that use twisted-wire pairs employ a special form of twisted-wire-pair cable that uses a higher-quality protective sheath, called *shielded-twisted-wire-pair cable*. This type of cable is less subject to electrical interference and can more reliably support high transmission rates over long distances.

COAXIAL CABLE   Figure 2.2 shows the construction of a typical coaxial cable. Coaxial cable consists of a central conducting copper core that is surrounded by insulating material. The insulation is surrounded by a second conducting layer, which can consist of either a braided

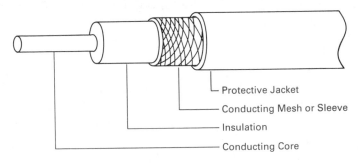

Figure 2.2   Coaxial cable

wire mesh or a solid sleeve. A protective jacket of nonconducting material protects the outer conductor. Coaxial cable is less subject to interference and crosstalk than twisted-wire pairs and is able to support data rates of up to 100 Mbps. As with local area networks that use twisted-wire pairs, much lower data rates than 100 Mbps are usually employed using coaxial cable.

Coaxial cable has been used for many years for television transmission. The same cable and electronic components that are used by the cable television industry are used in some local area network implementations. Others use an entirely different type of coaxial cable.

FIBER-OPTIC LINKS   Optical fibers can be used to carry data signals in the form of modulated light beams. An optical fiber consists of an extremely thin cylinder of glass, called the *core,* surrounded by a concentric layer of glass, known as the *cladding.* The construction of a typical optical fiber is shown in Fig. 2.3. The refractive index of the cladding is lower than that of the core, which causes light that is traveling down the core to be reflected back into the core when it strikes the cladding. In practice, a number of such optical fibers are often bound together into a cable, with all of the fibers surrounded by a protective sheath.

Optical fiber cables support very wide bandwidths. Transmission rates of up to 565 Mbps are routinely employed in commercially available systems, and data rates of up to 200,000 Mbps have been demonstrated. Signals transmitted over optical fiber are not subject to electrical interference, and the cable is smaller and lighter than electrical cable. However, optical fiber is typically more expensive to install than electrical cable.

WIRING FOR LOCAL AREA NETWORKS   A major factor in choosing a particular local area network implementation is type of physical cabling system that the LAN uses. In a very simple case, a local area network may be used to link a number of computers and other intelligent devices that are in close physical proximity, sometimes in the same room. In

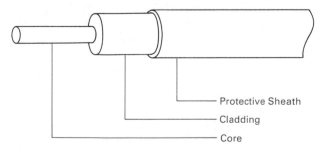

Protective Sheath

Cladding

Core

Figure 2.3   Optical fiber construction

such a case, the type of wiring the local area network employs may be of little concern. In more advanced applications, an enterprise might want to interconnect devices in an entire building or even throughout a group of buildings. In such cases, the type of cabling the LAN employs may be the most important characteristic of the network.

Some types of LAN implementations today use ordinary telephone twisted-wire pairs for data transmission. Several commercially available local area network products permit data transmission at bit rates of up to 10 Mbps over ordinary telephone wiring. Such a LAN implementation may be of interest to an enterprise that already has its offices interconnected with sufficient telephone wiring that can be used for local area network communication. Installing a LAN is then a matter of gaining access to the various wiring closets in which the telephone wiring terminates and locating the telephone circuits that are to be used for installing the local area network (no small feat in some situations).

CABLING SYSTEMS

In many cases, an enterprise may decide to install wiring specifically for the purpose of handling the data communication needs of the organization. Various equipment vendors now market general-purpose cabling systems that can serve a wide range of communication needs. These cabling systems provide the capability for handling voice, low-speed data communication, high-speed local area network communication, fiber-optic communication, and sometimes also video signal distribution. Cabling systems are particularly attractive to those constructing new facilities who wish to provide for flexible data communication and for future growth.

We will next introduce two widely used cabling systems: the IBM Cabling System and Digital Equipment Corporations's DECconnect Communication System.

IBM CABLING SYSTEM

In 1984, before it even offered local area network products in its product line, IBM recognized the future importance of local area networks. At that time it began marketing the *IBM Cabling System*. The IBM Cabling System offers several types of physical cables, including the following:

- **Type 1 Cable.** Type 1 cable consists of two solid, #22 AWG twisted-wire pairs surrounded by an outer braided shield. Both twisted-wire pairs are suitable for data use. Several varieties of Type 1 cable are available, including cable for indoor use in conduits, cable suitable for installation in wiring plenums, and cable for outdoor installation.

- **Type 2 Cable.** Type 2 cable also contains two solid, #22 AWG twisted-wire pairs surrounded by an outer braided shield. Between the braided shield and the outer protective sheath are four additional solid #22 AWG twisted-wire pairs suitable for use in telephone communication. Several varieties of Type 2 cable are also available for indoor use in conduits or in wiring plenums.

- **Type 5 Cable.** Type 5 cable contains two optical fibers within a single outer cover. Type 5 cable can be installed indoors, outdoors, and in dry, waterproof underground conduits.

- **Type 6 Cable.** Type 6 cable is similar to Type 1 cable, except that it uses stranded #26 AWG wire. Type 6 cable is typically used for constructing patch cables that interconnect longer lengths of Type 1 and Type 2 cable.

In addition to these types of cable, the IBM Cabling System includes a variety of accessories, such as connectors, wiring faceplates, surface-mounted outlets, distribution panels, and patch cables. IBM recommends that cable be installed so that the wiring from each individual office or workplace terminates in a central *wiring closet,* thus creating a star configuration, as shown in Fig. 2.4. Since all wiring terminates in easily accessible wiring closets, patch cables can be used to create networks having any desired structure. The networks that are typically constructed using the IBM Cabling System are physically star structured, due to the wiring closets, and logically ring structured, as shown in Fig. 2.5. The various network structures, or topologies, to which local area networks conform are introduced in Chapter 3.

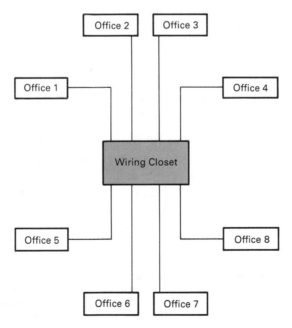

Figure 2.4   Star configuration using a wiring closet

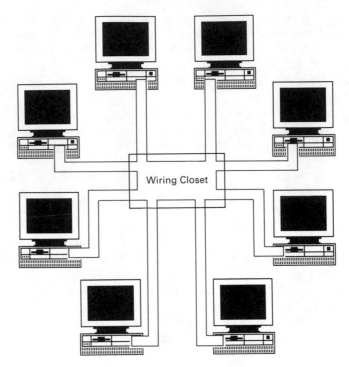

Figure 2.5   Star-wired logical ring structure

DECCONNECT COMMUNICATION SYSTEM

The cabling system offered by the Digital Equipment Corporation for interconnecting its equipment is called the *DECconnect Communication System*. The DECconnect system uses the following types of cable to interconnect offices and workplaces:

- **ThinWire Ethernet Cable.** ThinWire Ethernet cable is a flexible coaxial cable, about ¼-inch thick, that is similar to the type of coaxial cable that is used for closed-circuit television transmission. It is used for relatively short distance communication at 10Mbps over an Ethernet type of local area network. Ethernet is described in detail in Chapters 6 and 20.

- **Standard Ethernet Cable.** Standard Ethernet cable is relatively rigid, ½-inch-thick coaxial cable that is typically used to interconnect several smaller networks that use the ThinWire Ethernet cable.

- **Twisted-Wire-Pair Data Communication Cable.** This cable is unshielded and contains four twisted-wire pairs. It is used for connecting terminals and other types of computer equipment to a network using slow-speed, non-LAN types of data communication.

- **Telephone Cable.** This is standard telephone cable that contains four un-shielded twisted-wire pairs. It is used for ordinary voice telephone communication.
- **Video Cable.** This is standard closed-circuit television coaxial cable and is used for video applications.

The DECconnect system centers around a single type of faceplate that serves all the communication needs of a particular office or workplace. As shown in Fig. 2.6, the DECconnect faceplate has the following four connectors:

- A BNC connector that gives access to a ThinWire Ethernet network
- A modified modular connector, similar to a telephone connecter, that is used to connect computer equipment to the twisted-wire-pair data communication cable
- A standard modular telephone jack that is used to connect telephone equipment to the telephone system
- An F-type connector for connecting video equipment to the video cable

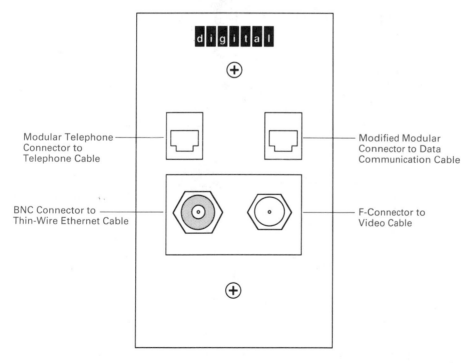

Figure 2.6   DECconnect faceplate

   DEC recommends that the four types of cable that terminate in the faceplate be installed between each office or workplace and a central *satellite equipment room* (SER). One or more satellite equipment rooms can be installed on
each floor of a building, interconnected using standard, thick Ethernet cable (see
Fig. 2.7). Like the IBM Cabling System, since all wiring terminates in easily
accessible wiring closets, patch cables can be used to create networks having
any desired structure. The DECconnect system includes a variety of accessories,
such as connectors, wiring faceplates, surface-mounted outlets, patch panels,
and patch cables.

   Like the IBM Cabling System, the DECconnect system uses a physical
star configuration to interconnect workplaces with the satellite equipment room.
However, the DECconnect system is typically used to construct Ethernet local
area networks that use a bus structure. Again, local area network structures, or
topologies, are introduced in Chapter 3.

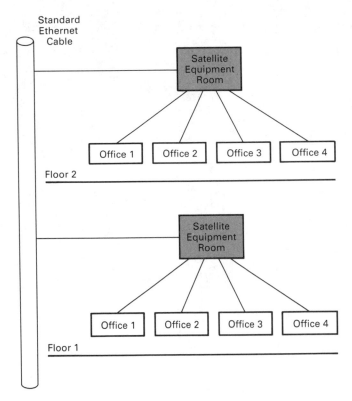

Figure 2.7   Interconnecting satellite equipment rooms with standard Ethernet
cable

TRANSMISSION TECHNIQUES

Now that we have discussed the physical wiring that is used to construct local area networks, we next discuss the techniques that are used for transmitting signals over those facilities. Two techniques can be used for transmitting signals over a physical communication medium: *baseband* and *broadband*. Baseband transmission uses *digital signaling,* and broadband transmission uses *analog techniques*. Equipment can be designed to transmit either digital or analog signals over any of the physical media used in telecommunications.

In discussing transmission techniques, we will often refer to the medium over which data is transmitted as simply a communication channel. By this we mean a link of arbitrary construction that has certain characteristics. These characteristics can be defined apart from the physical methods that are used to implement the channel. Equivalent channels can be constructed using any desired media, and in many cases the physical methods that are used to transmit data can be made transparent to the communicating stations.

In the following sections we will discuss the differences between baseband and broadband transmission and the related differences between digital and analog signaling.

BASEBAND TRANSMISSION

With baseband transmission, data signals are carried over the physical communication medium in the form of discrete pulses of electricity or light. With this form of transmission, a sending device sends data pulses directly over the communication channel, and the receiving device detects them.

As the data pulses travel along the communication medium, they become distorted. The pulses received at the other end are far from their original shape, and if the line is too long, the signals too weak, or the transmitting speed too great, the received signal may be unrecognizable and interpreted wrongly by the machine at the other end. To overcome these difficulties, devices called *repeaters* can be used that receive the digital signals and retransmit them at their original strength and sharpness. Since the repeater totally regenerates the signal, the result of any noise that might have crept into the signal is nullified. Noise and interference are not a problem with baseband transmission unless they corrupt the signal sufficiently to prevent a bit from being correctly identified as a 0 or 1. Communicating stations attached to the network may themselves act as repeaters in some LAN implementations, receiving a signal and then retransmitting it at its original strength, so that separate equipment is not needed for signal regeneration.

With baseband transmission, the entire channel capacity is used to transmit a single data signal. Multiple devices attached to a network using baseband transmission share the communication channel by means of *time-division multiplexing* (TDM). With TDM the devices take turns transmitting, only one device

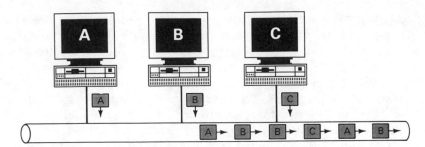

Figure 2.8   Time-division multiplexing

transmitting at a time. Data from different devices is then interleaved on the communication channel, as illustrated in Fig. 2.8. Since only one station can transmit at a time, there must be a way of determining which station is allowed to transmit. Local area networks use a variety of techniques, called *access control methods,* to control access to the transmission medium. The various access control methods used with local area networks are discussed in Chapter 3.

BROADBAND TRANSMISSION   Broadband transmission typically employs analog transmission using a wider range of frequencies than baseband transmission. With analog transmission, the signals employed are continuous and nondiscrete. Signals flow across the transmission medium in the form of *electromagnetic waves*. Figure 2.9 illustrates the characteristics of an electromagnetic wave.

Electromagnetic waves have three characteristics that are useful in telecommunications: *amplitude, frequency,* and *phase.* In an electrical wire, a wave's *amplitude* is associated with the *level of voltage* carried on the wire; in

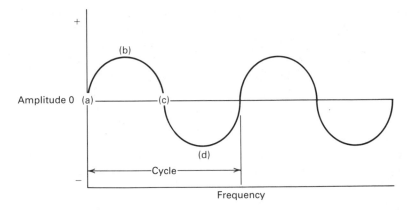

Figure 2.9   Characteristics of an electromagnetic wave

an optical fiber, the wave's amplitude is concerned with the *intensity of the light beam*. The *frequency* of a wave concerns the number of cycles or oscillations that the wave makes per second. A frequency rate of one oscillation per second is defined as one *hertz*. A wave's *phase* refers to the point to which the wave has advanced in its cycle. In Fig. 2.9, (a) identifies the beginning of the cycle, (b) is one-fourth of the cycle, (c) is half the cycle, and (d) is three-fourths of the cycle. A wave's phase is generally described in terms of degrees, with the beginning of the cycle being $0°$; one-fourth of the cycle, $90°$; half the cycle, $180°$; three-fourths of the cycle, $270°$; and completion of the cycle, $360°$.

Modulation Techniques

With analog transmission, a data signal is superimposed on a *carrier signal* by varying, or *modulating*, any one of the three wave characteristics of the carrier signal. For example, a particular value of the carrier signal's amplitude, frequency, or phase might represent the value 0, and some other amplitude, frequency, or phase value might represent the value 1. In this way a data signal can be *carried* by the carrier signal.

Measurements of Channel Capacity

In general, the higher the frequency of the carrier signal, the greater its information-carrying capacity. In telecommunications literature, the term *bandwidth* is often used to refer to the capacity of a communication channel. A channel's bandwidth is the difference between the highest and the lowest frequencies that are carried over the channel. The higher the bandwidth, the more information can be carried. For example, a telephone channel supporting voice communication transmits frequencies ranging from about 300 hertz (Hz) to 3100 Hz. So the range of frequencies, or bandwidth, supported is $3100 - 300 = 2800$ Hz, or about 3 kHz. The transmission media used with local area networks support bandwidths much larger than this.

A channel's bandwidth has a direct relationship to its *data rate,* or the number of bits per second that can be carried over it. Since local area networks deal mainly with data transmission, we will find bits per second to be a more useful measure of a channel's capacity than bandwidth.

Another term that is used to express channel capacity is *baud*. Baud is a measurement of the *signaling speed* of a channel; a certain communication channel is said to have a speed of so many baud. This refers to the number of times in each second the line condition changes. Suppose that we are using amplitude modulation and that one amplitude value is used to represent binary 0 and another to represent binary 1. In this particular case, the line's signaling speed in baud is the same as the line's data rate in bits per second. Suppose, however, that we use four different amplitudes to represent the binary value 00, 01, 10, or 11 (called *dibits*). In this case the data rate in bits per second will be twice the signaling speed in baud. If the signals are coded into eight possible states, then one line condition represents a *tribit,* and the data rate in bits per second is three times the signaling speed in baud. Some literature mistakenly uses the term *baud* to mean *bits per second.* Since the term *baud* can be confusing, we will avoid using it in this book.

Signal Amplification

Another issue that must be dealt with as part of physical data transmission is that of signal strength. When an electrical signal is transmitted along a wire, it gradually decreases in strength—a process known as *attenuation.* With analog transmission, *amplifiers* may be included as part of the network. An amplifier receives a signal and then retransmits at its original strength. Placing amplifiers at appropriate points along the physical transmission medium allows devices to be more widespread geographically and still be able to detect the signals that are transmitted over the physical medium. However, if any noise or interference has crept into the signal along the way, the noise is typically amplified along with the signal. Thus in analog transmission, the quality of the signal tends to deteriorate with distance even when amplifiers are used.

Frequency-Division Multiplexing

When analog transmission is used, the available bandwidth of the physical transmission medium is often divided up into multiple channels. Different transmissions can then take place simultaneously over the different channels using a technique called *frequency-division multiplexing* (FDM; see Fig. 2.10).

With broadband transmission, the multiple channels are often used in entirely different ways. For example, data can be transmitted on some, video signals on others, voice telephone calls on others, and so on, all simultaneously. For data transmission, one channel can be used by devices to transmit data and another channel to receive data. When multiple devices share the same channel

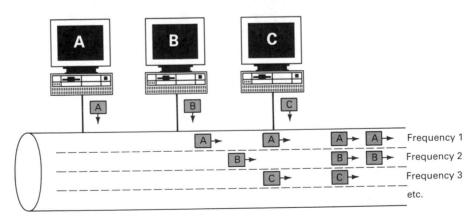

Figure 2.10   Frequency-division multiplexing

for data transmission, time-division multiplexing can be used to divide up access to the channel, as shown in Fig. 2.11. As with baseband transmission, a method of determining when a device is allowed to transmit must be employed.

A limited form of broadband transmission is possible where the entire bandwidth is used to make up a single channel. This is known as single-channel broadband. As with regular broadband, single-channel broadband uses analog signaling. Single-channel broadband provides a relatively inexpensive way to construct an initial network that can later be converted to multichannel or full broadband without requiring rewiring.

Direction of Transmission

Another difference between baseband and broadband transmission is in the direction of signal flow. With baseband transmission, signal flow is bidirectional; that is, the signal travels away from the sending device in both directions on the physical medium; as illustrated in Fig. 2.12. When device B transmits data, the signal goes out in both directions and eventually reaches all other devices along the wire or cable. When the signal reaches either end of the cable, terminators absorb it. Generally, the single-channel broadband technique also uses bidirectional transmission.

With full broadband signaling, transmission is unidirectional; the signal moves in one direction along the cable. In order for a signal to reach all devices on the network, then, there must be two paths for data flow. Figure 2.13 shows the two most common approaches used to provide the two paths.

The configuration shown at the top of Fig. 2.13 is known as *mid-split broadband*. The bandwidth of the cable is divided into two channels, each using a different range of frequencies. One channel is used to transmit signals, the other to receive. When a signal is transmitted, it travels to one end of the cable, known as the head end. At the head end, a frequency converter changes the

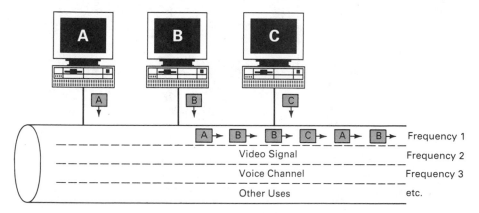

Figure 2.11 Frequency-division multiplexing with time-division multiplexing

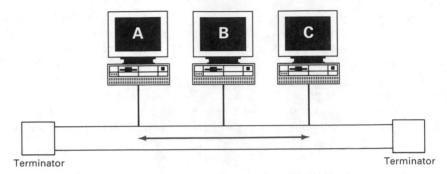

Figure 2.12 Bidirectional flow

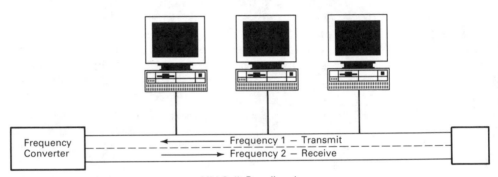

Mid-Split Broadband

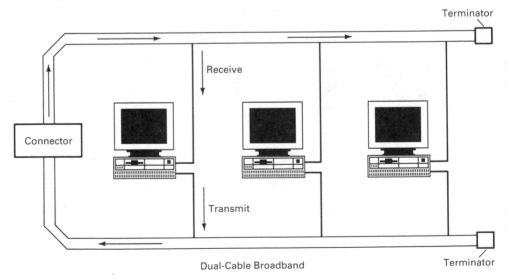

Dual-Cable Broadband

Figure 2.13 Unidirectional flow

frequency of the signal from the send channel range to the receive channel range and retransmits it in the opposite direction along the cable. The signal can now be received by all the devices on the cable.

The second configuration is known as dual-cable broadband. In this configuration, each device is attached to two cables. One cable is used to send and the other to receive. When a signal is transmitted, it reaches the head end and is passed on via a connector to the other cable, without any change in the frequency of the signal. The signal can then be received by any of the devices it passes along the second cable.

DIGITAL TRANSMISSION OVER AN ANALOG CHANNEL

We have discussed the differences between analog and digital signaling. Although analog transmission is often used over a communication medium, it is important to realize that the communicating stations that are attached to the network are digital, regardless of whether the network uses baseband (digital) or broadband (analog) signaling.

Modems

When analog transmission techniques are used to implement the communication channel, the digital signals that communicating stations generate must be converted to and from analog form. This conversion is performed by using a device called a *modem,* short for *modulator-demodulator.* Modems are routinely employed in conventional data transmission for transmitting digital data over ordinary analog telecommunications channels. Modems are also employed on local area networks when analog transmission techniques are used over the physical communication medium.

With broadband transmission, the carrier frequencies employed are very high frequency radio waves. Thus radio frequency (RF) modems must be used to attach devices to the transmission medium. Commonly available equipment for cable television, including coaxial cable, amplifiers, and signal distribution equipment, can be used in constructing broadband data networks. Employing existing technology can help to keep down the cost of network components.

Virtual Channel

Figure 2.14 shows the configuration that might be used in order for two digital devices to communicate over a physical communication medium that uses analog transmission. It is important to realize that the use of modems and analog transmission techniques is transparent to the two communicating devices. The two communicating stations send and receive digital bit streams whether the physical transmission medium uses digital or analog techniques. The modems automatically convert these digital bit streams to and from analog form. To the

Figure 2.14   Digital transmission over an analog communication facility

two communicating devices, it appears as though a digital channel connects them. This apparent digital channel is often referred to as a *virtual channel*.

ENCODING   Communicating stations can use a variety of encod-
SCHEMES   ing schemes to represent binary values for transmis-
                      sion over the communication channel. With one sim-
ple encoding scheme, used for many years over some telegraph circuits, the
presence of a pulse indicates the value 1 and the absence of a pulse represents
the value 0 (see Fig. 2.15).

Local area networks generally use a more sophisticated encoding scheme
than this for representing binary values. The two most commonly used LAN
encoding schemes are *Manchester encoding* and *differential Manchester encoding*. A number of commonly used encoding schemes, including the two Manchester variations, are described in Box 2.1.

SYNCHRONIZATION   For communication to take place between two digital
                      devices, a particular length of time is generally as-
sociated with the transmission of each bit. This is known as the *bit duration* or
bit time. Both the sending and receiving stations must be in synchronization and
must be able to determine when the beginning and the end of each bit time
occurs. To process data being transmitted properly, the receiving device must
be able to recognize when data is being transmitted and identify the portion of
the signal that corresponds to each bit. There are several ways in which this can
be done.

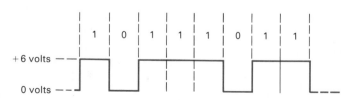

Figure 2.15   Telegraph signaling

BOX 2.1   Encoding schemes

RS-232-C Encoding

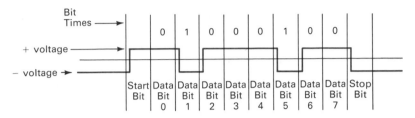

The technique most often used with low-speed data communication over an ordinary telecommunications channel is defined in a standard called *RS-232-C,* which is published by the Electronics Industry Association (EIA). With RS-232-C transmission, a negative voltage on the line for a bit time represents the value 1 and a positive voltage the value 0.

Zero-complemented Differential Encoding

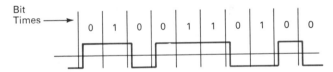

Many high-performance line control procedures, such as IBM's Synchronous Data Link Control (SDLC), often employ a more complex encoding scheme called *zero-complemented differential encoding* to represent bit values. With this technique, a transition on the line from negative to positive or from positive to negative within a bit time indicates the value 0; the lack of a transition during a bit time represents the value 1.

Manchester Encoding

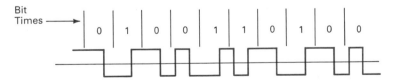

For electrical purposes, it is desirable in many local area network implementations that transitions from positive to negative and from

(Continued)

BOX 2.1 *(Continued)*

negative to positive occur often with predictable regularity. *Manchester encoding* produces the desired number of transitions and is used in many local area network implementations. With a typical implementation of Manchester encoding, a negative voltage for the first half of the bit time followed by a positive voltage for the second half of the bit time represents the value 1; a positive voltage followed by a transition to a negative voltage represents the value 0. Thus with Manchester encoding, a transition from negative to positive or from positive to negative occurs *every* bit time.

With Manchester encoding, bit times in which the signal is held either positive or negative for the entire bit time are used to represent something other than a bit value, for example, the beginning or end of a transmission block.

Differential Manchester Encoding

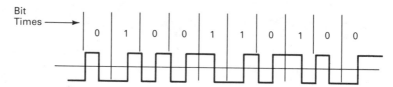

A form of Manchester encoding called *differential Manchester encoding* is used in some local area network implementations. With this technique, a transition occurs during each bit time, as with conventional Manchester encoding. However, the interpretation of the transition from positive to negative or from negative to positive depends on whether the previous bit time represented a 0 or a 1. To represent the value 1, the polarity remains the same as it was at the end of the previous bit time and then changes in polarity at the midpoint of the bit time only. To represent the value 0, the polarity changes at the beginning of the bit time and also at the midpoint of the bit time. With this form of encoding, a change from positive to negative can represent either a 0 or a 1 depending on the state of the line at the end of the previous bit time. Whether a transition occurs or does not occur indicates the value. No transition at the beginning of the bit time indicates the value 1; a transition at the beginning of the bit time indicates the value 0.

As with conventional Manchester encoding, bit times in which no transition occurs at the midpoint of the bit time are often used for control purposes.

Start and Stop Bits

When a simple encoding scheme is used, such as with RS-232-C transmission (see Box 2.1), *start bits* and *stop bits* are employed to identify the beginning and end of sequences of data. When start and stop bits are employed, each group of bits generally corresponds to a single character, usually 7 or 8 bits in length.

RS-232-C transmission uses start and stop bits to control transmission. This type of transmission is referred to as *asynchronous* or *start-stop transmission*. Between transmissions of each individual data character, the line is kept in an idle state, normally indicated by the continuous transmission of a signal having a negative voltage. A start bit precedes any group of data bits and consists of a change to a signal of positive voltage. A predetermined number of data bits (on which both sender and receiver must agree) then follow, where a negative voltage level indicates a 1 bit and a positive signal level a 0 bit. Following the data bits there will be at least one stop bit, which is indicated by at least one bit time at which the line remains at the negative voltage. This guarantees that there will be a transition in the signal level when the next start bit is sent.

The occurrence of start bits at the beginning of each data character allows the communicating devices to establish synchronization to ensure that the receiver samples the signal at appropriate points to identify data bit values correctly. If long strings of data bits were sent between start and stop bits, the receiver might slip out of synchronization with the sender, and the data bit values would be interpreted incorrectly.

With some types of transmission, the receiver uses the occurrence of transitions in the signal to help in maintaining synchronization. In such a system, it is important that transitions occur relatively frequently. If long strings of 0 or 1 bit values are sent, it is difficult for the receiver to remain in synchronization with the sender. Various schemes have been used to insert transitions into the transmitted data at intervals in the event that long strings of 0 or 1 bits occur in the data.

However, start-stop transmission is typically used with low data rates and when only a single data character at a time is transmitted. Under these conditions, start and stop bits are sent frequently enough so that lack of adequate transitions does not occur.

Delimiter Bits

In more advanced data transmission systems, signal patterns other than a 0 or a 1 bit are typically used to identify the beginning and end of data blocks being transmitted. These signal patterns are known as *delimiter bits,* or *delimiters*. For example, with Manchester encoding, values of 0 and 1 are both associated with a transition in signal level occurring at the midpoint of the bit time. Bit times in which a transition does not occur can represent delimiters that mark the beginning and the end of a data block, with no possibility of data bits being confused with delimiters. These delimiters can also be used to synchronize processing initially. Since Manchester encoding employs a signal transition for every data bit, it is easy for the receiver to maintain synchronization even when long strings of data are transmitted.

Synchronization Characters

Another approach to synchronization is to use a group of bits having a predefined bit configuration as a synchronization character. In this case, a data block is preceded by one or more of these synchronization characters. The receiving device looks for this pattern and, when it finds it, recognizes that data will follow. The receiving device uses the synchronization characters to synchronize its processing with that of the sender. The synchronization characters are discarded before the data is actually processed. Synchronization characters may also be inserted within a message, if needed for the receiver to maintain synchronization.

SUMMARY

Data signals are carried in a local area network by a physical transmission medium. Commonly used transmission media employed with local area networks include twisted-wire pairs, coaxial cable, and optical fiber. A number of physical transmission characteristics are concerned with the way a signal is transmitted across a physical medium.

Transmission can be baseband or broadband. In baseband transmission, the entire bandwidth is used to transmit a single digital signal. In broadband transmission, analog techniques are used whereby the available bandwidth is sliced up into a number of channels. For digital transmission, data is carried on the transmission medium in its original form. For analog transmission, data is superimposed on a carrier signal that is modulated by varying either its amplitude, its frequency, or its phase. Amplifiers and repeaters can be used to amplify or regenerate signals.

A variety of encoding schemes, such as Manchester encoding, can be used to encode data signals. Depending on the encoding scheme that is used, synchronization can be accomplished using start-stop bits, delimiters, or synchronization characters.

3 ACCESS CONTROL METHODS

A characteristic common to all local area networks is that multiple devices, typically called *stations,* must share access to a single physical transmission medium. Several methods can be employed to control the sharing of access to the transmission medium. One feature by which local area networks can be classified is the particular access control method used. Principal issues for the choice of an access control method include the network topology employed and whether control is centralized, random, or distributed. Let us examine the various topologies that networks can use.

NETWORK TOPOLOGIES   The topology of a network concerns the physical configuration of the devices and the cable that connects them. Three principle topologies are employed for local area networks: the *star,* the *bus,* and the *ring.*

Star Topology

A *star* configuration, shown in Fig. 3.1, features a central controller, to which all nodes are directly connected. All transmissions from one station to another pass through the central controller, which is responsible for managing and controlling all communication.

Often the central controller acts as a switching device. When one node wishes to communicate with another node, the central controller, in this case a switch, establishes a circuit, or dedicated path, between the two nodes that wish to communicate. One such path is represented by the dotted line in Fig. 3.1. Once a circuit is established, data can be exchanged between the two nodes as if they were linked by a dedicated point-to-point link. The star topology has been employed for many years in dial-up telephone systems, in which individual

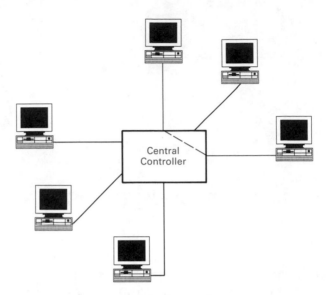

Figure 3.1   Star topology

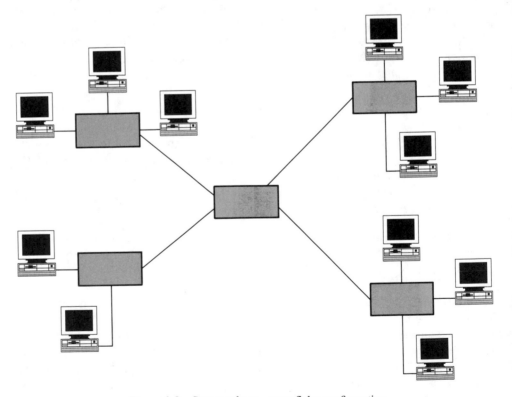

Figure 3.2   Star topology—snowflake configuration

telephone sets are the nodes and a *private branch exchange* (PBX) acts as the central controller.

Figure 3.2 illustrates a more complex version of the star topology, known as a snowflake configuration. Here a station in the basic star configuration is a star itself, with subsidiary stations attached to it.

Bus Topology

In the *bus* topology, shown in Fig. 3.3, each station is directly attached to a common communication channel. Signals that are transmitted over the channel take the form of messages. As each message passes along the channel, each station receives it. Each station then determines, based on an address contained in the message, whether to accept and process the message or simply to ignore it.

A more complex form of the bus topology, known as a *tree,* is shown in Fig. 3.4. In the tree topology, the common communication channel takes the form of a cable with multiple branches and the stations attached like leaves to the branches. In the tree structure, all stations still receive all transmissions.

Ring Topology

The *ring* topology is illustrated in Fig. 3.5. Here the cable forms a loop, with stations attached at intervals around the loop. Signals that are transmitted around the ring take the form of messages. Messages are received by each station in turn. As with the bus topology, a station determines, on the basis of an address contained in the message, whether to accept and process a given message. However, after receiving a message, each station acts as a repeater, retransmitting the message at its original signal strength. Figure 3.6 shows a more complex form of ring topology in which multiple rings are interconnected.

TRANSMISSION CONTROL

The various access control methods can be characterized by where in the network the transmission control

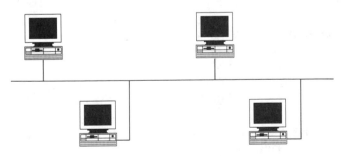

Figure 3.3 Bus topology

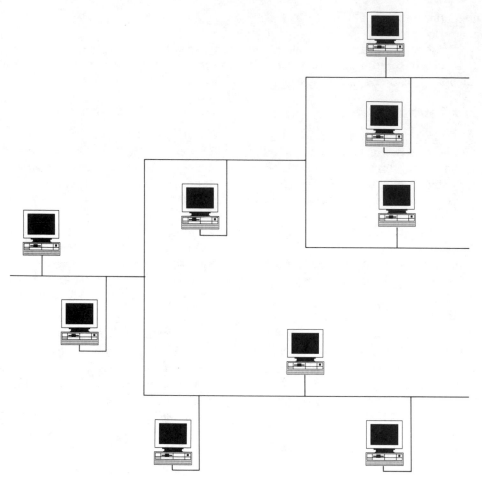

Figure 3.4   Tree topology

function is performed. An access control method can use the following forms
of transmission control:

- **Random Control.** With *random control,* any station can transmit, and specific
  permission is not required. A station may check the medium to see if it is free
  before beginning to transmit.

- **Distributed Control.** With *distributed control,* only one station at a time has
  the right to transmit, and that right is passed from station to station.

- **Centralized Control.** With *centralized control,* one station controls the entire
  network, and other stations must receive permission from the controlling station
  in order to transmit.

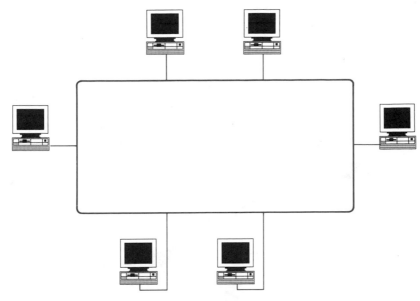

Figure 3.5 Ring topology

We will examine each of these forms of transmission control. First, however, it is important to point out that there is no one *best* method for handling transmission control. Rather, the various methods each offer different advantages, and trade-offs must be made by the local area network implementer in choosing a particular form of transmission control. Here are some of the advantages centralized control may offer:

- Fewer problems in coordinating the activities of multiple stations
- More options in terms of prioritizing access or guaranteeing access to each station
- Less logic circuitry in individual stations, thus simplifying their interface to the network

But there may also be disadvantages, including higher risk of a failure affecting the entire network and reduced efficiency if the central control point becomes a bottleneck. The choice of an access method, like the choice of physical characteristics for the network, must be made on the basis of processing requirements.

Many access method control methods have been devised by the implementers of local area network products. They can be categorized according to whether control of access to the physical medium is *random, distributed,* or *centralized*. We shall discuss the following methods:

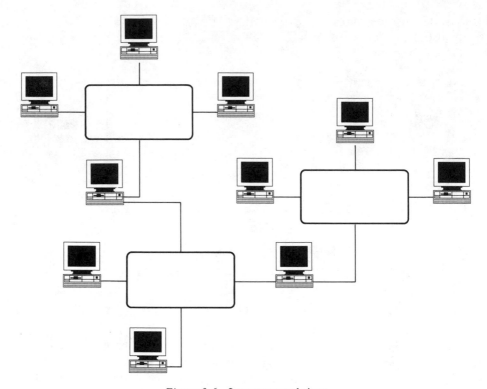

Figure 3.6   Interconnected rings

Random Transmission Control

- Carrier sense multiple access with collision detection (CSMA/CD)
- Slotted ring
- Register insertion

Distributed Transmission Control

- Token passing: token ring, token bus
- Carrier sense multiple access with collision avoidance (CSMA/CA)

Centralized Control

- Polling
- Circuit switching
- Time-division multiple access (TDMA)

Of these techniques, three are of primary importance because they are the basis of the IEEE standards for local area networking and hence the basis for most LAN implementations:

- **Carrier Sense Multiple Access with Collision Detection (CSMA/CD).** This is the protocol used by Ethernet.

- **Token Ring.** This is the basis for IBM's predominant local area networking architecture.

- **Token Bus.** This is the basis for General Motors' MAP architecture.

In subsequent chapters we discuss these three access control methods, and the architectures that use them, in detail.

Much mathematical analysis has been done of the various possible types of access control to determine which are the most efficient. The optimum choice depends on factors such as the number of stations served, message lengths and message length distribution, the speed of the channel, and the ratio of propagation time to message transmission time.

We will discuss first the access control methods that employ a random transmission control technique.

RANDOM TRANSMISSION CONTROL

With access control methods that control access to the physical transmission medium in a *random* fashion, any station is allowed to transmit whenever the transmission medium is available. The three access control methods discussed next that employ random control are *carrier sense multiple access with collision detection* (CSMA/CD), *register insertion,* and *slotted ring.*

Carrier Sense Multiple Access with Collision Detection (CSMA/CD)

The CSMA/CD access method has been in use for a number of years and is the most commonly used access method for local area networks that employ a bus or tree topology. It is used as the access control method in Ethernet and is one of the methods defined in the local area network standards developed by the IEEE, which we begin discussing in Chapter 5. CSMA/CD and Ethernet are discussed more fully in Chapters 6 and 20.

Under CSMA/CD, before a station transmits, it first "listens" to the transmission medium to determine whether or not another station is currently transmitting a message. If the transmission medium is "quiet," that is, if no other station is transmitting, the station sends its message. The term *carrier sense* indicates that a station listens before it transmits.

When a message is transmitted, it travels to all other stations on the network. As the message arrives, each receiving station examines the address attached to the message. If the address applies to that station, the station receives and processes the message.

With CSMA/CD, it occasionally happens that two (or more) stations send their messages simultaneously, resulting in a garbled transmission known as a *collision*. All stations on the network, including the transmitting stations, continually listen to the transmission medium and are able to detect a collision. Receiving stations ignore the garbled transmission, and the transmitting stations immediately stop transmitting as soon as they detect the collision.

Following a collision, each transmitting station waits for a period of time and then attempts to transmit again. If all transmitting stations were to wait the same amount of time before retransmitting, they would be very likely to have another collision. To avoid this, each station first generates a random number that determines how long it should wait before retransmitting after a particular collision. The algorithm used to calculate the wait time is designed to minimize the time spent waiting when traffic is light and to minimize the occurrence of successive collisions when traffic is heavy.

A key advantage of the CSMA/CD method is that access to the physical medium is typically very fast as long as traffic is not heavy, since a station can transmit anytime the carrier is idle. However, under heavier traffic loads, the number of collisions increases, and the time spent responding to collisions and retransmitting may cause performance to deteriorate.

As mentioned earlier, the CSMA/CD technique is employed with bus- or tree-structured networks, where a message that a station transmits reaches all other stations virtually simultaneously. The other two access control techniques that use random control are better suited to a network that uses a ring topology.

Slotted Ring

With the slotted-ring technique, the various stations on the ring continuously send several fixed-length transmissions, called *slots,* from one station to the next around the ring. Each slot has a marker at the beginning that indicates whether the slot is empty or contains data. If a station has a message to transmit, it waits for an empty slot, changes the marker, inserts the destination address and as much of the message as will fit in the slot, and transmits the slot to the next station on the ring. When a slot containing data is received by a station, the station checks the destination address to see if it should process this message. If so, the station accepts the data and then retransmits it to the next station on the ring. When the message returns to the original sender, the sender removes the message from the ring and transmits an empty slot. With this method, a station cannot transmit at any time; it must wait until it receives an empty slot.

As we have seen, it is the responsibility of the sending station to mark a slot as empty. However, transmission errors may affect a slot such that the sending station no longer recognizes a message, or a station failure may make it unable to perform its job. To prevent problems like these from causing a slot to remain marked as full indefinitely, one of the stations on the ring is designated as a monitor and watches for a slot that has traversed the entire ring and has not been reset properly.

The slotted-ring technique has the advantage of simplicity, thus making the interface required for each station relatively simple, and it works well for short messages. For messages that require multiple slots to transmit, the need for addressing and control information in each slot can drive overhead up and make the method less efficient than it is for short messages.

Register Insertion

The *register insertion* method is another technique used with the ring topology. Each station has a shift register equal in size to the maximum-length data unit that is used on the network. It also has a buffer of the same size that is used for storing a data unit that it wishes to send. The use of these registers is illustrated in Figs. 3.7 and 3.8.

In Fig. 3.7, a data unit is received from the ring and sent on to the next station. The input pointer initially points to the rightmost position in the shift register. As each bit in the data unit is received, it is stored in the shift register, and the input pointer moves to the left. When enough bits have been received to identify the destination address, the station determines if it needs to process this data unit. If not, the station begins sending bits to the next station on the ring. The rightmost bit is sent, and the other bits are shifted one to the right. The next incoming bit then is inserted in the spot indicated by the input pointer, which now remains stationary. When the end of the data unit is reached, bits continue to shift right, and the input pointer moves with them.

If, however, the station recognizes the address in the data unit as its own, the station accepts the data unit for processing. The data unit may be erased from the shift register at this point and thus removed from the ring, or it may be retransmitted. Retransmission may be necessary if the message is to be pro-

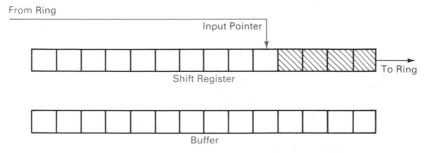

Figure 3.7 Receiving and transmitting a packet from the ring

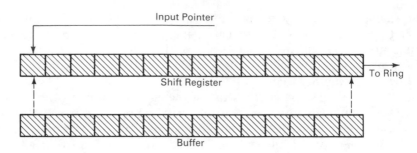

Figure 3.8 Sending a new packet to the ring

cessed by more than one station or if the sending station is responsible for removing it from the ring.

Figure 3.8 illustrates the process used when a station has a data unit to transmit. When the station's shift register is empty, the contents of the station's buffer are transferred in parallel to the shift register. Bits are then shifted out to the ring, just as if a data unit had been received from the ring. When a data unit is of less than the maximum size, it can be placed in the shift register before the shift register is completely empty. The transmitting station waits until the shift register has a large enough empty portion following the end of a data unit that it is already sending. The new data unit then shifts out and is transmitted following the data unit just received.

With register insertion, a station is allowed to transmit whenever its shift register has enough empty space for the message. This method is very efficient in its use of the transmission medium, since a station may transmit whenever the ring is idle at its location. However, since there may be several messages on the ring, a data unit must be positively identified before it can be removed. With this technique, a transmission error that damages the address portion of a message can cause problems with message removal, and various techniques are used to handle this type of situation.

Now that we have examined some of the access control methods that use random transmission control, we will discuss access control methods that use distributed transmission control.

DISTRIBUTED TRANSMISSION CONTROL

With access control methods that use *distributed* transmission control, all stations on the network co-operate in performing the job of controlling access to the transmission medium. Two common access control methods use distributed techniques: *token passing* and *carrier sense multiple access with collision avoidance* (CSMA/CA).

Token Ring

With networks that employ a ring topology, the most commonly used access method is token passing, which involves the passing of a token from one station to the next along the ring. The IBM Token Ring Network, described in Chapters 8 and 15, uses this method.

With token passing, a small message, called a *token*, constantly circulates around the ring. If the token is marked as free, a station that receives it can transmit a message. It then transmits the message, marks the token as busy, and appends the token to the message. The message, with the attached busy token, circulates around the ring, passing from station to station. Each station that is to receive it copies it as it comes past and sets bits in it indicating whether or not it has been received properly. When the message reaches the station that originally sent it, that station changes the token back to a free token and removes the message. The free token then circulates around the ring again until another station wishes to transmit.

As with the slotted-ring and register insertion techniques, error conditions might prevent a sending station from recognizing and being able to remove its message when it comes back around. To handle this, one of the stations on the ring is designated as a monitor and it is responsible for detecting a busy token that is not being reset properly. Other stations are designated as passive monitors. They are responsible for monitoring the status of the active monitor, taking over its role if the active monitor is unable to function.

The token ring approach has the advantage of allowing greater control over transmission among the stations on the ring. Each station is always guaranteed a chance to transmit a message within some predetermined period of time. The method allows for different priorities to be assigned to stations on the ring, and high-priority stations can be given the opportunity to transmit before lower-priority stations. The optional priority system used with the token ring access method is discussed in detail in Chapter 8. A station can also be allowed to send multiple messages while it has the token. In this case, there is usually a time limit on how long a station can continue transmitting messages. The principal disadvantage with the token ring technique is the complexity and overhead involved in token processing and monitoring.

Token Bus

Token passing can also be used on a network that has a bus or tree topology. This is known as the *token bus* method. This method is more commonly used in factory floor local area networks, where process control and robotics devices are interconnected. The token bus method is the basis of General Motors' MAP protocol, described in Chapters 7 and 10.

With this method, a short message or token is transmitted from one station to the next. When a station receives the token, it is allowed to transmit messages until a maximum amount of time has been reached. It then transmits the token to the next station. If it has no messages to transmit, the token is passed on immediately.

With token bus, stations have a *physical* bus or tree topology but a *logical* ring topology as far as passing of the token is concerned. This is illustrated in Fig. 3.9. Physically, the stations are attached to the transmission medium in a linear sequence of *A, B, C, D,* and *E*. The token, however, is passed in the sequence shown by the dashed line. It goes from *A* to *C* to *D* to *E* to *B* and back to *A,* forming a logical ring. The logical ring is implemented on the basis of descending station address values. The token is always passed to the station with the next lowest address until the station with the lowest address on the network receives it. The token is then passed to the station with the highest network address, and the cycle begins again.

As with the token ring technique, the token bus method can provide for a high degree of control over each station's access to the transmission medium. Also as with token ring, there is additional complexity. Removing messages from the network is not a problem because messages do not circulate from station to station as they do in a physical ring. However, monitoring is required to detect problems with the token, including loss, duplication, or monopolization by one station. Also, as stations are added to or removed from the network, adjustments must be made to the logical sequence of token passing to include or remove these stations.

Carrier Sense Multiple Access with Collision Avoidance (CSMA/CA)

Another distributed control method is known as *carrier sense multiple access with collision avoidance* (CSMA/CA). With CSMA/CA, each station "listens" to the carrier while a transmission is in progress. After the transmission ends, each station waits for a specified period of time, based on its position in a

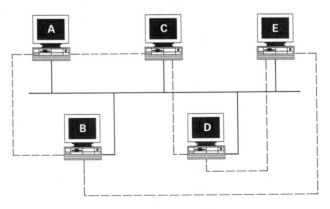

Figure 3.9 Token bus

logical list of stations. If no other station has started transmitting by the time a particular station's waiting time has elapsed, it may begin transmission.

Different methods are used to handle the situation that can occur when the end of the allotted time is reached and no station has a message to send. In one approach, the highest-priority station (highest in the list) sends a dummy data unit, which then triggers another time period when stations have an opportunity to transmit. Another approach allows the stations to enter a free-for-all mode, where any station can transmit, and collision detection techniques are employed to handle conflicting transmissions.

Variations also relate to prioritization. With one variation, the first transmission slot is reserved for the station that has just received a message. This allows the station to send a response and the two stations to maintain an efficient dialog. In another variation, a station that has just transmitted must wait until all the other stations have had an opportunity to transmit before it can transmit again. This ensures that the stations lower in the list have an opportunity to transmit.

CENTRALIZED CONTROL

Although centralized control techniques are more commonly associated with wide area networks than with local area networks, there are some LANs in which control is *centralized* in a single network device. The access control methods that employ a centralized approach are *polling, circuit switching,* and *time-division multiple access* (TDMA).

Polling

One centralized way of controlling access to the transmission medium is through *polling*. With polling, one station is designated the *master* station; all other stations are *secondary* stations. The master station sends a message to each of the secondary stations in turn, notifying the station that it has the opportunity to transmit. If the polled secondary station has a message to transmit, it sends the message to the master station, which in turn relays it to the station or stations indicated by the message's destination address. If a polled station has no message to transmit, it responds negatively to the poll. When the master station completes its processing with one station, it consults a polling list to determine the next secondary station to poll.

The polling method allows for flexibility of control, since a station can be permitted to send a number of messages before the next station is polled. Also, priorities can be assigned to stations, with higher-priority stations being polled more frequently than lower-priority stations. Secondary stations have very simple requirements, and their interface to the network can be implemented more simply and for less cost. However, the master station is more complex, and if the master station fails, the entire network fails. Also, the fact that messages may need to be sent twice, first to the master station and then on to the receiving station, can increase transmission delays. This method is most commonly used with a star topology, where the central station is the master station and consists of a more powerful processor than the secondary stations.

Circuit Switching

Another centralized control technique, which can be used with a star-structured network, is *circuit switching*. This technique is used by private branch exchanges (PBX) for conventional telephone systems and hence is sometimes not classed as a LAN technique. With circuit switching, a station wishing to begin transmitting requests the establishment of a connection, or *circuit,* with another station. The central controller station determines if the connection can be made. If so, the sending and receiving stations are physically connected. They can then transmit messages back and forth, and the path or circuit they are using remains dedicated to their use. When the two stations finish their dialog, they are disconnected, and the circuit is released.

The central controller is typically able to support multiple circuits between pairs of stations that can be used simultaneously. This is illustrated in Fig. 3.10 by the dashed lines between stations B and F and between stations D and E. If the controller uses digital techniques, there are mechanisms that allow a large

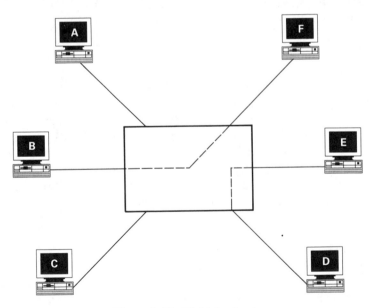

Figure 3.10   Multiple circuits

number of circuits to share access to the transmission facilities managed by the controller. Transmission access is switched among the different circuits at very high speed relative to the data transmission rates, giving each circuit the appearance of having continuous access.

With circuit switching, as with polling, stations other than the central controller have simpler requirements and can be implemented less expensively. However, there can be higher overhead associated with the establishment and disconnection of circuits and the risk of entire network failure if the central controller fails.

Time-Division Multiple Access (TDMA)

Time-division multiple access (TDMA) is a centralized control method that can be used with a bus-structured network. With the TDMA technique, each station on the bus has a specific time slot during which only it can transmit. If a station has nothing to transmit during its time slot, that transmission time goes unused.

The cycle is started by a master station sending out a short timing message. Each station synchronizes itself with the master station and then transmits when its time interval arrives. If a new station is added to the network, the master station lengthens the total time interval, assigns the new station the time interval at the end of the cycle, and then waits that much longer before sending out the next timing message.

Prioritization can be implemented by assigning different priorities to different stations and inserting a priority value in the timing message. Only stations with a priority equal to or higher than the priority value contained in the timing message participate in the sequence of transmissions following that timing message.

The TDMA technique does allow for centralized control over access to the transmission medium. However, large amounts of transmission capacity may go unused if only a few stations have messages to transmit. Also, a station that miscalculates the timing interval because of some malfunction may cause interference with another station's transmission. The TDMA method is also vulnerable to failure on the part of the master station and may require alternate master stations that can be activated if the current master fails.

SUMMARY

The three principal topologies used for local area networks are bus, ring, and star. Control of access to the transmission medium can be random, distributed, or centralized. Carrier sense multiple access with collision detection (CSMA/CD) uses random control on a bus- or tree-structured network. The slotted-ring and register insertion methods use random control on a ring-structured network. Token ring uses token passing, a form of distributed control, on a network that has a ring topology. Token bus is a distributed-control method that uses token passing on a bus-structured network. Polling and circuit switching provide centralized control on networks that have a star topology. Time-division multiple access (TDMA) provides centralized control on bus-structured networks.

4 NETWORK ARCHITECTURES

Part of the power of local area networks is their ability to support a wide variety of devices. Supporting a wide variety of devices, however, can present substantial compatibility problems. For varying devices to be linked together, the hardware and software of these devices need to be compatible, or else complex interfaces have to be built for meaningful communication to take place. To facilitate this compatibility, *network architectures* are being developed that allow complex networks to be built using a variety of equipment.

GOALS OF A NETWORK ARCHITECTURE

A network architecture defines protocols, message formats, and standards to which machines and software packages must conform to achieve given goals. When new products are created within the architecture, they will be compatible—they can be employed in networks and interconnected with existing devices and software.

The goals and standards of a network architecture are important to both users and vendors. The architecture must provide users with a variety of choices in the configuration of networks, and it must allow them to change a configuration with relative ease as their systems evolve. It should provide the precise coordination between intelligent machines required if the advantages of local area networks are to be realized.

Architectures should permit mass production of hardware or software building blocks that can be used in a variety of networks. They also provide standards and definitions that allow development laboratories to create new devices and software that will be compatible with existing systems. These new products can then be integrated into existing networks without the need for costly interfaces and program modifications.

THE NATURE OF ARCHITECTURE

Although architectures provide rules for the development of products, these rules can change. This is because the term *architecture* in the computer industry often implies an overall scheme or plan that has not necessarily been fully implemented. It is the goal toward which its implementers strive. Thus architectures are bound to evolve and change as new hardware, software, and techniques are developed.

The term *architecture* is often used to describe database management systems, operating systems, and other highly complex software-and-hardware mechanisms. It is a particularly important concept in describing local area networks because in these networks so many potentially incompatible hardware devices and software packages must fit together to form an easily used and easily modified whole.

For many complex systems, an *architectural definition* states the eventual requirements. For database systems, for example, CODASYL (the committee that developed COBOL) defined a long-range database architecture and specified in great detail some of the protocols involved in database systems. This is contrasted with the relational database architecture. As with network architectures, individual implementations of CODASYL-type or relational-type database management systems often provide only some of the functions defined in the complete architecture. The architecture remains independent of any particular hardware and software products used to implement it.

A good architecture ought to relate primarily to the needs of the users rather than to enthusiasms for particular techniques. A well-architected house is one that reflects the desired life style of its owners, not one designed to exploit a building technique that is currently in vogue. Fred Brooks, author of *The Mythical Man-Month*, defined architecture in a way that makes a clear distinction between architecture and engineering:

> Computer architecture, like other architecture, is the art of determining the needs of the user of a structure and then designing to meet those needs as effectively as possible within economic and technological constraints. Architecture must include engineering considerations, so that the design will be economical and feasible; but the emphasis in architecture is upon the needs of the user, whereas in engineering the emphasis is upon the needs of the fabricator.

DEVELOPERS OF ARCHITECTURES

Because of the importance of network architectures, several types of organizations have gotten involved in developing standards, including standards organizations, common carriers, and computer manufacturers. Architectures designed by these organizations have many characteristics in common. They all define the rules of a network and how the components of a network can interact. But there are also differences.

Standards Organizations

Standards organizations, by their very nature, have as their primary purpose the development of standards. However, a standards organization is empowered only to describe or recommend an architecture. It cannot implement the architecture or build the products it describes. Implementation is the responsibility of vendors and user organizations.

The *Consultative Committee on International Telegraphy and Telephony* (CCITT) is an international standards organization based in Geneva, Switzerland. It has developed standards for various complex aspects of telephone transmission and data transmission. Data communication standards are described in a series of recommendations with names like X.3, X.25, X.28, and X.29. The *International Standards Organization* (ISO), also based in Geneva, has a seven-layer "reference model" for computer networking called the Open Systems Interconnect (OSI) architecture. This, in cooperation with the CCITT, is the basis for evolving standards for computer networking. As mentioned in Chapter 1, The *Institute of Electrical and Electronics Engineers* (IEEE) has been active in the development of network standards. The IEEE Computer Society Local Network Committee has focused on standards related to local area networks and has produced a set of proposed LAN standards known as IEEE Project 802. The IEEE Project 802 standards will be covered in detail in Part II of this book.

Common Carriers

A common carrier, such as AT&T, MCI, or Western Union, is a company that furnishes communications services to the general public. (In many countries, providers of telecommunications facilities are referred to by other names, such as the postal, telegraph, and telephone administrations, or PTTs, in many European countries; in this book, we will refer to all such organizations as *common carriers*.) For communication between data processing machines, common carriers employ protocols devised by standards organizations like the CCITT. Common carriers also offer advanced features like electronic mail that go far beyond simply transporting raw data back and forth between user machines.

A common carrier data network is basically the data processing equivalent of the telephone network. It allows machines to send data to one another and provides a standard set of features. Common carrier networks may be used when multiple local area networks, or local and wide area networks, are interlinked.

Computer Manufacturers

Computer manufacturers are active in the development of network architectures. These architectures are specifically designed for corporate data processing systems and can be installed in configurations designed to meet the user's specific needs.

Although computer network architectures facilitate interconnectability among the products of one manufacturer, they may make it difficult to interconnect products of different manufacturers. The protocols used within the architecture are highly complex and often different from one manufacturer to another. Many manufacturers are developing architectures that are compatible with the standards developed by standards organizations, such as ISO, CCITT, and IEEE, or are at least providing interfaces to networks that conform to these standards. The standards, however, such as ISO's OSI standards, are still evolving and incomplete, so the proprietary architectures of manufacturers such as IBM (with SNA) and DEC (with DECnet) are very important and are the basis for most corporate networks.

CHARACTERISTICS OF NETWORK ARCHITECTURES
The various network architectures that have been developed do share some characteristics. One that they all have in common is a similar set of high-level objectives. The high-level objectives that most network architectures are designed to achieve are listed in Box 4.1. They may seem simple and straightforward, but designing an architecture that achieves all of them is both difficult and complex. Striving to meet these objectives has led to the development of architectures that support communications systems that are

BOX 4.1   High-level objectives of network architectures

- **Connectivity.** Permit diverse hardware and software products to be connected to form a unified networking system.
- **Modularity.** Permit the use of a relatively small set of mass-produced general-purpose building blocks in a wide diversity of network devices.
- **Ease of Implementation.** Provide a general solution to network communication that can be easily installed in a variety of configurations to meet the needs of all types of users.
- **Ease of Use.** Provide communication facilities to network users in a way that frees them from concerns about or knowledge of network structure or implementation.
- **Reliability.** Provide appropriate error detection and correction facilities.
- **Ease of Modification.** Permit the network to evolve and be easily modified as user needs change or new technologies become available.

highly modular, can be installed without requiring significant investment of technical expertise or programming on the part of the user, and can be modified without requiring changes to the application systems that make use of the systems.

Another characteristic common to the different architectures is the use of a layered approach. A network architecture encompasses a wide range of functions that must be performed. These functions are organized into groups, which are then allocated to various *functional layers*. A given layer is responsible for performing a specific set of *functions* and for providing a specific set of *services*.

A network architecture can, then, be defined in terms of the services provided by each layer and the interfaces between layers. *Protocols* define the services offered across a layer interface and the rules that are followed in the processing performed as part of a service. *Data formats* for the data exchanged across an interface are also defined as part of the architecture.

Two types of interfaces are addressed as part of a network architecture, as illustrated in Fig. 4.1. One set of interfaces exists between the layers in a given station, or *network node*. These interfaces are represented by the solid vertical arrows in the figure. When data is being processed in a node, it passes up or down from one layer to the next. When a message is being sent by a network node, it starts at the highest layer in that node and moves successively down to the lowest layer in that node, which then transmits it across the physical transmission medium. When a message is received by a network node, it passes from the lowest layer up to the highest. The various protocols and data formats describe the processing to be performed by each layer.

The second set of interfaces exists between comparable layers in different nodes. These interfaces are represented by the horizontal dashed arrows in Fig. 4.1. Here the protocols and data formats are used to coordinate the processing to be performed by any given layer in the sending and receiving nodes.

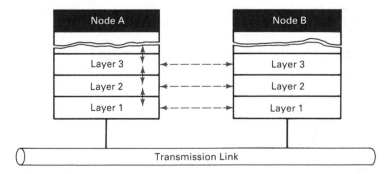

Figure 4.1 A network architecture defines two different types of interface between layers.

The layered approach offers two key advantages. The first is *ease of modification*. If, for example, a new technology became available to use in layer 1, it could be incorporated without affecting any other layers, as long as the interfaces to layer 2 are maintained unchanged. The second advantage is *diversity*. Node A and node B can be implemented using completely different hardware and software, as long as both nodes use the same protocols and data formats. This makes it easier to incorporate diverse hardware and software products in the same network.

We will next discuss three network architectures that are extremely important in today's data processing environment and have much influence over the way in which LANs are being developed and implemented: The OSI model, IBM's SNA, and the IEEE Project 802.

THE OSI MODEL

As mentioned earlier, ISO has been very active in developing a generalized model of system interconnection, known as the *Reference Model of Open Systems Interconnection* (OSI model). The OSI model has also been adopted by the CCITT and is used to coordinate all of its standards efforts. The primary purpose of the OSI model is to provide a basis for coordinating development of standards that relate to the flexible interconnection of systems using data communications facilities. In OSI terminology, a *system* is defined as follows:

> A set of one or more computers and the associated software, peripherals, terminals, human operators, physical processes, transfer means, etc., that forms an autonomous whole capable of performing information processing and/or information transfer.

The OSI model is concerned with the *interconnection* between systems—the way they exchange information—and not with the internal *functions* that are performed by a given system. The OSI model provides a generalized view of a layered architecture. With the broad definition that has been given to the term *system,* the architecture can apply to a very simple system, such as the connection of a terminal to a computer, or to a very complex system, such as the interconnection of two separate computer networks. It can also be used as a model for a network architecture; as we will see, the OSI model is particularly important to the technology of local area networks, and many LAN architectures are in conformance with it. The development of the OSI model is still in progress. For some layers, specific standards have been defined in support of the model; for other layers, standards still need to be developed.

The OSI model uses a layered approach, where sets of functions have been allocated to different layers. Box 4.2 shows the seven OSI layers and describes the general functions performed by each.

BOX 4.2 Layers of the OSI model

Application
Presentation
Session
Transport
Network
Data Link
Physical

- **Physical Layer.** The *physical* layer is responsible for the transmission of bit streams across a particular physical transmission medium. It involves a connection between two machines that allows electrical signals to be exchanged between them.

- **Data Link Layer.** The *data link* layer is responsible for providing reliable data transmission from one node to another and for shielding higher layers from any concerns about the physical transmission medium. It is concerned with the error-free transmission of frames of data.

- **Network Layer.** The *network* layer is concerned with routing data from one network node to another. It is responsible for establishing, maintaining, and terminating the network connection between two users and for transferring data along that connection. There can be only one network connection between two given users, although there can be many possible routes from which to choose when the particular connection is established.

- **Transport Layer.** The *transport* layer is responsible for providing data transfer between two users at an agreed on level of quality. When a connection is established between two users, the transport layer is responsible for selecting a particular class of service to be used, for monitoring transmissions to ensure the appropriate service quality is maintained, and for notifying the users if it is not.

- **Session Layer.** The *session* layer focuses on providing services used to organize and synchronize the dialog that takes place between users and to manage the data exchange. A primary concern of the session layer is controlling when users can send and receive, based on whether they can send and receive concurrently or alternately.

- **Presentation Layer.** The *presentation* layer is responsible for the presentation of information in a way that is meaningful to the network users. This may include character code translation, data conversion, or data compression and expansion.

(Continued)

BOX 4.2   *(Continued)*

• **Application Layer.** The *application* layer provides a means for application processes to access the system interconnection facilities in order to exchange information. This includes services used to establish and terminate the connections between users and to monitor and manage the systems being interconnected and the various resources they employ.

IBM'S SNA

A vendor-developed network architecture in widespread use is IBM's *Systems Network Architecture* (SNA). SNA is a mainframe-oriented network architecture that also uses a layered approach. The layers defined as part of SNA are shown and described in Box 4.3. Generally, the services included as part of the SNA architecture are similar to those defined in the OSI model. However, there are some differences in the way that the services are organized and grouped into layers, so there is not an exact one-to-one correspondence between the layers in the two architectures.

BOX 4.3   SNA layers

Transaction Services
Presentation Services
Data Flow Control
Transmission Control
Path Control
Data Link Control
Physical Control

• **Physical Control Layer.** *Physical control* handles the transmission of bits over a physical circuit. Although the physical control layer is addressed in the architecture, SNA does not actually define specific protocols for this layer. Rather, the SNA architecture assumes the use of various existing international standards at this level.

BOX 4.3   *(Continued)*

- **Data Link Control Layer.** *Data link control* is responsible for the transmission of data between two nodes over a particular physical link. A primary function of this layer is to detect and recover from transmission errors.

- **Path Control Layer.** *Path control* is concerned with routing data from one node to the next in the path that a message takes through the network. This path often crosses through several nodes as a message moves from the source node to its destination.

- **Transmission Control Layer.** *Transmission control* keeps track of the status of connections, or sessions, between network users, controls the pacing of data flow within a session, and sees that the units of data that make up a message are sent and received in the proper sequence. This layer also provides an optional data encryption/decryption facility.

- **Data Flow Control Layer.** *Data flow control* is concerned with the overall integrity of the flow of data during a session between two network users. This can involve determining the mode of sending and receiving, managing groups of related messages, or determining the type of response mode to use.

- **Presentation Services Layer.** *Presentation services* is responsible for formatting data for different presentation media used in a session. This can involve converting messages from one character code to another and formatting data for display on various types of devices.

- **Transaction Services Layer.** *Transaction services* provides application services to end users of the network. These application services include operator control over sessions, document distribution and interchange, and distributed data access.

No local area networks conform completely to the SNA architecture. However, SNA is important to LAN technology because in many situations, a local area network must connect to, and be made a logical part of, an SNA mainframe network.

IEEE PROJECT 802   As discussed in Chapter 1, the IEEE has undertaken a major role in developing standards for local area networks. IEEE Project 802 has defined a flexible network architecture oriented specifically to the implementation of local area networks. The approach the IEEE has taken in the definition of this LAN architecture is in complete conformance with the OSI model; however, IEEE Project 802 addresses only the lowest two layers, the physical and data link layers. The functions performed by higher-level layers in a local area network is left up to the individual LAN implementers and, in many cases, to the users of the network. Figure 4.2 illustrates the relationships between the OSI, SNA, and IEEE Project 802 architectures.

Data Link Layer

The data link layer is responsible for transmission of data from one network node to another. In the OSI model, a protocol known as *High-Level Data Link Control* (HDLC) has been defined that describes the operation and interfaces of this layer. In the SNA architecture, a subset of HDLC known as *Synchronous Data Link Control* (SDLC) is employed. Local area networks use different forms of link control.

In the IEEE 802 architecture, the data link layer is divided into the following two sublayers:

- **Logical Link Control.** This sublayer is responsible for medium-independent data link functions. It allows the network layer above to access the services of the local area network without regard to how the network is implemented.

- **Media Access Control.** This sublayer is concerned with the access control method that determines how use of the physical transmission medium is controlled.

Physical Layer

As with the OSI model, the lowest layer in the IEEE model is concerned with the physical transmission of signals across a transmission medium. It is concerned with the types of cabling and with the plugs and connectors. Since the

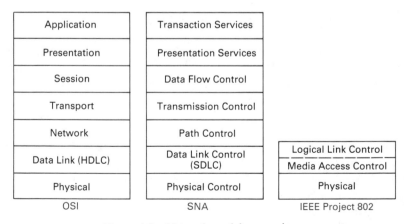

Figure 4.2   Network model comparison

IEEE model addresses local area networks, the transmission medium is assumed to be some form of electrical or fiber-optic cable; the architecture does not address the complex transmission methods typically employed by common carriers for long-distance signal transmission.

A FAMILY OF STANDARDS

Early in its work on the development of local area network standards, IEEE Project 802 determined that it would not be able to develop a LAN architecture that documented a single standard to meet the needs of all LAN requirements. In recognition of this, the project has taken the approach of developing sets, or families, of standards. This was done in the hope of still encouraging compatibility within a given set of standards while allowing the different sets of standards to meet the widely varying needs of different types of users.

Box 4.4 illustrates the families of standards currently being addressed by

BOX 4.4   IEEE Project 802 layers and sublayers

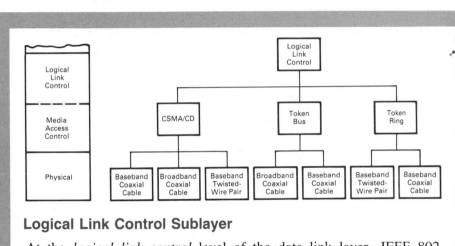

Logical Link Control Sublayer

At the *logical link control* level of the data link layer, IEEE 802 defines a single standard; the standard at this level of the architecture is a common element in all the IEEE 802 standards. This layer shields the higher level layers from concerns with the specific LAN implementation. The logical link control sublayer initiates control signal interchange, organizes data flow, interprets commands, generates responses, and carries out error control and recovery functions.

(Continued)

BOX 4.4 *(Continued)*

Media Access Control Sublayer

Any local area network must support multiple devices that all contend for access to a single physical transmission medium. The standard defining the functions of the *media access control* sublayer of the data link layer defines the way in which this sharing of access is managed. Many access control methods can be used at this level in a LAN implementation. Of these, IEEE Project 802 chose the CSMA/CD, token bus, and token ring access control methods for standardization.

The media access control sublayer is primarily concerned with defining the rules that must be followed for stations to be able to share the transmission medium. Four functions make up a media access control sublayer standard:

- **Medium Access Management.** The rules or procedures used by network stations to control the sharing of the transmission medium.

- **Framing.** The addition of header and trailer information necessary to identify the beginning and end of a message, to synchronize sender and receiver, to route the message, and to provide for error detection.

- **Addressing.** The determination of the appropriate network addresses to use to identify the devices involved in sending and receiving a message.

- **Error Detection.** The checking done to ensure that a message has been transmitted and received correctly.

Physical Layer

IEEE Project 802 has standardized on three physical media that can be used at the physical layer of the architecture: *twisted-wire pairs, coaxial cable,* and *fiber-optic cable.* The physical standard includes such information as the type of cable, the type of transmission, the encoding method, and the data rate.

The physical layer is responsible for establishing, maintaining, and releasing physical connections between two pieces of equipment and for transmitting bits over the transmission medium. This includes encoding the data into the proper form for transmission, generating the signal, and controlling the timing of the devices so that they are synchronized with the signal being transmitted and received.

IEEE Project 802. It also introduces the functions of the three layers and sub-layers defined by the architecture. Each of the four currently defined IEEE 802 standards is described in Part II of this book.

SUMMARY

A network architecture defines protocols, message formats, and standards to which products must conform in order to connect properly with the network. Architectures are developed by standards organizations, common carriers, and computer and network vendors. Network architectures use a layered approach, whereby functions are organized into groups and assigned to specific functional layers in the architecture. Network architectures define the interfaces between layers in a given network node and within the same layer in two different nodes.

OSI provides a generalized model of system interconnection. It encompasses seven layers: application, presentation, session, transport, network, data link, and physical. IEEE Project 802 has developed a set of standards for local area networks. These standards specify in detail protocols and data formats for the physical and data link layers. In the IEEE approach, the data link layer is divided into two sublayers: logical link control and media access control. IEEE Project 802 documents families of standards that define the functions performed by the three layers and sublayers described by the architecture.

PART **II** IEEE PROJECT 802 ARCHITECTURE

5 IEEE 802.2: LOGICAL LINK CONTROL

The logical link control (LLC) sublayer of the IEEE 802 architecture provides services to the layer above it in the same manner that a conventional data link protocol provides in a wide area network. If you are familiar with the bit-oriented protocols used in modern wide area computer networks, such as ISO's High-Level Data Link Control (HDLC) or IBM's Synchronous Data Link Control (SDLC), you will find many similarities in the services that are provided by the logical link control services.

SERVICE INTERFACE SPECIFICATIONS The standards for the LLC sublayer include specifications of the services that are provided at the interfaces between layers and sublayers of the IEEE 802 architecture. The IEEE 802 standard documents two *service interface specifications,* indicated by the vertical arrows in Fig. 5.1:

- **Network/LLC Service Interface Specification.** This service interface specification describes the services that define the interface between the LLC sublayer and software operating above the LLC sublayer that requests LLC services and thus services of the network as a whole. In a LAN implementation that conforms to the OSI reference model, the software layer *above* logical link control is the *network* layer.

- **LLC/MAC Service Interface Specification.** This service interface specification describes the services that define the interface between the LLC and the sublayer *below* it, the media access control (MAC) sublayer.

The IEEE LLC standard also defines the control information attached to the data units that are passed between the LLC sublayer and the MAC sublayer. This control information is added to the data unit by the LLC sublayer prior to

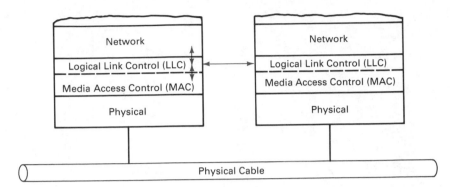

Figure 5.1   Logical link control specifications

transmission, used by the LLC for its processing functions, and then removed from the data unit before it is passed to a higher layer at the receiving station.

PEER-TO-PEER PROTOCOLS   The LLC standard also defines interactions that take place between the LLC sublayer at the transmitting station and the LLC sublayer at the receiving station. These interactions, indicated by the horizontal arrow in Fig. 5.1, are defined by a set of *peer-to-peer protocols,* which are defined as sequences of message exchanges that take place between the LLC sublayers in the two stations in transferring data and control information from one station to another.

We will examine both service interface specifications and peer-to-peer protocols in detail in this chapter. However, before we begin discussing service interface specifications, we must have a clear understanding of what IEEE 802 standards calls *service access points,* and we must define the data unit that the LLC sublayer works with.

SERVICE ACCESS POINTS   Logical link control has the overall responsibility for the exchange of data units between stations. In a local area network, the logical link required to exchange data units can be established between any pair of stations in the network. Also, in some LAN applications, a single station can be involved with data exchanges between any number of other stations.

To distinguish between different exchanges that involve the same station, the term *service access point* (SAP) is used to identify a particular element in a network station that is involved in a single data exchange. A service access point can be considered to be the address of a *port,* or *access point,* to a higher-level layer in that station.

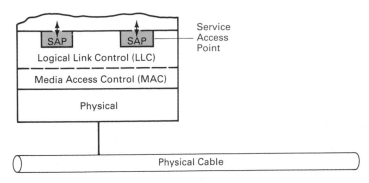

Figure 5.2   Service access points

Figure 5.2 illustrates a station that implements two SAPs. The device in the diagram can be using one SAP to send data units to one device and the other to send data units to another device. A device can also use several SAPs to process data units that are received from several sources. A service access point involved in *sending* a data unit is known as a *source service access point* (SSAP). A service access point involved in *receiving* a data unit is known as a *destination service access point* (DSAP).

LLC DATA UNIT

The data unit that is logically passed from the logical link control sublayer in the source station to the logical link control in the destination station is called an *LLC protocol data unit* (LLC PDU). In this chapter, when we use the term *data unit,* we mean the LLC PDU.

In transmitting a data unit from the source station to the destination station, the data unit is passed by the destination station from its logical link control layer down to its media access control layer. An LLC protocol data unit conforms to the basic format shown in Fig. 5.3.

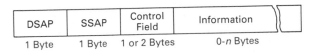

Figure 5.3   Logical link control protocol data unit format. DSAP = Destination Service Access Point; SSAP = Source Service Access Point.

COMMANDS AND RESPONSES

Some data units, called *commands,* are sent by the station that initiates an information exchange and are used to control message processing in the network; commands can also carry user data. Other data units, called *responses,* are sent in response to a command and are used as positive or negative acknowledgments; responses can also carry user data. Each data unit contains a control field that is used to identify the particular type of command or response that a data unit contains. The control field can be followed with information that is being sent as part of the command or response. In some cases, a data unit can consist only of control information and will not have an information field following the control field.

SERVICE ACCESS POINT ADDRESSES

A data unit contains two addresses, identifying both the data unit's *destination* service access point and its *source* service access point. As we will see in Chapters 6, 7, and 8, the medium access control sublayer is responsible for appending additional information to the data unit to form a new data unit called a *transmission frame,* or simply a *frame.* The resulting transmission frame includes the network addresses of the sending and receiving stations. The combination of station address and service access point address is required to identify uniquely the source and the destination of the data, since a given station may be involved in several transmissions, using several service access points.

The source SAP address is always an individual address that identifies a single SAP—the one responsible for originating the data unit. The destination SAP address can be either an *individual* address, which identifies a single SAP, or a *group* address. A group SAP address specifies a group of destination SAPs within one destination station that are all to receive the data unit. A particular group address, known as a global address, specifies all DSAPs in the destination station.

STATION ADDRESSES

Although, as we have mentioned, it is the responsibility of the MAC sublayer to append station addresses to the transmitted data unit, we will discuss station addresses here because addressing considerations are the same for all three of the MAC methods discussed in Chapters 6, 7, and 8.

For data units to be sent and received properly, each device or station on the network must have an address that identifies it uniquely. When networks are interconnected, the issue arises of how to ensure that device addresses are unique across the interconnected networks so that there will be no confusion about the device for which a message is intended. IEEE Project 802 has developed two forms of addressing that can be used for specific LAN implementation.

Under one form of addressing, it is the responsibility of the organization installing the network to assign addresses to network devices. Typically this form of addressing is used for isolated networks, where each device is assigned an address that is unique within the network. Addresses can be either 16 or 48 bits in length. Addresses handled in this manner are referred to as being *locally administered.*

The second form of addressing uses a 48-bit address and a scheme of addressing that is called *universal*. An address field with 48 bits gives 281.475 trillion unique addresses—so many that with universal addressing, every mainframe, minicomputer, and microcomputer that is manufactured can be assigned a unique address by its manufacturer. This guarantees that there will be no duplication of addresses when devices are added to a network or when networks are interlinked. Different blocks of addresses are assigned to different manufacturers, who are then responsible for assigning addresses to the products they manufacture. The use of universal addresses simplifies address management for networks but increases transmission overhead, since more addressing bits must be sent in each transmitted data unit. Vendors of network products can choose whether to support one or both forms of addressing. Users of a given network product may be allowed to choose the form of addressing, or it may be fixed by the manufacturer.

We will next discuss the interface between the network layer and the logical link control sublayer. After that, we will introduce the interface between the LLC sublayer and the MAC sublayer. Finally, we will end this chapter by discussing peer-to-peer protocol procedures that the LLC in a sending station uses for communicating with the LLC in the receiving station.

NETWORK/LLC INTERFACE SERVICE SPECIFICATION

Two types of operation are defined as part of the interface service specification for the interface between the network layer and the logical link control sublayer. The first, called *Type 1 operation*, provides a facility called *connectionless service*. With Type 1 operation, there is no need to establish a logical connection between the sending and receiving station, and each data unit sent is processed independently. No sequence checking is done to ensure that data units are received in the same sequence in which they were sent, and the receiving station sends no acknowledgment that it has received a data unit. No flow control or error recovery is provided as part of connectionless service. With Type 1 operation, data units can be sent to either individual or group addresses. Type 1 operation is sometimes referred to as *datagram* service.

Type 2 operation is a *connection-oriented service*. A logical connection between the sending and the receiving stations must be established before Type 2 operation can begin, the connection must be maintained while Type 2 operation proceeds, and the connection is terminated when Type 2 operation ends. During Type 2 operation, sequence checking is performed to ensure that data units are received and processed in the sequence in which they were sent. Flow control is provided, as is error recovery, which consists of the retransmission of data units that are not correctly received. Only individual addresses can be used with Type 2 operation. The LLC standard identifies connection-oriented service as an optional feature of the standard. A station that supports only connection-less service is a *Class I station;* a station that supports both types of service is a *Class II station*.

SERVICE PRIMITIVES

Interface service specifications define the way in which the network layer requests services of the logical link control sublayer and thus of the local area network as a whole. The LLC standard documents these interface service specifications by defining a number of *service primitives* and listing the *parameters* that can be associated with each service primitive. A particular LLC service can have one or more service primitives associated with the interface activity related to that service. Three types of service primitives are defined by the LLC standard:

- **Request.** A *request* primitive is used to request that a particular service be performed.

- **Indication.** An *indication* primitive is used to notify a service user that a significant event has occurred.

- **Confirm.** A *confirm* primitive is used to notify a service user of the results of one or more service requests.

All the defined service primitives logically represent the collection of services that are provided by the LLC sublayer. It is important to realize that the IEEE 802 LLC standard defines service primitives in an abstract manner; it does not specify a particular coding syntax that must be used to invoke a particular service, nor does it define how a service is to be implemented. Issues of coding

Connectionless Service

```
    L_DATA.request
    L_DATA.indication
```

Connection-Oriented Service

```
    L_CONNECT.request
    L_CONNECT.indication
    L_CONNECT.confirm

    L_DATA_CONNECT.request
    L_DATA_CONNECT.indication
    L_DATA_CONNECT.confirm

    L_DISCONNECT.request
    L_DISCONNECT.indication
    L_DISCONNECT.confirm

    L_RESET.request
    L_RESET.indication
    L_RESET.confirm

    L_CONNECTION_FLOWCONTROL.request
    L_CONNECTION_FLOWCONTROL.indication
```

Figure 5.4   Network/LLC interface service primitives

syntax and implementation details must be determined as part of product implementation by the vendors that build LAN hardware and software products. Figure 5.4 shows the service primitives associated with the interface between the
network layer and the LLC sublayer.

PRIMITIVES FOR   For connectionless service (Type 1 operation), only
TYPE 1 OPERATION   two service primitives are defined:

- **L_DATA.request.** Passes a data unit to LLC and requests that it be transmitted.

- **L_DATA.indication.** Notifies the network layer that a data unit has been received and passes it from the LLC sublayer to the network layer.

BOX 5.1   Establishing a logical link connection

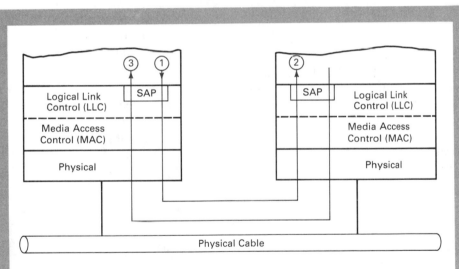

1. An **L_CONNECT.request** is passed from the network layer in the
   source station to the LLC sublayer to request that a connection be established.
2. Once the connection request has been processed, an **L_CON-
   NECT.indication** notifies the network entity in the destination station of
   the results of the attempt to establish the connection.
3. An **L_CONNECT.confirm** notifies the original network entity of the
   results of its request.

PRIMITIVES FOR TYPE 2 OPERATION

For connection-oriented service (Type 2 operation), the LLC standard defines several sets of primitives. **L_CONNECT** primitives are used to establish a logical link connection between two service access points. Box 5.1 shows how the three **L_CONNECT** primitives are typically used to establish a connection.

L_DATA_CONNECT primitives are used to transmit data over the connection once it has been established. **L_DISCONNECT** primitives terminate the link connection. **L_RESET** primitives are used to reset a link connection to its initial state. Finally, **L_CONNECTION_FLOWCONTROL** primitives can be used to control the amount of data that is passed between the network layer and the LLC sublayer.

SERVICE PRIMITIVE PARAMETERS

Each primitive has a set of parameters associated with it. The parameters define the pieces of information that are passed across the interface as part of the service request. For example, Box 5.2 shows the semantics of the **L_DATA.request** primitive.

Note that the box shows the *semantics* of the **L_DATA.request** service primitive as the IEEE 802 documentation describes it and is not meant to represent a *coding syntax*. The semantics of the command describes the parameters that can be included with the service primitive, not how the command that represents the primitive and its parameters is actually coded. As discussed earlier, the way service primitives are actually coded and the way their parameters are passed from the network layer to the LLC sublayer is dependent on the LAN implementer. Box 5.2 does not show all the parameters that can be included with a service primitive. Here are some other parameters that can be included with some service primitive:

- **status.** Provides information on whether a request was successfully processed or why it failed.

- **reason.** Indicates why disconnection or resetting of a link connection was requested.

- **amount.** Used with the **L_CONNECTION_FLOWCONTROL** service primitive to indicate the amount of data that is allowed to be passed.

The IEEE LLC standard specifies the parameters that can be included with each primitive and thus the information that must be made available by the network layer as part of the service request.

Now that we have examined the interface between the network layer and the LLC sublayer, we will briefly describe the interface between the LLC sublayer and the MAC sublayer below it. This interface is described in detail in Chapters 6, 7, and 8.

BOX 5.2 L_DATA.request service primitive semantics

Semantics

```
L_DATA.request(
                local_address,
                remote_address,
                l_sdu,
                service_class
                )
```

Parameter Descriptions

local_address. Specifies a combination of the source service access point (SSAP) address and the sending station address.

remote_address. Combines the destination service access point (DSAP) address with the destination station address. The **remote_address** parameter can specify either an individual address or a group address. All the network/LLC interface service primitives include **local_address** and **remote_address** parameters. These parameters provide the values needed to determine the values for the SSAP and DSAP fields in the LLC data unit and the station addresses added by the MAC sublayer.

l_sdu. Specifies the data unit to be transmitted.

service_class. Specifies the priority desired for the transmission.

LLC/MAC INTERFACE SERVICE SPECIFICATION

To provide the services requested by the next higher layer, the LLC sublayer must request certain services of the layer below it—the media access control sublayer. These services are documented in the standard and together define the interface between the logical link control sublayer and the media access control sublayer (LLC/MAC interface). The LLC/MAC interface services allow an LLC sublayer entity in one network station to exchange data units with peer LLC sublayer entities in other network stations. The service primitives that define the LLC/MAC interface are described in Box 5.3.

So far, we have examined the LLC service interface specifications, which discuss the *services* that define the interface between the LLC sublayer and the software layer both above and below it. Another important part of the IEEE 802 standards for the LLC sublayer concerns the *procedures* that enable the LLC sublayer in one network node to communicate with the LLC sublayer in another network node.

BOX 5.3   LLC/MAC interface service primitives

```
MA_DATA.request        (
                        destination_address,
                        m_sdu,
                        requested_service_class
                       )

MA_DATA.indication     (
                        destination_address,
                        source_address,
                        m_sdu,
                        reception_status
                        requested_service_class
                       )

MA_DATA.confirm        (
                        transmission_status,
                        provided_service_class,
                       )
```

Service Primitives

MA_DATA.request. Requests that a data unit be sent to one or more peer LLC entities.

MA_DATA.indication. Notifies an LLC entity that a data unit has been received and transfers it from the MAC sublayer to the LLC sublayer.

MA_DATA.confirm. Provides information about the success or failure of a particular **MA_DATA.request.**

Service Primitive Parameters

destination_address. Provides the information needed to determine the address of the destination station or stations.

source_address. Specifies the address of the sending station.

m_sdu. Specifies the data unit being transmitted.

requested_service_class. Indicates the priority requested for data transmission.

provided_service_class. Indicates the priority actually used.

reception_status. Indicates whether or not a data unit was received successfully.

transmission_status. Provides status information about a previous **MA_DATA.request.**

LLC PEER-TO-PEER PROTOCOL PROCEDURES   In addition to defining specifications for the interfaces between adjacent layers, the LLC standard also defines the operations involved in transferring data and control information between the LLC sublayer in a sending network node and the LLC sublayer in the receiving network node.

The protocols involved in these operations are known as *peer-to-peer protocols*. The standard defines different procedures for Type 1 operation (connectionless service) and Type 2 operation (connection-oriented service). The procedures are defined in terms of the way in which commands and responses are processed.

PROTOCOLS FOR TYPE 1 OPERATION

As discussed earlier, with Type 1 operation there is no error checking or acknowledgment of data units received. Delivery of data units is handled on a *best efforts* basis. Three commands are defined for Type 1 operation: Unnumbered Information (UI), Exchange Identification (XID), and Test (TEST). All three are *unnumbered,* or *U-format,* commands.

UNNUMBERED COMMANDS

Unnumbered commands conform to the format shown in Fig. 5.5. All unnumbered commands have a control field one byte in length. (Much of the IEEE 802 documentation uses the term *octet* to refer to a collection of 8 binary digits; we will use the popular term *byte* for this.) The value 11 in the first two bits of the control field identifies these as unnumbered, or U-format, commands. Dif-

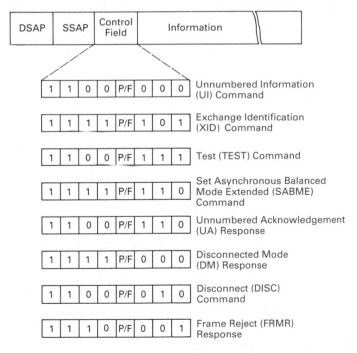

Figure 5.5 U-format commands and responses. DSAP = Destination Service Access Point; SSAP = Source Service Access Point; P/F = Poll/Final bit.

ferent values in the rest of the control field identify which command the data unit represents. The poll/final bit is used only with the XID and TEST commands. It is used to indicate that the receiver of the command must send back a response. The following describes the purpose of the three most commonly used U-format commands.

- **Unnumbered Information (UI).** Sends a data unit to one or more LLC entities. The destination SAP address can be an individual address, a group address, or a global address. When a UI command is received, no sequence checking is done, and no acknowledgment is sent. With Type 1 operation, it is possible for a data unit to be lost when errors occur, unless error checking is performed by higher layers.

- **Exchange Identification (XID).** Exchanges information about the types of services the two stations support and the amount of information that can be sent without a response under Type 2 operation. One LLC entity sends an XID command with its information. Each recipient of that command responds by sending back an XID response with its information. Possible uses for the XID command and response include determining if a particular station is available on the network, determining the stations that make up a particular group address, checking for duplicate addresses, determining service types supported by a station, and announcing the presence of a station on the network. The exact way in which the XID command is used is left as an implementation option.

- **Test.** Elicits a TEST response from the destination LLC entity. An information field is optionally included in the TEST command. If one is included, the TEST response should include it. The TEST command and its response are used to perform a basic test of the LLC-to-LLC transmission path.

PROTOCOLS FOR TYPE 2 OPERATION

With Type 2 operation, or connection-oriented service, a logical connection is established between the sending and receiving stations. Sequence checking is used to ensure that all data units arrive in the proper sequence, and acknowledgments are sent back to the sending station. Unacknowledged data units are retransmitted. Flow control is also used, to prevent overloading of the receiving station.

Connection-oriented service supports two functions related to error checking and correction: *sequence checking* and *message acknowledgment*. Every information data unit sent is assigned a sequence number. When the information data unit is received, the sequence number of each data unit is checked to ensure that all data units have arrived in the sequence sent. Periodically, the receiving LLC entity sends an acknowledgment so that the sending LLC entity knows that information data units have arrived successfully. If problems occur and the receiving LLC entity informs the sending LLC entity that information data units were not successfully received, the sending LLC entity is able to retransmit them or take other required actions.

Once a data link connection has been established, each LLC entity maintains a send counter, called *N(S)*, and a receive counter, called *N(R)*. Each counter is 7 bits in length, allowing for sequence values that range from 0 to 127.

ESTABLISHING AND TERMINATING CONNECTIONS

U-format commands and responses are also used to establish and terminate the logical connection over which data transmission takes place. The functions of these commands and responses (also shown in Fig. 5.5) are as follows:

- **Set Asynchronous Balanced Mode Extended (SABME).** Sent by one LLC entity to another as a request to establish a data link connection between them. The second LLC entity responds with an *unnumbered acknowledgment* (UA) response if it accepts the request. Both LLC entities reset their send and receive counters to zero and begin exchanging information over the connection. A *disconnected mode* (DM) response indicates that the other LLC entity is not able to make the data link connection. No connection is established, and information transfer does not take place.

- **Disconnect (DISC).** Terminates a data link connection. Either LLC entity can initiate disconnection by sending a DISC command. Either a UA or DM response causes the link to be disconnected.

- **Frame Reject (FRMR).** Sent when an LLC entity receives an invalid data unit. Conditions that cause a data unit to be considered invalid include these:
  —Invalid N(R) or N(S) value
  —Invalid presence of an information field
  —Exceeding the maximum allowable length for a data unit
  —Receiving an unanticipated response
  A FRMR response is sent when a data unit error condition exists that cannot be corrected by retransmitting one or more data units. Following receipt of a FRMR response, the LLC entity can issue a DISC command to terminate the connection. The LLC entity can also issue a SABME command. In this case, the SABME command requests that the data link connection be reset, by setting send and receive counters to zero, before continuing data transmission. Responses to the SABME command have the same effect here as with a SABME command used to establish a connection.

INFORMATION TRANSFER COMMANDS

When an information data unit is sent by an LLC entity, it is sent in the form of an *information transfer command* (I-format command), having the format shown in Fig. 5.6. A value of zero in the first bit of the control field identifies the data unit as an I-format command. The command has a 2-byte control field, which contains the current value of both the LLC

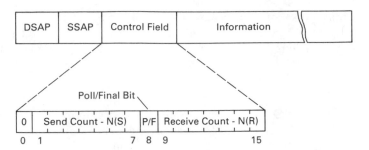

Figure 5.6 I-format commands. DSAP = Destination Service Access Point; SSAP = Source Service Access Point; P/F = Poll/Final bit.

entity's send and receive counters. The send counter contains the sequence number of the data unit the LLC entity is sending, and the receive counter contains the sequence number the LLC entity expects to find in the next data unit it receives. After an LLC entity sends each I-format command, it updates its send counter. After each LLC entity receives an I-format command that has a sequence number that matches the value in the LLC entity's receive counter, the LLC entity updates its receive counter. Box 5.4 demonstrates the use of send and receive counters when information data units are being sent in both directions.

SUPERVISORY COMMANDS

In the example in Box 5.4, information commands were being sent in both directions and were used to acknowledge receipt of data units. There may be times when an LLC entity needs to send an acknowledgment but does not have an information data unit to send. There are commands, called S-format, or supervisory, commands, that can be used for acknowledgment as well as providing various types of control information. These commands have the format shown in Fig. 5.7. A value of 10 in the first two bits of the control field identifies a data unit as containing an S-format command. S-format commands use a 2-byte control field, which contains a receive count value in the control field as well as other information. The supervisory function bits identify the particular type of command the data unit contains. Here are some commonly used S-format commands:

- **Receive Ready (RR).** Used to acknowledge received data units and also indicates that the LLC entity is able to receive additional data units.

- **Receive Not Ready (RNR).** Acknowledges received data units and indicates that the LLC entity is temporarily unable to receive more data units, possibly due to an internal constraint, such as lack of buffer space. When the busy condition clears, the LLC entity may send another command, possibly an RR, to indicate it is now able to receive again.

BOX 5.4 Updating send and receive counters

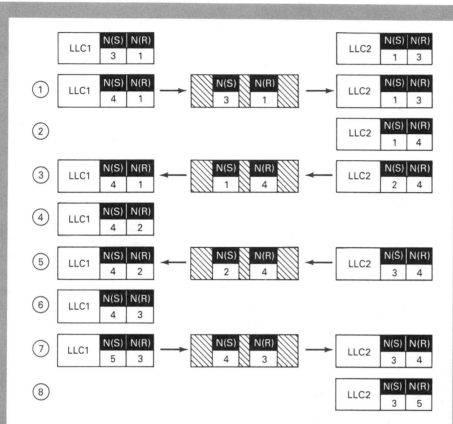

1. LLC1 sends an I-format command containing the current values of its send counter [NS(R) = 3] and receive counter [N(R) = 1]. LLC1 adds 1 to the current value of its send counter, making the new counter value 4.

2. LLC2 receives the I-format command, checks that the send counter value [N(S)] in the received command matches its receive counter value [N(R)], and updates its receive counter. The value of 1 in the N(R) counter in the data unit indicates that LLC1 expects the next data unit it receives to have a sequence number of 1. This data unit acknowledges receipt of the data unit having the sequence number value of 0.

3. LLC2 sends a data unit with a send sequence number value of 1 and receive sequence number value of 4; LLC2 then adds 1 to its send counter.

(Continued)

BOX 5.4 *(Continued)*

4. LLC1 receives the data unit, sequence-checks it, and adds 1 to its receive counter. This data unit acknowledges receipt of data unit 3 sent by LLC1.

5. LLC2 sends a data unit with a send sequence number value of 2 and updates its send counter.

6. LLC1 receives the data unit, sequence-checks it, and updates its receive counter.

7. LLC1 sends data unit 4 and updates its send counter.

8. LLC2 receives the data unit, sequence-checks it, and updates its receive counter. This data unit acknowledges receipt of data units 1 and 2 sent by LLC2.

- **Reject (REJ).** Used to request retransmission of I-format commands. Reject requests retransmission starting with the data unit corresponding to the N(R) receive count value specified in the REJ command. The Reject command is considered to be a positive acknowledgment of data units that have N(S) send count values lower than the Reject command's N(R) value.

SENDING ACKNOWLEDGMENTS   Several factors determine when an acknowledgment is sent. One is the *poll/final bit* carried in the data unit's control field. When an LLC entity sends an I-format command that has its poll/final bit set to 1, this requests that an acknowledgment be sent back immediately. If the receiving LLC entity does not have an information data unit ready to send when it receives the command, it responds by sending a supervisory, or S-format, command.

There is a limit to the number of data units an LLC entity can send before it must wait for an acknowledgment. This value is known as the *window size*. The window size has a maximum value of 127, reflecting the 7-bit size of the N(S) and N(R) counter fields. Window sizes can be set smaller than this. LLC entities can use XID commands prior to establishing a data link connection to exchange window size values. When an LLC entity sends the number of data units specified by the window size without receiving an acknowledgment, it stops sending until it receives an acknowledgment.

Whenever an LLC entity receives an I-format command that has its poll/final bit set to 1, the LLC entity sends an acknowledgment immediately. If the LLC entity receives an I-format command that does not have the poll/final bit set to 1, the action the LLC entity takes depends on several factors. If the LLC

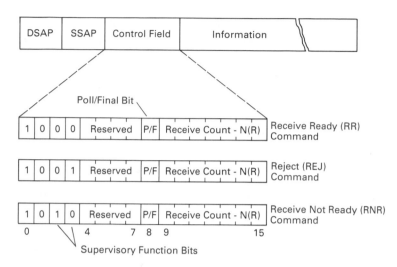

Figure 5.7 S-format commands. DSAP = Destination Service Access Point; SSAP = Source Service Access Point; P/F = Poll/Final bit.

entity has received a number of data units that is equal to the current window size, the LLC entity sends an acknowledgment; otherwise, the LLC entity waits for additional data units to arrive. If no additional data units arrive immediately, the LLC entity waits a period of time before sending an acknowledgment. The length of time is based on an *acknowledgment timer* that the LLC entity starts each time it receives a new I-format command.

When an LLC entity starts sending data units, it also starts an acknowledgment timer. If no acknowledgment is received before the timer runs out, it sends a supervisory data unit with the poll/final bit set to 1 to request an acknowledgment. Depending on the response received, the LLC entity may resume sending, retransmit previously sent data units, or perform a reset procedure.

FLOW CONTROL

The window size value that sending and receiving LLC entities maintain acts as a flow control mechanism. The window size limits the number of data units the sending LLC entity transmits and thus prevents the receiving LLC entity from being overloaded. If the LLC entity waits for several data units to arrive, the number of data units that are allowed to accumulate before a response is sent depends on the window size. The receiving LLC entity can also use acknowledgments and the Receive Not Ready (RNR) command to control the rate at which it receives data units. In this way the receiving LLC entity can ensure that it does not receive more data than it has the resources to handle.

SUMMARY   The logical link control sublayer of the IEEE 802 architecture performs for a local area network a set of functions that are comparable to those performed in a wide area network by a conventional bit-oriented data link protocol. The LLC standard defines both service interface specifications and peer-to-peer protocols. LLC is responsible for the exchange of protocol data units between stations. Service access points represent individual processes within a station that are involved in communication. The data units exchanged by LLC contain the destination SAP, source SAP, control field, and, optionally, an information field.

Two types of service are defined. Type 1 operation provides connectionless service that delivers data units on a best-efforts basis; no error handling or flow control is provided. Type 2 operation provides a connection-oriented service that can be used for reliable data transmission. With Type 2 operation, a logical connection is established between the sending and receiving stations. Sequence checking is performed, and acknowledgments are sent. Flow control and error recovery based on retransmission are also provided.

Logical link control can be used with any of the three media access control standards defined by IEEE Project 802. Higher-level network layers interface with LLC rather than directly with the MAC sublayer; thus higher-level layers are shielded from any concern about LAN implementation details.

6 IEEE 802.3: CSMA/CD

A media access control (MAC) sublayer operates below the level of the logical link control sublayer and provides services to it. At the MAC level, three standards have been defined by IEEE Project 802. These standards address three different approaches to controlling access to the physical transmission medium: *CSMA/CD, token bus,* and *token ring*. All three interface to the same LLC standard, which we discussed in detail in Chapter 5. The subject of this chapter is the MAC method called *carrier sense multiple access with collision detection* (CSMA/CD).

CSMA/CD OPERATION

As we discussed in Chapter 3, CSMA/CD is the most commonly used access method for local area networks that employ a bus or tree topology. It is used as the MAC method in Ethernet, a popular LAN architecture.

With CSMA/CD, a transmitting station first "listens" to the transmission medium to determine whether or not another station is currently transmitting a message. If the transmission medium is "quiet," the station transmits. When two or more stations all have messages to send, they may all listen at exactly the same time and then send their messages simultaneously, resulting in a *collision*. Receiving stations ignore the garbled transmission, and the transmitting stations immediately stop transmitting as soon as they detect the collision. Following a collision, each transmitting station waits for a random period of time and then attempts to transmit again.

CSMA/CD FUNCTIONS

The IEEE CSMA/CD standard defines a model that comprises six functions, as shown in Fig. 6.1. Three of the functions are associated with transmitting data, and three parallel functions are concerned with receiving data. The *data encap-*

81

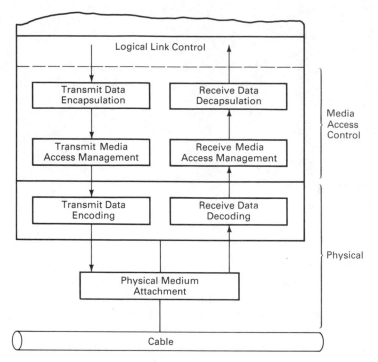

Figure 6.1 CSMA/CD functions

sulation/decapsulation and *media access management* functions shown in Fig. 6.1 are performed by the media access control sublayer itself; the *data encoding/ decoding* function is performed by the physical layer, which operates below the MAC sublayer.

Data Encapsulation/Decapsulation

Data encapsulation applies to a sending station and provides for adding information to the beginning and end of the data unit to be transmitted, after the transmission frame is received from logical link control. This information is used to perform the following tasks:

- Synchronize the receiving station with the signal
- Delimit the start and end of the frame
- Identify the addresses of the sending and receiving stations
- Detect transmission errors

When a frame is received, a *data decapsulation* function in the receiving station is responsible for recognizing the destination address, determining if it matches the station's address, performing error checking, and then removing the control information that was added by the data encapsulation function in the sending station before passing the frame up to the LLC sublayer.

Media Access Management

In a sending station, the *media access management* function is responsible for determining whether the transmission medium is available for use and for initiating transmission when it is. This function also determines the actions to be taken when a collision is detected and when to attempt retransmission. In a receiving station, media access management performs validity checks on a frame before passing it on to the data decapsulation function.

Data Encoding

Data encoding, performed in the physical layer, is responsible for translating the bits being transmitted into the proper electrical signals to be sent across the transmission medium. For CSMA/CD, Manchester phase encoding is used to translate the bit stream into electrical signals (see Chapter 2). When the signal is received, *data decoding* translates it back from the electrical signals into the bit stream those signals represent. The data encoding function is also responsible for listening to the transmission medium and for notifying media access management whether the carrier is free or busy and whether a collision has been detected.

In addition to data encoding/decoding, the physical layer includes functions related to attaching a station to a particular physical transmission medium. These functions are generally performed in a physically separate device called a *medium attachment unit* that is used to connect a network station to the physical transmission cable.

THE LLC/MAC INTERFACE

As described in Chapter 5, the service specification of the interface between the LLC sublayer and the MAC sublayer defines three service primitives:

- **MA_DATA.request**
- **MA_DATA.indicate**
- **MA_DATA.confirm**

These service primitives allow the LLC and MAC sublayers to exchange LLC protocol data units. The protocol data unit exchanged at the LLC/MAC interface is described in Chapter 5 and contains the destination service access point address, source service access point address, control field, and, optionally, an information field.

As part of MAC sublayer processing, data encapsulation adds information to the LLC data unit to form a new data unit called a *transmission frame,* or simply a *frame,* that is transmitted across the network. On the receiving side, data decapsulation in the MAC sublayer removes the additional information from the frame before passing the LLC protocol data unit to the LLC sublayer. The information added by the MAC sublayer is described next.

CSMA/CD TRANSMISSION FRAME

The CSMA/CD standard defines a specific frame format to be used for the data being transmitted across the network. This format is shown and described in Box 6.1.

BOX 6.1   CSMA/CD frame format

Preamble	Start Frame Delimiter	Destination Address	Source Address	Length Count	Logical Link Control Information	Pad Bytes	Frame Check Sequence
7 Bytes	1 Byte	2 or 6 Bytes	2 or 6 Bytes	2 Bytes	0-n Bytes	0-p Bytes	4 Bytes

- **Preamble.** The frame begins with a *preamble,* which consists of 56 bits having alternating 1 and 0 values. The preamble is used for synchronization.

- **Start Frame Delimiter.** Following the preamble is the *start frame delimiter,* which consists of the bit sequence 10101011. The start frame delimiter indicates the start of a frame of data.

- **Address Fields.** The *destination address* field identifies the station or stations that are to receive the frame. The *source address* field identifies the station that sent the frame. If addresses are locally administered, the address fields can be either 2 bytes (16-bit addresses) or 6 bytes (48-bit addresses) in length; if universal addresses are used, 6-byte addresses must be used. (See Chapter 5 for a discussion of network addresses.) The address size to use is chosen by the vendor who develops the LAN equipment and software for a particular implementation of the CSMA/CD standard. For a given network, the source and destination address fields must be the same size, and addresses of the same size must be used by all stations on the network. The destination address can specify either an individual station or a group of stations. An address that refers to a particular group of stations is known as a *multicast group address.* An address that refers to *all* stations on the network is known as a *broadcast address.*

- **Length Count.** The *length count* field is a 2-byte field that indicates the length of the data field that follows. This field is used to determine the length of the information field when a pad field is included in the frame.

BOX 6.1 *(Continued)*

- **Information Field.** The *information* field contains the protocol data unit that was passed from the logical link control sublayer.

- **Pad Field.** To detect collisions properly, the frame that is transmitted must contain a certain minimum number of bytes. If a frame being assembled for transmission does not meet this minimum length, a *pad* field is added to bring it up to that length.

- **Frame Check Sequence.** The frame ends with a *frame check sequence* field. When the sending station assembles a frame, it performs a cyclical redundancy check (CRC) calculation on the bits in the frame. The specific algorithm that is used is described in the IEEE documentation and always results in a 4-byte value. The sending station stores this value in the frame check sequence field and then transmits the frame. When the receiving station receives the frame, it performs the identical CRC calculation and compares the results with the value in the frame check sequence field. If the two values do not match, the receiving station assumes that a transmission error has occurred and can request that the frame be retransmitted.

Figure 6.2 shows the relationship between the logical link control protocol data unit and the CSMA/CD transmission frame. The protocol data unit created by the LLC sublayer, including the destination service access point, source service access point, and control field, are treated by CSMA/CD simply as data. CSMA/CD software or firmware in the sending station adds its control information before transmitting the frame, and complementary CSMA/CD software

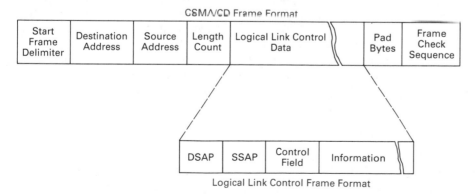

Figure 6.2 CSMA/CD versus logical link control frame formats. DSAP = Destination Service Access Point; SSAP = Source Service Access Point; P/F = Poll/Final bit.

or firmware in the receiving station removes that control information after receiving the frame and before passing it to the LLC sublayer in the receiving station.

CSMA/CD MEDIA ACCESS MANAGEMENT

A key responsibility of the media access control sublayer is to manage the sharing of the transmission medium among the different stations on the network. In CSMA/CD, this is known as *media access management*. The media access management function receives a frame from the data encapsulation function once the necessary control information has been added. Media access management is then responsible for seeing that the data is physically transmitted. The approach used by CSMA/CD involves *carrier sensing,* or listening for a free transmission medium before transmitting.

Media access management determines, through the services of the physical layer, whether or not the transmission medium, or *carrier,* is currently being used. If not, media access management passes the frame to the physical layer for transmission. If the carrier is busy, media access management continues monitoring the carrier until no other stations are transmitting. Media access management then waits a specified time, to allow the network to clear, and begins transmission.

COLLISION DETECTION

Media access management continues to monitor the carrier after transmission of the frame starts. If two stations have begun transmission at the same time, their signals will collide, causing them to become garbled. When this happens and the transmitting station detects the collision, the station ceases transmitting data and sends out a jamming signal. The jamming signal ensures that all other stations on the network detect the collision. All stations that have been transmitting cease their transmission, wait a period of time, and, if the carrier is free, attempt retransmission of the frame.

A station must listen while it is transmitting long enough to ensure that a collision has not taken place. The length of time this takes varies, depending on whether baseband or broadband transmission is being used.

Baseband Collision Detection

Figure 6.3 illustrates worst-case collision detection on a baseband network. Stations A and B are the two stations farthest apart on the network. Station A begins transmission, and just before its signal reaches station B, station B begins transmission. The collision occurs near station B, causing a signal that must travel back the length of the network to reach station A. The frame that station

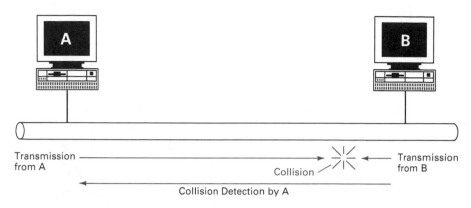

Figure 6.3   Baseband collision detection

A is transmitting must be large enough to ensure that station A is still transmitting when it detects the collision with station B's transmission.

Propagation time is the length of time it takes a signal to reach the far end of the network. So here the maximum time it may take to detect a collision is twice the propagation time from station A. This represents the time it takes station A's signal to reach the far end plus the time it takes the collision signal to travel the length of the network to reach station A.

Broadband Collision Detection

For broadband transmission, the worst case involves two stations that are farthest from the head end. This is illustrated in Figure 6.4, using a dual-cable system. Station B begins transmission just before it receives a transmission from station A, and a collision occurs. The collision signal must then travel to the head end and down the other cable until it is received by station A.

Here the time to detect the collision is approximately four times the propagation time from station A to the head end. Station A's signal travels to the head end and back almost to the far end before station B begins transmitting and the collision occurs. The collision signal must then travel to the head end and back to the far end for station A to receive it.

The maximum time it will take to detect a collision determines minimum frame size, since a station must continue transmitting long enough to be able to detect a collision. Frame size is also a factor in network efficiency. When a station has a frame to send, it monitors the carrier continuously until it detects that the carrier is free. If frames are large, it is more likely that there will be more than one station waiting for the carrier to become free. They will all begin transmitting as soon as it is free, and a collision is guaranteed. However, if frame size is long relative to collision detection time (i.e., propagation time), the time lost to processing collisions is not critical.

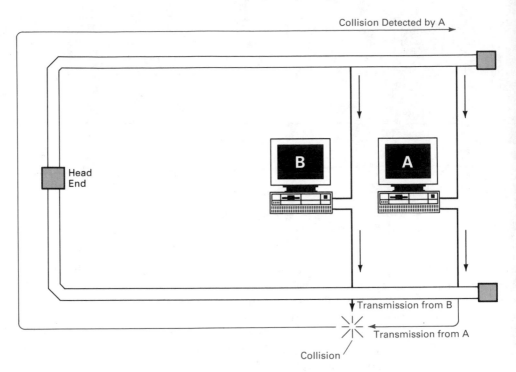

Figure 6.4   Broadband collision detection

BACKOFF AFTER COLLISION   When a collision occurs, all stations that have been transmitting stop, wait a certain length of time, and then, if the carrier is free, start transmitting again. If all stations waited the same length of time before checking the carrier and starting transmission again, another collision would occur. To avoid this, each station generates a random number that determines the length of time it must wait before testing the carrier. This time period is known as the station's *backoff delay*. Backoff delay is calculated in terms of multiples of *slot time,* which is the time it takes a signal to travel from one end of the network to the other and back again.

Each station generates a random number that falls within a specified range of values. It then waits that number of slot times before attempting retransmission. The smaller the range of values from which the random number is selected, the greater the likelihood that two stations will select the same number and have another collision. However, if the range of numbers is large, all the stations may wait for several slot times before any station transmits, causing transmission time to be wasted.

To achieve a balance between these two considerations, the CSMA/CD standard uses an approach known as *binary exponential backoff*. The range of numbers is defined as $0 \leq r < 2^n$, where n reflects the number of retransmission attempts that the station has made. For the first ten attempts, n ranges from 1 to 10. For subsequent attempts, n continues to have a value of 10. This means that for the first attempt at retransmission, the range is 0–1; for the second attempt, 0–3; for the third, 0–7; and so on. If repeated collisions occur, the range continues to expand until the station successfully transmits without collision. If a station is unsuccessful in transmitting after 16 attempts, it reports an error condition. Binary exponential backoff results in minimum delays before retransmission when traffic on the network is light. When traffic is high, repeated collisions will cause the range of numbers to increase, thus lessening the chance of further collisions. Of course, when the traffic is extremely high, repeated collisions could begin to generate error conditions.

CSMA/CD PHYSICAL LAYER STANDARDS

The specifications for the physical layer address issues such as the physical characteristics of the transmission medium (typically a wire or cable) and the mechanical connection from the network station to the transmission medium. These specifications address physical issues, including plug dimensions, the number of pins in the plug, and the placement of the pins. They also address electrical issues, such as the voltage levels of the signals that flow on the wire, and functional issues, such as the meaning of a particular voltage level on a given wire.

A detailed model of the physical layer has been defined as part of the CSMA/CD standard. Figure 6.5 illustrates this model. One portion of the phys-

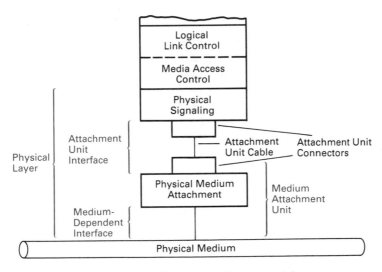

Figure 6.5 CSMA/CD reference model

ical layer, known as *physical signaling* (PLS), resides in the device, or station, that is attached to the network. Physical signaling is responsible for the data encoding/decoding function. This involves transforming the bit stream being transmitted into binary signals using the Manchester encoding scheme and transforming signals received from the network back into its corresponding bit stream. Physical signaling is also responsible for signaling media access management as to the status of the transmission medium.

A *medium attachment unit* (MAU) is a device used to attach a station to a particular transmission medium. This unit handles all the functions that are dependent on the specific transmission medium being used. By having a medium attachment unit that is separate from the station itself, the same station can be used with different transmission media simply by changing the medium attachment unit used to attach it.

An *attachment unit interface* (AUI) defines the interface between the network device, or station, and the medium attachment unit. It consists of the cable and connectors used to attach the device to the medium attachment unit.

PHYSICAL SIGNALING FUNCTIONS

The primary functions of the physical signaling (PLS) sublayer are as follows:

- Accept a bit from the MAC sublayer, encode it, and transmit it.
- Receive a bit signal from the MAU, decode it, and pass it to the MAC sublayer.
- Provide the MAC sublayer with status information on the state of the carrier, the occurrences of collisions, and the success or failure of transmissions.

Encoding and decoding involve the conversion between bit streams and binary signals. The Manchester encoding scheme used with CSMA/CD is illustrated in Fig. 6.6. With Manchester encoding, the signal state always changes

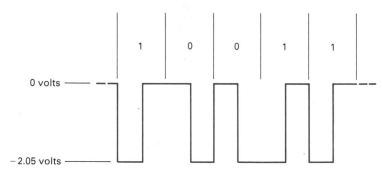

Figure 6.6   Manchester encoding for CSMA/CD

at roughly the midpoint of each bit time. For a 1 bit, the signal changes from low to high; for a 0 bit, from high to low. This type of signaling allows data and clocking signals to be combined into a single transmission, since the receiving station can use the state change that occurs during each bit time to stay synchronized.

PHYSICAL SIGNALING INTERFACES

The 802.3 standard defines detailed specifications for the various elements of the physical layer. For physical signaling, these include MAC/PLS interface service specifications, PLS service and functional specifications, and PLS/PMA (physical medium attachment) interface specifications. For the attachment unit interface, the standard defines signal characteristics, electrical characteristics, interchange circuits, and mechanical characteristics. For the medium attachment unit and physical medium, it defines functional specifications, electrical characteristics, coaxial cable characteristics, coaxial cable connector and repeater specifications, and environmental specifications.

THE MAC/PLS INTERFACE

The MAC/PLS interface service specification defines the services that are provided by the physical layer to the MAC sublayer. These services consist of a single *function*, two *procedures*, and three *Boolean variables*. The elements of the interface are listed, along with their functions, in Box 6.2. Functionally, these

BOX 6.2 MAC/PLS interface service primitives

The interface between the MAC sublayer and the physical layer consists of a function, two procedures, and three Boolean variables.

Function:

ReceiveBit   Each invocation retrieves one bit from the physical layer and passes it to the MAC sublayer.

Procedures:

TransmitBit   Each invocation passes one bit from the MAC sublayer to the physical layer, where it is transmitted across the network.

(Continued)

BOX 6.2 *(Continued)*

Wait	This procedure allows the MAC sublayer to wait a specified number of bit times. The slot time used for backoff following a collision is defined in bit times. This procedure is used to wait the appropriate number of slot times following a collision.

Boolean Variables:

collisionDetect	This Boolean variable is used to signal the MAC sublayer that a collision has been detected by the physical layer.
carrierSense	This Boolean variable is used to inform the MAC sublayer whether or not data is currently being transmitted on the transmission medium.
transmitting	This Boolean variable is used by the MAC sublayer to signal the physical layer that it has bits ready to transmit.

services allow the MAC sublayer to determine if the carrier is currently busy, to transfer data—one bit at a time—to PLS for transmission, to determine if a collision has occurred, to wait a specified number of bit times, and to receive data from PLS—one bit at a time.

THE PLS/PMA INTERFACE

The interface between the physical signaling (PLS) sublayer and the physical medium attachment (PMA) sublayer is logically defined in terms of *messages*. Box 6.3 lists the messages and their meaning. Two modes of operation have been defined for the medium attachment unit (MAU) in the 802.3 standard. In normal mode, the MAU is able both to send and to receive. In monitor mode, the MAU is unable to send but is still able to receive signals from the carrier. The optional messages are primarily related to the monitor mode, which is an optional feature.

ATTACHMENT UNIT INTERFACE

The *attachment unit interface* (AUI) passes signals between physical signaling (PLS) in the device and the physical medium attachment (PMA) unit. It is used to provide the network stations with independence from the particular transmission medium used, thus allowing the same station to be used with base-

BOX 6.3   The PLS/PMA interface

Messages Sent from PLS to PMA:

output   PLS sends PMA this message whenever PLS receives a data bit from the MAC sublayer.

output_idle   PLS sends PMA this message at all times when the MAC sublayer is not sending PLS data bits to transmit.

normal   PLS sends PMA this message to indicate that the MAU should operate in normal mode and both transmit and receive data.

isolate   PLS sends PMA this message to indicate that the MAU should operate in monitor mode and should only receive data. This is an optional function.

mau_request   PLS sends PMA this message when PMA has indicated that the MAU is not available and PMA wants it to be made available because the MAC sublayer has a data bit to transmit. This is an optional function.

Messages Sent from PMA to PLS:

input   PMA sends PLS this message when it has received a bit from the transmission medium and wants to transfer it to PLS.

input_idle   PMA sends PLS this message whenever it does not have a data bit ready to transfer to PLS.

signal_quality_error PMA sends PLS this message whenever PMA detects a collision or an improper signal on the transmission medium.

mau_available   PMA sends PLS this message to indicate that the MAU is available for transmission.

mau_not_available   PMA sends PLS this message whenever the MAU is not available for transmission. This is an optional function.

band coaxial cable, broadband coaxial cable, or baseband fiber optics. The AUI also allows a device to be located up to 50 m from the transmission cable.

Very detailed and specific standards are defined for the signal characteristics, electrical characteristics, cable requirements, interchange circuits, and mechanical characteristics associated with the attachment unit connectors and attachment unit cable that make up the AUI. Standard components that will meet these specifications are twisted-wire-pair cable and 15-pin connectors.

AUI standards are designed to encompass signaling rates from 1 to 20 Mbps. All devices attached to a given network must operate at a single signaling rate. Network devices and MAUs, however, may be designed to operate at more than one possible rate, with the ability to be manually set to a specific rate when attached to a particular network.

BASEBAND MEDIUM ATTACHMENT UNIT   The 802.3 standard allows for the definition of multiple medium attachment unit standards. One standard defined is for baseband transmission over coaxial cable at a data rate of 10 Mbps. This standard allows for up to 500 m of coaxial cable without use of a repeater. The rate (10 Mbps), transmission technique (baseband), and cable length (500 m) are sometimes published using a shorthand notation, as 10BASE5. With this MAU standard, 50-ohm coaxial cable is used, and the maximum path length for the network is 2500 m.

MAU functional specifications include the five functions shown in Box 6.4. Through these functions, the MAU sees that signals received from PLS over the AUI are placed on the coaxial cable and that signals received from the coaxial cable are passed over the AUI to PLS. The MAU also detects collisions and notifies PLS when one occurs.

Collisions are detected when the signal level on the cable equals or exceeds the combined signal level of two transmitters. As a signal travels along

BOX 6.4   MAU functions

Function	Purpose
Transmit	Transmit serial data bit streams on the baseband medium.
Receive	Receive serial data bit streams from the baseband medium.
Collision Presence	Detect the presence of two or more stations transmitting concurrently.
Monitor	Inhibit the transmit function while the receive and collision presence functions remain operational.
Jabber	Interrupt the transmit function when an abnormally long data bit stream is being transmitted.

the cable, it gradually attenuates, or weakens. If the signal is allowed to weaken too much, then when it combines with the signal from another transmitter, the combined signal might not be recognized as a collision. To prevent this, repeaters must be used at least every 500 m, to regenerate the signal to its original level.

Another collision detection problem can arise if stations are not spaced properly. Signal reflection may give a false collision indication. To avoid this, stations must be placed in such a way that the distance between them is a multiple of 2.5 m, and no more than 100 stations can be attached to any one 500-m cable segment.

Electrical characteristics are defined for the MAU and for its interface to the coaxial cable. Electrical, mechanical, and physical characteristics are also defined for the coaxial cable and the connectors, terminators, and repeaters used with it. Environmental specifications related to safety, electromagnetic environment, temperature and humidity, and regulatory requirements are also included in the standard.

There are many variations of the CSMA/CD standard. For example, one supports baseband transmission over coaxial cable with a data rate of 10 Mbps and a maximum segment length of 200 m (10BASE2). This variation allows lower-cost LAN implementations to be constructed using the CSMA/CD access control method.

Another variation of the standard uses baseband transmission on an unshielded twisted-wire pair, at a rate of 1 Mbps with a maximum cable length of 500 m (1BASE5). The use of a lower speed and twisted-wire-pair cable makes this also a lower-cost alternative. This form of transmission is used with AT&T's STARLAN local area network, described in Chapter 24.

Yet another variation of the CSMA/CD standard now being marketed is an implementation of Ethernet that supports a data rate of 10 Mbps over twisted-wire-pair cable. Ethernet is described in Chapter 20.

BROADBAND MEDIA ACCESS UNIT

Another CSMA/CD standard variation is for broadband transmission using the CSMA/CD access control method. With this standard, 75-ohm coaxial cable is used. Different data rates are supported, including 2 Mbps and 10 Mbps. Maximum length for the network can be several kilometers from the head end to the farthest station.

Collision detection is performed by the sending station's medium attachment unit. It keeps a copy of the frame transmitted and compares the bits it receives to the bits it sent. (Every station on the network receives a transmission, including the station that sent it.) If the bits match for the time interval required for all other stations to have received the signal, the sending station assumes that no collision has occurred.

SUMMARY   CSMA/CD functions include data encapsulation/decapsulation, media access management, and data encoding/decoding. A CSMA/CD frame contains a preamble, start frame delimiter, destination address, source address, length count, data, optional padding, and a frame check sequence. Media access management is based on stations listening for a free transmission medium before transmitting. If two or more stations begin transmitting at the same time, a collision occurs. The transmitting stations stop sending, wait a period of time, and then attempt transmission again.

CSMA/CD uses Manchester encoding and supports several forms of transmission. Baseband transmission can be used at data rates of from 1 Mbps to 20 Mbps. Broadband transmission can be used with various data rates, including 2 Mbps and 10 Mbps.

7 IEEE 802.4: TOKEN BUS

The IEEE 802 standards include two access control methods based on the token-passing technique. One of the methods is used on a network with a bus topology and the other on a network with a ring topology. The token passing standard employing the bus topology, known as *token bus,* is defined in IEEE standard 802.4. This is the basis of the General Motors MAP architecture that is used extensively in factory automation. With the token bus approach, control of the transmission medium is determined by possession of a token, which is passed from station to station in a logical ring.

TOKEN BUS OPERATION

With the token bus access control method, a *token* is transmitted from one station to the next. When a station receives the token, it is allowed to transmit data units until a maximum amount of time has been reached. It then transmits the token to the next station. If a station that receives the token has no data units to transmit, it passes the token on immediately. Although the network must take the form physically of a *bus,* the network is logically arranged as a *ring* with respect to passing the token from one station to the next.

TOKEN BUS FUNCTIONS

The token bus standard employs the logical model shown in Fig. 7.1. The token bus standard addresses the media access control sublayer and the physical layer. The primary functions addressed as part of the MAC sublayer are:

- **Interface to the LLC Sublayer.** The MAC sublayer must receive data units from the LLC sublayer and prepare them for transmission. On the receiving

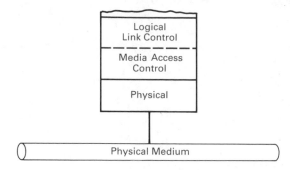

Figure 7.1   Token bus reference model

side, the MAC sublayer must receive data units that have been transmitted across the network and pass them to LLC.

- **Token Handling.** This includes passing the token from one station to the next, recognizing a token when it is received, and, optionally, providing for the prioritization of data units.

- **Ring Maintenance.** The logical ring that the stations form needs to be initialized when the network is powered up and modified as stations are added or deleted.

- **Fault Detection and Recovery.** Possible faults include multiple tokens, lost tokens, token pass failures, stations with inoperative receivers, and duplicate station addresses. These must be detected and, where possible, corrected.

- **Sending and Receiving Data.** In a sending station, data units must be passed from the MAC sublayer to the physical layer for transmission across the network; in a receiving station, data units must be received by the MAC sublayer from the physical layer. These functions include adding and removing the control information necessary to form data units in the format described as part of the token bus standard.

TOKEN HANDLING   Access to the transmission medium is based on a short control data unit called a *token* being passed in a logical sequence from one station to the next. The token represents the *right to transmit*. When a station receives the token, it is allowed to transmit, for a predetermined length of time, data units it has waiting. When the station has transmitted all its data units or the end of the time period has been reached, the station transmits the token to the next station. If a station that receives the token has no data units to transmit, it passes the token immediately to the next station on the logical ring.

The token bus architecture can be described as a combination of a *logical ring* with a *physical bus*. This is illustrated in Fig. 7.2. The network stations are physically attached in a bus topology. However, the token, as indicated by

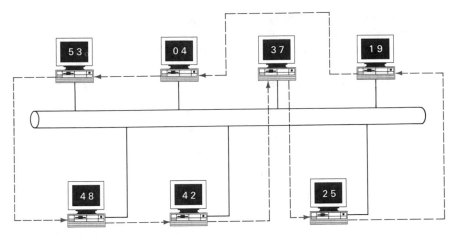

Figure 7.2 Token passing

the dashed line in the diagram, follows a logical ring around the network. The token is passed from one station to the next in descending order of station addresses. When the station with the lowest address value is reached, the token passes back to the station with the highest network address.

Because the physical topology takes the form of a bus, the token and all other data units are sent in a broadcast fashion and are received by all stations on the network. Every data unit contains an address field that identifies each station that is to receive it. A station then accepts and processes only data units that are addressed to it. It passes the token by changing the address field in the token to that of the next logical station in the ring before it transmits the token.

Since a station transmits only when it has received the token, two stations can never transmit at the same time, and collisions cannot occur. Because there can be no collisions, there is no minimum length requirement for data units, and the token can be a very short data unit, containing only the control information required for proper processing.

SERVICE CLASSES AND ACCESS CLASSES With token passing, every station on the ring is guaranteed an opportunity to transmit within some predetermined maximum length of time, assuming no transmission delays and no network problems. When the optional priority scheme is not implemented, every station has an equal opportunity to transmit, and each station is given the opportunity to transmit for a predetermined maximum length of time each time the token circulates all the way around the ring.

The token bus standard provides for the assignment of *service classes* to different types of data units, where a given service class has one of eight different priority values, from 0 through 7. The LLC sublayer assigns a service class to each data unit as it passes the data unit from the LLC sublayer to the MAC sublayer. The MAC layer recognizes four different priority values called *access classes* having the values 0, 2, 4, and 6. The eight service classes are mapped by the MAC sublayer into access classes in the following fashion:

Service Classes		Access Class
0	1	0
2	3	2
4	5	4
6	7	6

If the optional priority scheme is not implemented, the MAC sublayer treats all data units as if they were assigned to access class 6, the highest-priority access class. When a station receives the token, it transmits data units from its queue, on a first-in, first-out basis, until a network-determined time limit expires. This time limit, called the *high-priority token hold time,* is the same for all network stations. Thus no matter how long it takes for the token to circulate around the ring, each station receives the same opportunity to transmit. The high-priority token hold time limit prevents a single station from monopolizing the network should that station happen to have a long queue of data units waiting to be transmitted. When the time limit expires, the station passes the token, whether it has more data units to send or not.

OPTIONAL PRIORITY SCHEME

When the optional priority scheme is implemented, the MAC sublayer stores data units that it receives from the LLC sublayer into four queues according to the access class that the LLC sublayer assigns to each data unit as it passes that data unit to the MAC sublayer. Data units that are held in the queue for access class 6 are treated as though the priority system were not in operation. Each station that receives the token is allowed to transmit data units from access class 6 until the network-determined time limit expires.

Each of the three lower-priority access classes has a *target token rotation time* assigned to it, with higher-priority classes having longer target token rotation times than the lower-priority classes. Each station also sets three rotation timers to the three target rotation times each time it transmits the token. These timers all begin to count down as the token circulates around the ring.

Let us suppose that a station has transmitted all the data units that it had queued up in access class 6. It then examines the rotation timer for access class 4 to see if that time limit has expired. If the timer for access class 4 has not yet expired, the station is able to transmit data units from access class 4 queue, until either no more data units are available in that queue or the rotation timer assigned to that queue expires. If the station transmits all the data units in access class 4 and the timer for that queue has still not expired, it checks the timer for access class 2 and then transmits data units from that queue if any are available. The station then moves down to access class 0 if the timer for access class 2 has not yet expired.

Note that the priority algorithm is designed so that network bandwidth is assigned to the highest-priority data units as long as there are data units in access class 6 available for transmission by any station on the network. Lower-priority data units are sent only when there is sufficient bandwidth available for them. If there are many stations that have data units in access class 6 to transmit, it is likely that by the time a station finally receives the token, all its rotation timers will already have expired and the station will be allowed to transmit only data units assigned to access class 6. If traffic on the network is light, a station may receive the token before any of its rotation timers have expired, and the chances are better that lower-priority data units will be transmitted.

RING MAINTENANCE

To control the operation of the ring, each station knows the address of its *predecessor,* the station from which it received the token, and its *successor,* the station to which it must transmit the token. When a token bus network is initialized, or when it is reestablished following a catastrophic failure, each station must establish its predecessor and successor. As stations are added to or deleted from the ring, stations update their predecessor and successor values accordingly.

Adding a Station to the Ring

To allow for additions to the ring, each station must periodically give an opportunity for new stations to be added. To do this, a station that has received the token transmits a special control data unit, called a *solicit successor* data unit, that contains the address of the transmitting station and its current successor. Any station on the network that has an address that falls within the range of these two addresses can request that it be added to the ring. Ring maintenance procedures are designed so that new stations are added to the ring only when traffic on the network is relatively light. A station consults a timer called the maximum ring maintenance rotation time before transmitting a solicit successor data unit. If the current token rotation time is greater than the maximum ring maintenance rotation time, the station does not transmit a solicit successor data unit for that rotation of the token.

When a station holding the token transmits the solicit successor data unit, it then waits a period of time called the *response window* to see if any station responds. (The response window is the maximum amount of time it would take a response to reach the transmitting station and is equal to the *slot time*—twice the end-to-end propagation delay of the network.) If the token holder detects no response during the response window, it assumes that no new station wishes to be added to the ring.

A station that wishes to be added to the ring and has an address within the range specified in the solicit successor data unit responds to that data unit. If only one station responds, that station is added to the ring. The addition process involves the following steps:

1. The token holder changes its successor address to that of the station being added. The token holder also transmits the token to the station being added.

2. The station being added sets its successor and predecessor addresses appropriately and proceeds to process the token.

3. When the old successor receives a transmission from the station added, it saves that station's address as its new predecessor.

If more than one new station responds to the solicit successor data unit, their responses will collide and cause a garbled transmission. If the token holder detects a garbled transmission, it uses a contention resolution procedure to determine the station to be added. The token holder begins the contention resolution procedure by transmitting a *resolve contention* data unit. A station wishing to be added must wait 0, 1, 2, or 3 response windows before responding, depending on the value of its address. If a station detects a response from another station while it is waiting, that station does not respond.

If another conflict occurs and the token holder again detects a garbled transmission, it sends out another resolve contention data unit. This time, only stations that responded to the first resolve contention data unit are allowed to respond. They wait 0, 1, 2, or 3 response windows again based on the values of their addresses. This process continues until a single station responds or a maximum number of retries have been attempted. If the retry maximum is reached, the token holder passes the token to its successor without adding a station to the ring.

Deleting a Station from the Ring

The process for deleting a station from the ring is much simpler than the addition process. When a station wishes to be deleted, it waits until it receives the token. In then sends a *set successor* data unit to its predecessor, notifying it to change its successor address to the successor address of the station being deleted. Now its predecessor will pass the token directly to its successor, bypassing the station being deleted. When the new successor receives a transmission from its new predecessor, it saves that address as its predecessor address.

FAULT MANAGEMENT

The token bus standard also defines how certain error conditions are to be detected and corrected. Among these conditions are the following:

- Presence of multiple tokens on the ring
- Inactivity by a station when it is passed the token
- Loss of the token from the ring

Multiple Tokens

If a station that has received a token detects another transmission on the network, this indicates that another station is holding a token and is currently transmitting. To eliminate this condition, the station that received a token and has detected a transmission drops the token and reverts to a receiving state. This will reduce the number of token holders to either one or zero. If it is reduced to zero, the lost token procedure, described later, will start a new token circulating.

Station Inactive

After a station transmits the token, it listens for one response window to be sure its successor station has received the token and is transmitting. If it detects a transmission within the time period, it assumes that the successor station is processing properly.

If the issuing station does not detect a transmission within the window period, it retransmits the token. If there is no transmission following the second token passing, it assumes that the successor station has failed. The issuer then transmits a *who follows* data unit, asking the station that follows the failed station to identify itself. The station that follows the failed station issues a set successor data unit that identifies itself. The issuing station, when it receives the set successor data unit, changes its successor address and passes the token to its new successor. In this way, the failed station is automatically eliminated from the ring.

If there is no response to the who follows data unit, the issuer sends the data unit a second time. If no response is received the second time, the issuer sends out a solicit successor data unit in which the range of addresses covers the entire network. Responses to the solicit successor data unit are handled as described for additions to the ring. Assuming that a response is received and contention is resolved, a two-station ring is established. This process is repeated until the entire ring is reestablished.

If no response is received to the solicit successor data unit, the issuer transmits the data unit a second time. If no response is received after the second attempt, the issuing station reverts to listening mode.

Lost Token

If a station detects a lack of transmission that lasts longer than a predetermined period of time, it assumes that the token has been lost. When this happens, the station issues a *claim token* data unit that invites any station on the ring to claim the token and begin processing. Contending responses to the claim token data unit are handled in the same way as an addition to the ring. In this way, a single claimant is identified and is issued the token.

Several conditions can trigger lost token processing, including failure of the token-holding station or the network being initially powered up. When the network is being initially powered up, lost token processing provides the ring initialization necessary to start processing.

SENDING AND RECEIVING FRAMES

The primary purpose of the media access control sublayer is to accept data units from the logical link control sublayer in a sending station, to see that they are transmitted across the network, and to pass data units received back to the LLC sublayer in the station. On the sending side, the MAC sublayer adds header and trailer information to the protocol data unit that it receives from the LLC sublayer, forming a *transmission frame,* or simply a *frame*. The frame is then passed in the form of a bit stream to the physical layer. On the receiving side, a bit stream is passed up from the physical layer to the MAC sublayer. The MAC sublayer uses information in the header and trailer to check that the frame has been transmitted correctly, removes the header and trailer, and passes the resulting protocol data unit up to the LLC sublayer in the receiving station.

The MAC sublayer may also generate control frames that are transmitted across the network and are used by the MAC sublayer in the receiving station. In this case, no frames are exchanged with the LLC sublayer, either in the sending or the receiving station. Box 7.1 describes the format of a token bus transmission frame.

The frame control field is used to identify different types of frames. Control frames are used for token-passing and ring maintenance functions. Box 7.2 lists the control frames that are defined in the token bus standard. Each frame has a specific format. The frame control field is also used to identify three types of frames: LLC data frames, station management data frames, and special-purpose data frames.

BOX 7.1   Token bus transmission frame

Preamble	Start Delimiter	Frame Control	Destination Address	Source Address	Logical Link Control or Media Access Control Information		Frame Check Sequence	End Delimiter
1-*n* Bytes	1 Byte	1 Byte	2 or 6 Bytes	2 or 6 Bytes	0-819 Bytes		4 Bytes	1 Byte

- **Preamble.** Each frame begins with a *preamble* field that is used by the receiving station for synchronization. The length of this field and its contents vary with the modulation method and the data rate used in the particular implementation of the standard.

- **Start Delimiter.** The *start delimiter* is 1 byte long and contains a signaling pattern that is always distinguishable from data. (For example, with Manchester encoding, this might be a byte containing one or more bit times in which no transmission takes place. See Chapter 2 for a discussion of data encoding schemes.)

- **Frame Control Field.** The *frame control* field identifies the type of frame being sent. Possible types are LLC data frames, token control frames, MAC management data frames, and special-purpose data frames.

- **Address Fields.** Addresses can be either 2 bytes (16-bit addresses) or 6 bytes (48-bit addresses) in length. Two-byte addresses are locally administered; 6-byte addresses may be either locally administered or universal. The address length must be consistent throughout a given network. The source address is always an individual address. A destination address can be an individual address, a group address, or a broadcast address.

- **Information Field.** The *information field* may contain an LLC protocol data unit, token control data, management data, or special-purpose data, as indicated by the frame control field.

- **Frame Check Sequence.** The information field is followed by a *frame check sequence* field. When the sending station assembles a frame, it performs a cyclical redundancy check (CRC) calculation on the bits in the frame. The specific algorithm that is used is described in the IEEE documentation and always results in a 4-byte value. The sending station stores this value in the frame check sequence field and then transmits the frame. When the receiving station receives the frame, it performs the identical CRC calculation and compares the results with the value in the frame check sequence field. If the two values do not match, the receiving station assumes that a transmission error has occurred and can request that the frame be retransmitted.

- **End Delimiter.** Like the start delimiter, the *end delimiter* contains a signaling value that is always distinguishable from data. It marks the end of the frame and also identifies the position of the frame check sequence field.

BOX 7.2   MAC control frames

Frame Type	Control Field	Purpose
Claim_token	00000000	Used to initiate token-passing operations when a network is initialized or when the token is lost.
Solicit_successor_1	00000001	Used to allow new stations to be added to the network.
Solicit_successor_2	00000010	Used to allow a new station to be added to the ring when its address is lower than the lowest address or higher than the highest address currently on the network.
Who_follows	00000011	Used when a successor station does not respond to being passed the token. Based on the response to this, the station sending the token acquires a new successor.
Resolve_contention	00000100	Used when multiple stations respond to a solicit successor frame.
Token	00001000	Used as the token.
Set_successor	00001100	Used in response to a who follows frame or a solicit successor frame to supply the address of the new successor station.

LLC/MAC INTERFACE SERVICE SPECIFICATION

The interface between the LLC sublayer and the MAC sublayer is defined, as described in Chapter 5, using the following service primitives:

- **MA_DATA.request**
- **MA_DATA.indicate**
- **MA_DATA.confirm**

MA_DATA.request passes a protocol data unit from the LLC sublayer to the MAC sublayer for transmission over the network. **MA_DATA.indicate** notifies LLC that a frame has been received and then passes the resulting protocol data unit to the LLC sublayer. **MA_DATA.confirm** provides the LLC sublayer with status information about an **MA_DATA.request.**

STATION   The token bus standard also defines an interface be-
MANAGEMENT/MAC   tween the MAC sublayer and a *station management*
INTERFACE   function. The station management function is respon-
                         sible for control functions, such as resetting a MAC
sublayer entity and selecting its address, specifying values for constants (such
as timer values) used in the network, determining that a MAC entity's address
is unique within the network, and specifying group addresses. The interface
between the MAC sublayer and station management is defined in terms of a set
of service primitives, listed in Box 7.3.

BOX 7.3   Station manager/MAC interface primitives

MA_INITIALIZE_PROTOCOL.request. Resets the MAC sublayer and determines the MAC address, token protocol, and the station's role in the network.

MA_INITIALIZE_PROTOCOL.confirmation. Responds to an initialization request and indicates whether the specified protocol is available.

MA_SET_VALUE.request. Used by station management to set an MAC variable value.

MA_SET_VALUE.confirmation. Indicates whether or not a variable value was successfully set.

MA_READ_VALUE.request. Used by station management to request the value of a MAC variable.

MA_READ_VALUE.confirmation. Returns the requested variable value.

MA_EVENT.indication. Sent by station management to indicate that a significant event has occurred.

MA_FAULT_REPORT.indication. Sent to station management to indicate that an error has been detected by the MAC sublayer.

MA_GROUP_ADDRESS.request. Sent to the MAC sublayer to specify the set of group addresses this MAC entity should recognize and accept frames for.

MA_GROUP_ADDRESS.confirmation. Sent by the MAC sublayer to indicate whether or not a group address request was successfully processed.

(Continued)

BOX 7.3 *(Continued)*

MA_CDATA.request. Sent by station management to request that a station management frame be transmitted.

MA_CDATA.indication. Sent to station management to indicate the arrival of a station management frame.

MA_CDATA.confirmation. Sent to station management to indicate whether or not a data request was successfully processed.

PHYSICAL LAYER SPECIFICATION

The physical layer standards for the token bus standard include a specification of the interface between the MAC sublayer and the physical layer. The standard also documents specifications for the physical layer and describes three different transmission types. Two of the transmission types use baseband coaxial cable transmission and one uses broadband coaxial cable transmission.

MAC/PHYSICAL LAYER INTERFACE

The interface between the MAC sublayer and the physical layer provides for the passing of bits and control information between them. It is defined in terms of a set of service primitives, shown in Box 7.4. These primitives provide for the transmission and reception of 0 and 1 bits and also for nondata bits that are used in the start and end delimiter fields. They also allow for a station that is acting only as a repeater.

BOX 7.4 MAC/physical layer interface primitives

PHY_DATA.request. Passed to the physical layer to request that a symbol, which can be a 0 bit, 1 bit, or nondata bit, be transmitted.

PHY_DATA.indication. Passed to the MAC sublayer to indicate that a symbol has been received and to pass the symbol to the MAC sublayer.

PHY_MODE.request. Passed to the physical layer to select a mode of operation. The mode selected can be either normal or monitor mode.

PHY_NOTIFY.request. Passed to the physical layer to notify it that an end frame delimiter has been detected.

PHYSICAL LAYER/ STATION MANAGEMENT INTERFACE

An interface is also defined between the physical layer and the station management function. Its service primitives are shown in Box 7.5. These services relate primarily to determining, selecting, or changing the operating mode of the physical layer, including operation as a repeater.

BOX 7.5 Physical layer/station management interface primitives

PHY_RESET.request. Sent by station management to reset the physical layer and to verify the network's topology and the physical layer's role in the network.

PHY_RESET.confirmation. Sent by the physical layer to indicate the success or failure of a reset request.

PHY_MODAL_CAPABILITY_QUERY.request. Sent by station management to determine the physical layer's capabilities for a specific mode of operation.

PHY_MODAL_CAPABILITY_QUERY.confirmation. Sent by the physical layer to describe its capabilities in response to a query.

PHY_MODE_QUERY.request. Sent by station management to determine the physical layer's current mode of operation.

PHY_MODE_QUERY.confirmation. Sent by the physical layer, in response to a query, to specify its current mode of operation.

PHY_MODE_SELECT.request. Sent by station management to specify a particular mode of operation for the physical layer.

PHY_MODE_SELECT.confirmation. Sent by the physical layer to indicate whether the requested mode of operation has been selected.

PHY_MODE_CHANGE.indication. Sent by the physical layer to indicate that its mode of operation was changed by other than a request from station management.

TRANSMISSION TYPES

The token bus standard addresses three different types of transmission. For each transmission type, there is a specification for the physical layer and a description of the physical transmission medium. Physical layer specifications include detailed descriptions of functional, electrical, and physical characteristics as well as environmental specifications related to safety, electromagnetic and electric environment, temperature, humidity, and regulatory requirements. Transmission medium descriptions also specify functional, electrical, and physical characteristics and environmental considerations as well as transmission path delay considerations and, in some cases, network sizing considerations.

The three types of transmission defined by the standard are single-channel phase-continuous FSK, single-channel phase-coherent FSK, and broadband. These are described next.

Single-Channel Phase-Continuous FSK

The single-channel phase-continuous FSK specification uses baseband transmission. Frequency-shift keying (FSK) is used as the modulation technique, where the changes in frequency occur continuously (phase-continuous). For this approach, Manchester encoding is used.

With Manchester encoding, a low-high signal combination represents a 1 bit and a high-low combination represents a 0 bit. The other possible combinations, low-low and high-high, are used to represent nondata bits. These nondata bits are used as part of the start and end frame delimiters. By using signals that are not the same as data, the beginning and end of a frame are always clearly identifiable, and no combination of bits in a frame can be mistaken for a frame delimiter.

In addition to the basic signal transmission and reception functions, the physical layer specification includes a *repeater* function and a *jabber-inhibit* function. The repeater function allows a station to act as a repeater only, connecting two cable segments and regenerating the signal as it passes from one segment to the other. The jabber-inhibit function allows a station to interrupt a transmission and disable the transmitter if the transmission continues for too long a time.

A 75-ohm, CATV-type coaxial cable is used for the trunk cable in the network. Devices are attached to the trunk cable using a drop cable, which is 35- to 50-ohm cable, no more than 35 cm long. The data rate is 1Mbps. Carrier frequency ranges around 5 MHz, varying from 3.75 MHz to 6.25 MHz.

Single-Channel Phase-Coherent FSK

Single-channel phase-coherent FSK specification use baseband transmission and frequency modulation. Here, though, the frequency varies between two discrete values rather than varying continuously.

The encoding technique used is a variation on Manchester encoding. A low-low combination represents a 1 bit, a high-high combination a 0 bit. The other combinations, low-high and high-low, are used for nondata bits that are employed in the frame delimiters. The repeater and jabber-inhibit functions are also supported with this transmission specification.

This specification also uses 75-ohm, CATV-type coaxial cable for the trunk cable. Two data rates are supported: 5 Mbps and 10 Mbps. For the 5 Mbps rate, the frequencies used are 5 MHz and 10 MHz. For the 10 Mbps rate, the frequencies are 10 MHz and 20 MHz.

Broadband

The broadband specification uses broadband transmission over a bus-structured network. Either a single-cable, mid-split or a dual-cable configuration can be used, although the single-cable is recommended. The modulation technique used is called *multilevel duobinary AM/PSK*. This modulation technique uses amplitude modulation (AM) combined with phase-shift keying (PSK).

The signaling technique, multilevel duobinary, allows for three distinct amplitude levels. The three levels are symbolically represented as {0}, {2}, and {4}. Nondata bits are represented by the signal value {2}, 0 bits by {0}, and 1 bits by {4}. A scrambler function is also used when there is a long sequence of 0 bits or a long sequence of 1 bits, in which a pseudorandom function is used to convert certain 0 bits to 1 bits and vice versa. This prevents long sequences of a given bit value from affecting synchronization. On the receiving end, a descrambling function restores the bits to their original values.

Three data rates are supported: 1 Mbps, 5 Mbps and 10 Mbps. With 1 Mbps, a channel bandwidth of 1.5 MHz is required; with 5 Mbps, 6 MHz; and with 10 Mbps, 12 MHz.

SUMMARY

With token bus, a control data unit called a token is passed in a logical sequence from one station to the next. When a station receives the token, it is allowed to transmit for a specified period of time. Different priorities can be assigned to data units, and token rotation timers are used to allow transmission based on priority values. Each station knows the address of its predecessor and successor on the logical ring. When a station is added to or deleted from the network or the network is initialized, stations use special control data units to update these addresses. Fault management procedures are defined to detect multiple tokens, the loss of the token, or an inactive station.

A token bus transmission frame contains a preamble, start delimiter, frame control, destination address, source address, information field, frame check sequence, and end delimiter. The token bus standard supports three types of physical transmission: single-channel phase-continuous FSK bus, single-channel phase-coherent FSK bus, and broadband bus.

8 IEEE 802.5: TOKEN RING

The third media access control standard documented by IEEE 802 standards is for the *token ring* architecture. This is particularly important because it is the basis of IBM's main architecture for local area networking. Many other vendors market equipment and software that are compatible with IBM's token ring architecture. Token ring uses a logical model similar to that for token bus, as shown in Fig. 8.1. It defines the logical link control and media access control sublayers and the physical control layer. Devices are attached to the physical medium using a *trunk-coupling unit*. The MAC sublayer standard defines both an access protocol and a frame format.

TOKEN RING ACCESS PROTOCOL

The token ring network structure consists of a logical ring implemented using a physical ring topology, as shown in Fig. 8.2. Transmission flows in a single direction. Data units are passed from one station to the next in physical sequence along the ring. Each station transmits the data unit to the next station, acting as a repeater.

The right to transmit data units is controlled by a token, which is passed from one station to the next along the ring. When a station receives the token, it is allowed to transmit data units until a predetermined time limit is reached. A token with a configuration that indicates the right to transmit is called a *free token*. When a station receives a free token and has data units to transmit, it changes the configuration of the token to that of a *busy token* and includes the busy token as part of each data unit it then transmits. The data units travel from station to station around the ring. Each station that receives a data unit checks the address in the data unit to see if it should process that data unit. In either case, it sends the data unit on to the next station. When a data unit returns to

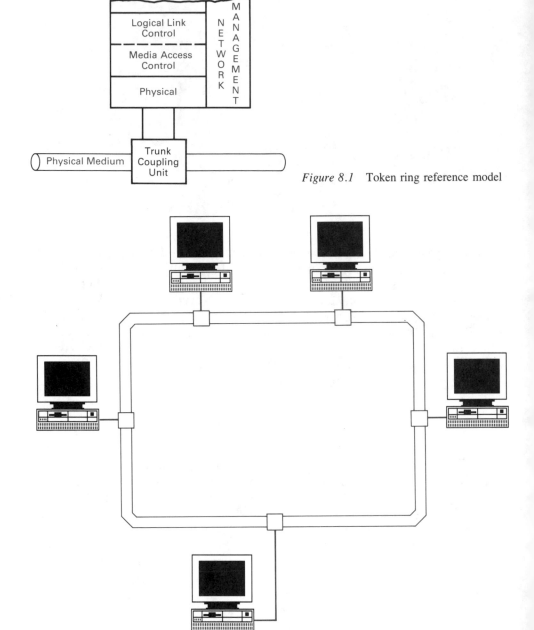

Figure 8.1 Token ring reference model

Figure 8.2 Token ring network structure

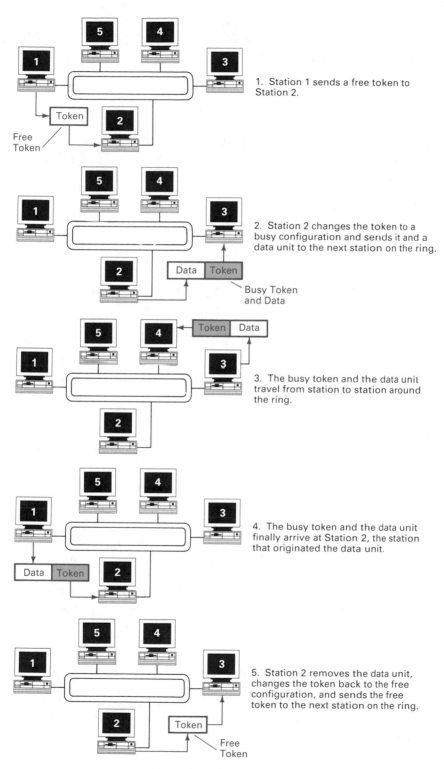

1. Station 1 sends a free token to Station 2.

2. Station 2 changes the token to a busy configuration and sends it and a data unit to the next station on the ring.

3. The busy token and the data unit travel from station to station around the ring.

4. The busy token and the data unit finally arrive at Station 2, the station that originated the data unit.

5. Station 2 removes the data unit, changes the token back to the free configuration, and sends the free token to the next station on the ring.

Figure 8.3   Token ring operation

the station that originally sent it, the station removes the data unit from the network and sends a free token on the next station. Figure 8.3 illustrates this procedure.

Since a data unit travels to all stations and then returns to the sending station, it is possible for destination stations to set control bits in the data unit as they pass it on to the next station, indicating whether or not the data unit was processed and whether any errors were detected. Three control bits have been defined for these purposes:

- **Address Recognized.** The destination station identified this data unit as being addressed to it.
- **Packet Copied.** The destination station passed a copy of the data unit up to the LLC sublayer for processing.
- **Error.** An error condition was detected. This bit can be set by any station on the ring, not only a station that has processed the data unit.

Different combinations of the address-recognized and packet-copied bits allow the source station to differentiate between different circumstances, such as these:

- The data unit was processed.
- The destination station recognized the data unit as being addressed to it but was not able to process it.
- The destination station either did not recognize the data unit or is nonexistent or inactive.

FAULT MANAGEMENT

Two error conditions can seriously affect the operation of a token ring network: loss of the token or a persistently busy token. The approach taken to detecting and correcting these conditions is to have one of the stations on the network function as an *active monitor*.

The station designated as the active monitor continuously monitors the network. If a predetermined period of time elapses with no token being detected, the monitor assumes that the token has been lost and issues a new token. To check for a persistently busy token, the monitor sets a monitor bit in a busy token as it passes. If a busy token returns to the active monitor station with the monitor bit still set, the monitor knows that the source station failed to remove the data unit from the network. This may have occurred either because a transmission problem garbled the data unit so that the source station did not recognize it or because the source station has failed. The monitor then changes the data unit to a free token and passes it on to the next station.

All other stations on the network act as *passive monitors*. They monitor the operation of the active monitor. If for some reason the active monitor fails, the passive monitors use a contention resolution procedure to determine which station should take over the role of active monitor.

Another type of failure that can seriously affect a token ring network is the failure of a station. If a station fails, it may no longer be able to transmit data units, thus causing the ring to be broken. The approach used to deal with this is to provide a *bypass switch* as part of each station. If a station fails, the bypass switch can be closed, either manually or automatically, removing the station from the ring and allowing data units to circulate again around the ring.

If the bypass switch is combined with a physical-star wiring configuration, physical failures in the ring can be much simpler to correct. Figure 8.4 illustrates the use of star wiring and bypass switches. With star wiring, each device is attached to a centrally located panel, which contains the bypass switches. If a failure occurs in a device or a disruption occurs in the cable attaching the device, the bypass switch is closed, and the ring remains unbroken. Notice that the topology of the network is still a ring and not a star, since the central panel

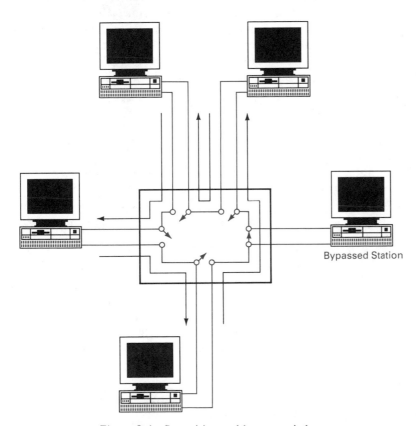

Figure 8.4   Star wiring and bypass switches

does not have the intelligence to act as a network station. It is simply a passive wiring concentrator. However, by having a portion of the wiring centrally located, it is much easier to attach a new device or to identify and isolate a fault. With a small number of devices, it may be desirable to attach devices directly to one another without using a central wiring concentrator. But with a large number of devices spread over many different offices and possibly even different floors, physically identifying and locating the connections from one device to another could become a major task.

OPTIONAL PRIORITY SCHEME

Token ring access control can be operated on either a nonpriority or a priority basis. When the optional priority scheme is not implemented, a station can send data units whenever it receives a free token. When the priority scheme is implemented, three bits in each data unit are used to represent the *current priority*. When a station receives a free token, it compares the priority value in the token against the priority of any data unit it has to transmit. If a data unit's priority is equal to or higher than the token priority, the data unit is transmitted. If the data unit's priority value is lower than that of the token, the data unit is not transmitted.

Each frame also contains three *reservation* bits. If a station has a data unit to transmit that has a priority greater than 0, when it receives and retransmits a frame, it can set the reservation bits in the token to the priority value of the data unit it has waiting to send. When the original sending station removes the data unit and generates a free token, it checks the reservation bits and the priorities of any additional data units it has waiting to send. If either the reservation bits in the token or the priority of the waiting data unit is higher than the current token priority, it sets the token priority to the higher value. If a station raises the token's priority value, it saves the previous lower value of the token's priority and is responsible for eventually restoring the token priority to the original lower value.

FRAME FORMAT

The format of the transmission frame used by the token ring access control method is shown in Box 8.1. Figure 8.5 shows two special frame formats. The first is the format used for the token, which contains only an access control field and the starting and ending delimiters. The other format is called the abort sequence and it is used to terminate the transmission of a frame prematurely.

An information frame can contain either a protocol data unit passed from logical link control or control information generated by medium access control. Box 8.2 lists some of the MAC control frames defined by the standard.

BOX 8.1   Token ring transmission frame

Starting Delimiter	Access Control	Frame Control	Destination Address	Source Address	Logical Link Control or Media Access Control Information	Frame Check Sequence	Ending Delimiter	Frame Status
1 Byte	1 Byte	1 Byte	2 or 6 Bytes	2 or 6 Bytes	0-4099 Bytes	4 Bytes	1 Byte	1 Byte

- **Starting Delimiter.** The *starting delimiter* is a unique signal pattern that identifies the start of a frame. Token ring uses differential Manchester encoding, which allows for signal values that do not correspond to either a 0 or a 1 bit. These are known as nondata values and are used as part of the starting and ending delimiters. This ensures that no data sequence will ever be mistaken for a delimiter.

- **Access Control Field.** The *access control* field identifies whether the frame is a data frame or a token. It also contains a bit used to identify a persistently busy token, priority bits, and reservation bits.

- **Frame Control Field.** The *frame control* field identifies the type of frame and, for certain control frames, the particular function to be performed.

- **Addresses.** Addresses can be either 2 bytes (16-bit addresses) or 6 bytes (48-bit addresses) in length, depending on whether they are locally administered or universal. The length used must be consistent throughout a given network. The *source address* must be an individual address. The *destination address* can be an individual address, a group address, or a broadcast address.

- **Information Field.** The *information* field can contain either a protocol data unit passed from logical link control or control information supplied by the media access control sublayer.

- **Frame Check Sequence.** The information is followed by a *frame check sequence* field. When the sending station assembles a frame, it performs a cyclical redundancy check (CRC) calculation on the bits in the frame. The specific algorithm that is used is described in the IEEE documentation and always results in a 4-byte value. The sending station stores this value in the frame check sequence field and then transmits the frame. When the receiving station receives the frame, it performs the identical CRC calculation and compares the result with the value in the frame check sequence field. If the two values do not match, the receiving station assumes that a transmission error has occurred and can request that the frame be retransmitted.

- **Ending Delimiter.** The *ending delimiter* identifies the end of the frame. As with the starting delimiter, it contains nondata values. In addition, it contains bits used to identify whether or not this is the last frame in a multiframe transmission and whether an error has already been detected by some other station.

- **Frame Status Field.** The *frame status* field contains the *address-recognized* and *frame-copied* bits that are used to indicate whether or not a frame was successfully received by a destination station.

Token Format

| Starting Delimiter | Ending Delimiter |

Abort Sequence

Figure 8.5   Special frame formats

SERVICE SPECIFICATIONS

The token ring standard defines service specifications for the interface between the LLC sublayer and the MAC sublayer, the MAC/physical layer interface, the MAC/network management interface, and the physical layer/network management interface. The LLC/MAC interface is defined, as it is in the LLC standard, by the service primitives **MA_DATA.request, MA_DATA.indication,** and **MA_DATA.confirmation.**

The MAC/physical layer interface uses the following service primitives:

- **PH_DATA.request.** This primitive defines the transfer of either one bit of data or a nondata value from the MAC sublayer to the physical layer for transmission.

- **PH_DATA.indication.** This primitive defines the transfer of either one bit of data or a nondata value from the physical layer to the MAC sublayer.

BOX 8.2   MAC control frames

Frame	Function
Claim Token	Used by a station to become the active monitor when no active monitor is present on the ring.
Duplicate Address Test	Used when a station is added to the ring to ensure that its address is unique.
Active Monitor Present	Used to notify all stations that an active monitor is present.
Standby Monitor Present	Used to notify all stations that a standby monitor is present.
Beacon	Sent when a serious ring failure occurs, to help identify the location of the failure.
Purge	Sent by the active monitor following claiming the token or to reinitialize the ring.

- **PH_DATA.confirmation.** This primitive defines a response sent from the physical layer to the MAC sublayer after the physical layer has received a **PH_DATA.request** and is ready to receive another bit or signal value.

The interfaces to the network management function provide access to services used to monitor and control the operation of the MAC sublayer and the physical layer. The MAC/network management primitives are listed in Box 8.3. The physical layer/network management primitives are shown in Box 8.4.

BOX 8.3   MAC/network management interface primitives

MA_INITIALIZE_PROTOCOL.request. Sent by network management to reset the MAC sublayer and change MAC operational parameters.

MA_INITIALIZE_PROTOCOL.confirmation. Sent by MAC to indicate the success or failure of an initialization request.

MA_CONTROL.request. Sent by station management to control the operation of the MAC sublayer.

MA_STATUS.indication. Sent by the MAC sublayer to report errors and significant status changes.

MA_NMT_DATA.request. Sent by network management when it has a data unit to transmit.

MA_NMT_DATA.indication. Sent to station management to notify it that a station management data unit has arrived and to transfer the data unit to station management.

MA_NMT_DATA.confirmation. Sent by the MAC sublayer to indicate the success or failure of a data request.

BOX 8.4   Physical/network management interface

PH_CONTROL.request. Sent by network management to request that the physical layer insert itself on or remove itself from the ring.

PH_STATUS.indication. Sent by the physical layer to inform network management of errors or significant status changes.

TOKEN RING PHYSICAL LAYER The token ring standard uses a form of encoding known as *differential Manchester encoding*. As with Manchester encoding, differential Manchester encoding always has a transition in the middle of a bit frame, which allows the encoded data to be self-clocking. The Manchester encoding system used with the token ring standard is illustrated in Fig. 8.6. (See Chapter 2 for a discussion of differential Manchester encoding.) A signal that does not make a transition during a bit frame is considered a code violation. There are two types of code violations, depending on whether or not there is a signal transition when the bit frame starts. These two types of code violations, illustrated in Fig. 8.7, are used in the starting and ending frame delimiters to distinguish the delimiters from data.

The standard currently has defined functional, electrical, and mechanical characteristics for baseband transmission using shielded, twisted-wire-pair cable. It uses 150-ohm, shielded, twisted-wire-pair cable and supports data rates of 1 Mbps or 4 Mbps. A variation of the token ring standard uses baseband transmission over coaxial cable and supports data rates of 4 Mbps, 20 Mbps, and 40 Mbps.

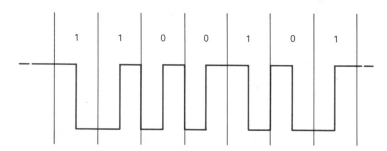

Figure 8.6 Differential Manchester encoding

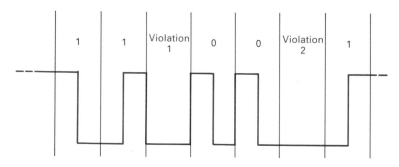

Figure 8.7 Code violations

SUMMARY
With the token ring access control method, a token is passed from one station to the next along a physical ring. When a station receives the token, it is allowed to transmit for a specified time. The station that transmits a data unit is responsible for removing it from the ring and then sending a free token to the next station. Stations around the ring that receive a data unit are able to set bits in the data unit that indicate whether the destination address was recognized, the data unit was copied, or an error was detected. Different priorities can be assigned to data units. The priority value associated with the token then determines when different data units can be transmitted.

A station designated as the active monitor is responsible for detecting and correcting the loss of the token or a persistently busy token. Stations designated as passive monitors monitor the active monitor station and take over its function if it fails.

A token ring transmission frame contains a starting delimiter, access control, frame control, address fields, information field, frame check sequence, and ending delimiter. The token ring standard uses differential Manchester encoding. Two transmission techniques are specified: baseband transmission over twisted-wire-pair cable at data rates of 1 Mbps or 4 Mbps and baseband transmission over coaxial cable at rates of 4 Mbps, 20 Mbps, or 40 Mbps.

PART III   OTHER LAN ARCHITECTURES

9 FIBER DISTRIBUTED DATA INTERFACE (FDDI)

One of the reasons for developing network standards, such as those developed by IEEE Project 802, is to make it easier to interconnect hardware and software from different vendors to form an operating network. The same need exists, even more strongly, when networks are interconnected to meet broader communication needs. In this chapter we examine the *Fiber Distributed Data Interface* (FDDI) standard that is designed to meet requirements both for high-performance individual networks and for high-speed connections between networks.

The Fiber Distributed Data Interface standard was developed by the American National Standards Institute (ANSI). It is based on the use of optical fiber cable and provides for a token-passing ring configuration operating at a data rate of 100 Mbps. The FDDI standard addresses the physical and MAC layers and assumes the use of the IEEE 802 logical link control (LLC) standard operating above the MAC layer. Although closely related to the local area network standards developed by the IEEE Project 802, it was felt that the experience of the Accredited Standards Committee (ASC) X3T9 in developing I/O interface standards made that committee better suited to deal with the high transmission speeds used in FDDI, and thus FDDI was assigned to the ASC X3T9.5 committee.

The FDDI standard is being developed to deal with the requirements associated with three types of networks: *backend local networks, high-speed office networks,* and *backbone local networks.*

- **Backend Local Networks.** Backend local networks are used to interconnect mainframe computers and large data storage devices where there is a need for a high-volume data transfer rate. Typically, in a backend local network there will be a small number of devices to be connected, and they will be close together.

- **High-Speed Office Networks.** The need for high-speed office networks has arisen from the increased use of image and graphics processing devices in the office environment. The use of graphics and document images can increase the amount of data that needs to be transmitted on a network by orders of magnitudes. A typical data processing transaction may involve 500 bits, whereas a document page image may require the transmission of 500,000 bits or more.
- **Backbone Local Networks.** Backbone local networks are used to provide a high-capacity network that can be used to interconnect lower-capacity local area networks.

All three types of networks have a requirement for the high transmission and data rates associated with the FDDI network.

FDDI ACCESS PROTOCOL

The FDDI media access control protocol is based on token passing in a ring configuration and is similar to the IEEE 802.5 token ring protocol. However, there are differences in token handling, priority, and management mechanisms. A frame with a specific format, called the *token,* is passed from one station to the next around the ring. When a station receives the token, it is allowed to transmit. The station can send as many frames as desired until a predefined time limit is reached. When a station either has no more frames to send or reaches the time limit, it transmits the token. Each station on the network retransmits the frames it receives and copies from the ring those that are addressed to it. When a frame returns to the sending station, that station is responsible for removing the frame from the ring. As stations copy frames, stations are able to set status bits in frames, indicating whether errors have been detected, addresses recognized, or frames copied for processing. Based on these status bits, a sending station is able to determine whether or not a frame was successfully received. However, error recovery processing and retransmission are not specified as part of the MAC protocol and are left to higher layers.

Since the token is transmitted as soon as a station is finished transmitting frames, it is possible that a station might transmit new frames while earlier frames it transmitted are still circulating around the ring. Thus it is possible that there may be multiple frames, from multiple stations, on the network at any given time. This is illustrated in Fig. 9.1.

CAPACITY ALLOCATION

FDDI does not use the priority mechanism documented in the IEEE 802.5 token ring standard. Instead, it uses a capacity allocation scheme based on the time it takes for the token to return. This scheme is designed to support a mixture of stream and burst transmissions and transmissions that involve dialogs between pairs of stations.

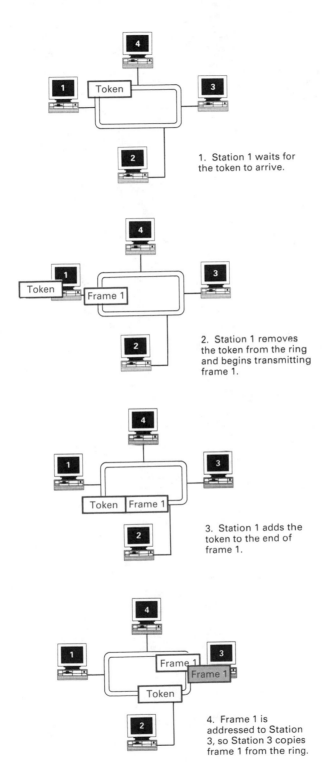

1. Station 1 waits for the token to arrive.

2. Station 1 removes the token from the ring and begins transmitting frame 1.

3. Station 1 adds the token to the end of frame 1.

4. Frame 1 is addressed to Station 3, so Station 3 copies frame 1 from the ring.

Figure 9.1   FDDI token-passing protocol

(Continued)

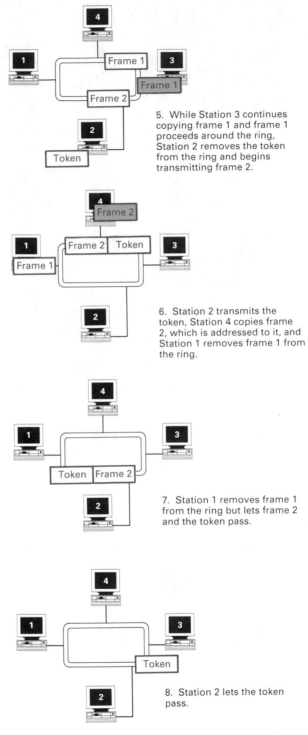

5. While Station 3 continues copying frame 1 and frame 1 proceeds around the ring, Station 2 removes the token from the ring and begins transmitting frame 2.

6. Station 2 transmits the token, Station 4 copies frame 2, which is addressed to it, and Station 1 removes frame 1 from the ring.

7. Station 1 removes frame 1 from the ring but lets frame 2 and the token pass.

8. Station 2 lets the token pass.

Figure 9.1   (Continued)

Two types of frames are defined: synchronous and asynchronous. Each station may be allocated a certain length of time during which it can transmit synchronous frames. This time interval is called its *synchronous allocation* (SA). A *target token rotation time* (TTRT) is also defined for the network. The TTRT must be large enough to accommodate the sum of all the station synchronous transmission times plus the time it takes for a frame of maximum size to travel around the ring. Each station keeps track of the time that has elapsed since it last received the token. When it next receives the token, it records the time elapsed since the last token. The station is then allowed to transmit synchronous frames for its synchronous allocation time. If the elapsed time as recorded when the token was received is less than the TTRT, it is allowed to send asynchronous frames for a time interval equal to that time difference. Thus stations that have a synchronous allocation are guaranteed an opportunity to transmit synchronous frames; the station sends asynchronous frames only if time permits. Asynchronous frames can optionally be subdivided using levels of priority that are then used to prioritize the sending of asynchronous traffic.

FDDI also provides a mechanism for implementing multiframe dialogs. When a station needs to enter into a dialog with another station, it can do so using its asynchronous transmission capacity. After the station transmits the first frame in the dialog, it transmits a *restricted token*. Only the station that receives the first frame is allowed to use the restricted token for transmitting asynchronous frames. The two stations can then exchange data frames and restricted tokens for the duration of the dialog. During this time, other stations will be able to send synchronous frames but no asynchronous frames.

FAULT MANAGEMENT

FDDI specifies general fault management techniques for handling token-related problems. All stations on the network are responsible for monitoring the functioning of the token-passing protocol and for initializing the ring if an invalid condition occurs. Invalid conditions can include an extended period of inactivity on the ring (lost token) or an extended period of data transmission without a token (persistent frame). When a station detects either condition, it begins a process of initializing the ring.

A station begins the ring initialization process by performing a *claim token* procedure. The station begins issuing a continuous stream of control frames called *claim frames*. Each frame contains a suggested target token rotation time (TTRT) value. If a station sending claim frames receives a claim frame from another station, it compares TTRT values. If its TTRT value is lower, it keeps transmitting claim frames. If the other station's value is lower, it transmits the other station's frames. If the values are the same, the station addresses are used to determine which station takes precedence. Eventually, the claim frame with the lowest TTRT value will be passed on by other stations and will return to the station that sent it. At this point the sending station recognizes itself as the winner in the claim token procedure.

The actual ring initialization procedure then follows. The station that was the winner in the claim token procedure sends out a token containing its TTRT value. The other stations recognize that ring initialization is now taking place because they previously received claim frames. Each station saves the TTRT value, performs initialization processing, and passes the token on the next station. No frames are transmitted until the token has passed once around the ring.

When a serious failure occurs, such as a break in the ring, a *beacon process* is used. When a station that has been sending claim frames recognizes that a defined time period has elapsed without the claim token process being resolved, it begins the beacon process by transmitting a continuous stream of beacon frames. If a station receives a beacon frame from another station, it stops sending its beacon frames and passes on the beacon frames it has received. Eventually, beacon frames from the station immediately following the break will be propagated through the network, allowing the network to be reconfigured. If a station receives its own beacon frames, it assumes that the ring has been restored and initiates the claim token procedure.

FRAME FORMAT

The frame format used for FDDI transmission is similar, but not identical, to that defined by the IEEE 802.5 token ring standard. In describing its frame format, FDDI uses the term *symbol* to refer to a group of 4 bits. Symbols are encoded in a way that allows both data and nondata values to be represented. The FDDI frame format is shown in Box 9.1. A special frame format is used for the token, consisting only of a preamble, starting delimiter, frame control field, and ending delimiter.

Four types of frames have been defined: logical link control (LLC), control, reserved for implementer, and reserved for future standardization. An LLC frame contains information passed from the LLC layer. A control frame includes the token; MAC frames, including the claim and beacon frames; and station management frames. The reserved frame types are used for implementation-specific purposes and for future versions of the standard.

MAC SERVICE SPECIFICATIONS

The FDDI standard defines a service specification for the LLC-MAC interface, which is close, but not identical, to the IEEE 802.2 LLC standard. The specification uses the primitives **MA_DATA.request, MA_DATA.indication, MA_DATA.confirmation,** and **MA_TOKEN.request.** The **MA_DATA** primitives serve the same purpose as those defined in the LLC standard. The **MA _TOKEN.request** primitive is used by LLC to request the capture of the next token. It can be used to minimize waiting time for the token when it has time-critical data that will be ready to send shortly.

BOX 9.1 FDDI transmission frame

Preamble	Starting Delimiter	Frame Control	Destination Address	Source Address	Logical Link Control or Media Access Control Information	Frame Check Sequence	Ending Delimiter	Frame Status
16 Symbols	2 Symbols	2 Symbols	4 or 12 Symbols	4 or 12 Symbols	0-n Symbols	8 Symbols	1 or 2 Symbols	1 Symbol

- **Preamble.** The *preamble* is used to synchronize each station's clock with the transmission. It consists of 16 idle symbols, or 64 bits.

- **Starting Delimiter.** The *starting delimiter* is a unique signal pattern that identifies the start of the frame. It consists of the J and K nondata symbols.

- **Frame Control.** The *frame control* field identifies the frame's type. It has the bit format CLFFZZZZ, where C identifies this as a synchronous or asynchronous frame, L specifies whether 16- or 48-bit addresses are used, FF indicates whether this is an LLC or MAC frame, and ZZZZ provides control information for MAC frames.

- **Addresses.** Addresses can be either 4 symbols (16-bit addresses) or 12 symbols (48-bit addresses) in length. A ring may contain a mixture of stations using 16-bit or 48-bit addresses. The *destination address* can be an individual address, a group address, or a broadcast address. The *source address* must identify an individual station.

- **Information Field.** The *information field* can contain data passed from the LLC layer or control information supplied by the MAC layer.

- **Frame Check Sequence.** The *frame check sequence* contains a 32-bit cyclic redundancy check value. The value is calculated on the basis of the contents of the frame control field, destination address, source address, and information field. The receiving station performs the same calculation and compares its calculated value to the stored value. If they are not the same, the frame is considered to be in error.

- **Ending Delimiter.** The *ending delimiter* identifies the end of the frame. It consists of either one or two nondata terminate, or T, symbols. The ending delimiter for a token uses two symbols. For all other frames, it uses one symbol.

- **Frame Status Field.** The *frame status field* contains information about the status of a frame, including whether an error was detected, the address recognized, and the frame copied. A separate symbol is used to represent each of the three conditions. An R symbol value indicates that the condition is true, or on, and an S symbol value indicates that the condition is off, or false. Additional implementation-defined indicators may be added to this field.

The MAC/physical layer service specification uses the following primitives:

- **PH_DATA.request.** This primitive transfers one 4-bit symbol from the MAC layer to the physical layer for transmission on the network.
- **PH_DATA.indication.** This primitive transfers one 4-bit symbol from the physical layer to the MAC layer.
- **PH_DATA.confirmation.** This primitive provides a response to the MAC layer signifying acceptance of the previous symbol and readiness to accept another symbol.
- **PH_INVALID.indication.** This primitive notifies the MAC layer that a symbol has been detected as invalid.

PHYSICAL LAYER SPECIFICATIONS

In the FDDI standard, the physical layer (PL) is divided into two sublayers, the *physical-medium-dependent* sublayer (PMD) and the *physical layer protocol* sublayer (PHY). PMD provides the services necessary to transport a suitably coded digital bit stream from station to station on the network and defines characteristics dependent on the physical nature of the medium, such as cables, connectors, power requirements, and optical bypass provisions. PHY provides services to the MAC layer and is concerned with data encoding and synchronization.

The interface between PHY and PMD uses the following primitives:

- **PM_DATA.request.** This primitive transfers properly encoded data from PHY to PMD.
- **PM_DATA.indication.** This primitive transfers encoded data from PMD to PHY.
- **PM_SIGNAL.indication.** This primitive notifies PHY of a change in status of the signal being received by PMD.

DATA ENCODING

The encoding system used by FDDI is designed to provide for synchronization as well as data transmission. It uses a two-part coding structure that ensures that transitions in the signal occur frequently. The first part of the encoding replaces a 4-bit symbol with a 5-bit value, using what is called a 4B/5B code. The 5-bit value is then represented using Nonreturn to Zero Inverted (NRZI) encoding. With NRZI, a 1 bit is represented by a transition in the signal and a 0 bit by no transition. The 5-bit values used to represent symbols are chosen so that there will never be more than three 0 bits in a row and thus no more than three bit times without a transition.

Symbol	5-bit Value
Data Symbols	
0000	11110
0001	01001
0010	10100
0011	10101
0100	01010
0101	01011
0110	01110
0111	01111
1000	10010
1001	10011
1010	10110
1011	10111
1100	11010
1101	11011
1110	11100
1111	11101
Control Symbols	
Quiet	00000
Idle	11111
Halt	00100
Starting Delimiter-J	11000
Starting Delimiter-K	10001
Ending Delimiter-T	01101
Control Reset (logical zero)	00111
Control Set (logical one)	11001

Figure 9.2   4B/5B code

The symbols being encoded can represent either 4-bit data values or control symbols. Figure 9.2 lists the symbols that have been defined and their corresponding 5-bit values.

PHYSICAL SPECIFICATIONS

The PMD portion of the FDDI standard specifies the use of optical fiber transmission operating at a data rate of 100 Mbps. The wavelength specified for data transmission is 1300 μm. Multimode fiber transmission is used, with core and cladding diameters of 62.5/125 or 85/125 μm. Alternative diameters of 50/125 and 100/140 μm are also included in the standard. Based on these physical characteristics, the maximum distance between repeaters is 2 km, the maximum number of physical connections is 1000, and the maximum total fiber path length is 200 km.

RELIABILITY

In addition to providing a high transmission rate, FDDI is designed to provide highly reliable communication. The PMD portion of the FDDI standard explicitly specifies certain reliability-enhancing techniques. These include the use of wiring concentrators and automatic optical bypass switches, which make it easier to locate faults and

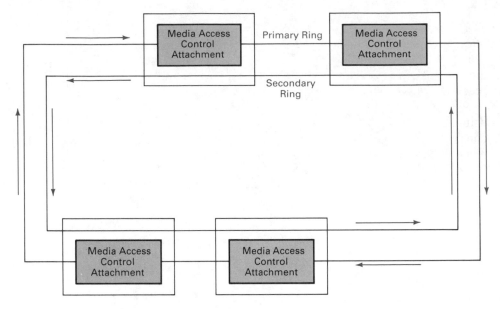

Figure 9.3   FDDI dual-ring configuration

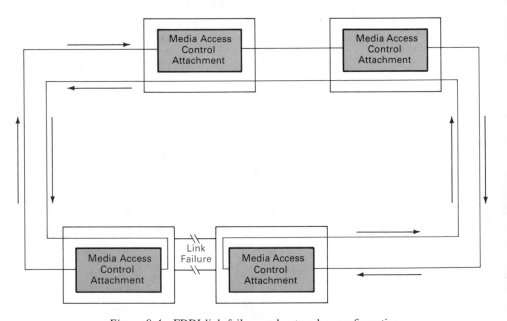

Figure 9.4   FDDI link failure and network reconfiguration

to bypass nonfunctioning stations, using the techniques described in Chapter 8. FDDI also allows a dual-ring configuration, in which two rings are used to interconnect stations with data flowing in opposite directions on the rings, as illustrated in Fig. 9.3. One of the rings is designated as the primary ring and the other as the secondary. Normally, data flows on the primary ring and the secondary ring is idle.

If a link failure occurs, the stations on either side of the link reconfigure using the secondary ring, as shown in Fig. 9.4. This restores the ring to a completed state and allows transmission to continue. If a station fails, a similar reconfiguration takes place, shown in Fig. 9.5.

FDDI defines two classes of stations:

- **Class A.** Class A stations connect to both the primary and secondary rings. A Class A station has the capability to reconfigure the network if a failure occurs.
- **Class B.** Class B stations connect only to the primary ring.

If a failure occurs and the network is reconfigured, it is possible for a Class B station to become isolated. This is shown in Fig. 9.6, where a link failure has caused a station to be isolated from the network. However, the single connection required for a Class B station typically makes it less expensive to attach to the network.

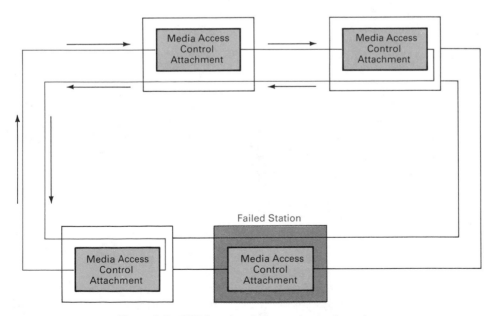

Figure 9.5 FDDI station failure and reconfiguration

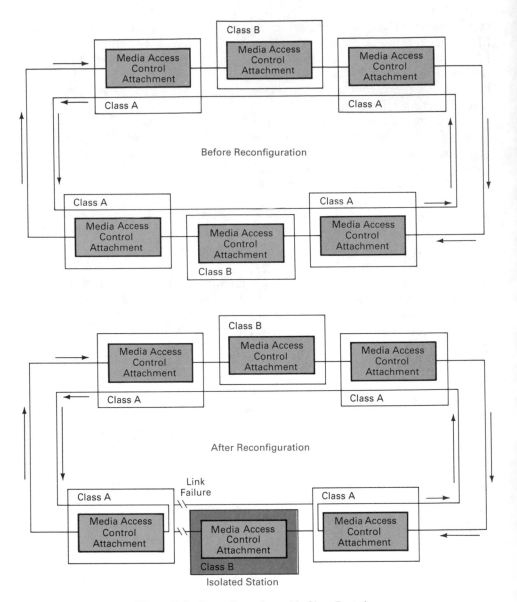

Figure 9.6   Reconfiguration with Class B stations

FUTURE OF FDDI   Development of a standard for the use of fiber optics
                       in local area networks should be critical in realizing
the potential that this technology offers. It will provide manufacturers with a
basis for designing products and will allow users to install fiber-based networks
with confidence that they will not become obsolete as the technology develops.

With the growing need for high-speed transmission in many networking environments, FDDI holds the potential to become the Ethernet of tomorrow.

The ASC X3T9.5 subcommittee has begun looking at a possible second-generation standard, sometimes called FDDI-II. A major feature of this second standard will be the addition of voice and video capability. FDDI-II will open new application areas for fiber-based local area networks of the future.

SUMMARY

The FDDI standard defines a token-passing, ring-structured network using optical fiber transmission with a 100 Mbps data rate. With the FDDI access control method, a token is passed from station to station. When a station receives the token, it can transmit frames until a time limit is reached. When a station finishes transmitting, it immediately passes on the token. Multiple frames may be on the ring at one time. The sending station is responsible for removing its frames from the ring when they return.

Frames are defined as synchronous or asynchronous. If a station has a synchronous allocation, it can transmit synchronous frames whenever it receives the token. It can then transmit asynchronous frames if time permits, based on the length of time that has elapsed since the station received the previous token. A restricted token is used to implement a multiframe dialog between two stations using the time available for asynchronous transmission. All stations monitor the network for error conditions, such as lost token or persistent frame. If either is detected, the station begins a claim token process. If the claim token process is successful, the ring is then initialized. A beacon process is used to locate a major failure, such as a break in the ring.

An FDDI frame contains a preamble, starting delimiter, frame control field, destination address, source address, information, frame check sequence, ending delimiter, and frame status field. FDDI encoding uses a 4B/5B code and replaces each 4-bit symbol with a 5-bit value. The 5-bit value is then further encoded using NRZI encoding. FDDI specifies a data rate of 100 Mbps, using multimode optical fiber transmission. Reliability specifications include automatic optical bypass switches, wiring concentrators, and a dual-ring configuration, in which the secondary ring can be used to reconfigure the network if a link or station failure occurs.

10 MAP AND TOP SPECIFICATIONS

One of the problems with network standards as defined by IEEE, ISO, and CCITT is that they permit many options. If different vendors implement different options, connectivity cannot be achieved even though all vendors adhere to the standards. A number of groups have been formed to address the development of network communications structures suitable for specific application areas. These groups define specific options from standards for their implementations. Among these are two groups that are having much influence in the development of standards for local area networks in two key application areas. The first group, the *Manufacturing Automation Protocol* (MAP) task force, was formed under leadership of General Motors to address the area of factory automation. The second group, the *Technical and Office Protocols* (TOP) task force, sponsored by the Boeing Company, was formed to address engineering, manufacturing, and general office applications.

Box 10.1 gives the addresses of the MAP and TOP organizations. These addresses can be used to obtain additional information about MAP and TOP or copies of the MAP and TOP specifications.

LAYER PROTOCOLS   The MAP and TOP task forces share a similar approach toward developing a networking environment in which there is a high degree of compatibility in the equipment offered by different vendors. The approach involves developing a specification that defines a uniform set of protocols to be used in the network structure. By having a common set of protocols to which all vendors can adhere, compatibility between them can be achieved.

Both groups use the OSI reference model as a basis for their architectures. The seven-layer OSI model is shown in Fig. 10.1. As discussed in Chapter 4, the OSI model provides guidelines within which specific standards and protocols

BOX 10.1　MAP and TOP information

For Information About MAP, Write to:

Attention: MAP Chairman
General Motors Technical Center
General Motors Corporation
Manufacturing Building A/MD39
30300 Mound Road
Warren, MI 48090–9040

For Information About TOP, Write to:

Boeing Computer Services
Network Services Group
P.O. Box 24346, M/S 7C-16
Seattle, WA 98124–0346

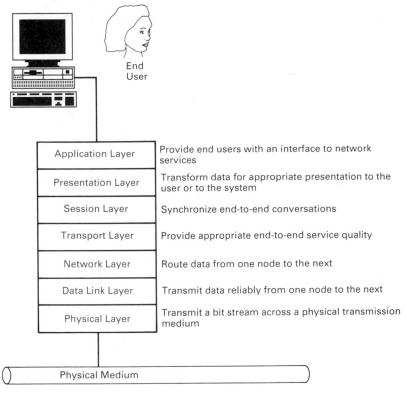

Application Layer	Provide end users with an interface to network services
Presentation Layer	Transform data for appropriate presentation to the user or to the system
Session Layer	Synchronize end-to-end conversations
Transport Layer	Provide appropriate end-to-end service quality
Network Layer	Route data from one node to the next
Data Link Layer	Transmit data reliably from one node to the next
Physical Layer	Transmit a bit stream across a physical transmission medium

Figure 10.1　OSI reference model

must fit. The model itself allows any number of standards and protocols to be created for any of the seven layers of the architecture. A wide range of protocols and features can be selected for any of the seven layers. Implementers of products that conform to the OSI architecture can then choose which protocols and features their products will use. This means that two different vendors could implement products that are consistent with the OSI architecture yet incompatible because they do not share common protocols and features.

The MAP and TOP approach is to define a selected set of protocols, implement selected features, and rigorously document these choices. By limiting the number of protocols and features available for implementation, MAP and TOP increase the likelihood that individual vendors will develop compatible products that can be interconnected as part of the same network. The two task forces have defined similar sets of protocols in their specifications, making it possible for MAP and TOP networks to be easily interconnected. Figure 10.2

OSI Layers	TOP V1.0 Protocols	MAP V2.1 Protocols
Application Layer	ISO FTAM (DP) 8571 File Transfer Protocol	ISO FTAM (DP) 8571 File Transfer Protocol, Manufacturing Messaging Format Standard ((MMFS), and Common Application Service Elements (CASE)
Presentation Layer	NULL (ASCII and Binary Encoding)	
Session Layer	ISO Session (IS) 8372 Basic Combined Subset and Session Kernel, Full Duplex	
Transport Layer	ISO Transport (IS) 8073 Class 4	
Network Layer	ISO Internet (DIS) 8473 Connectionless and for X.25 - Subnetwork Dependent Convergence Protocol (SNDCP)	
Data Link Layer	ISO Logical Link Control (DIS) 8802/2 (IEEE 802.2) Type 1, Class 1	
Physical Layer*	ISO CSMA/CD (DIS) 8802/3 (IEEE 802.3) CSMA/CD Media Access Control, 10Base5	ISO Token Passing Bus (DIS) 8802/4 (IEEE 802.4) Token Passing Bus Media Access Control

*Note that ISO is considering moving the IEEE-defined media access control (MAC) sublayer of the data link layer to the physical layer. This move would make the MAC sublayer conformant with the OSI reference model.

Figure 10.2   TOP and MAP common core of protocols

lists the protocols included in each specification. As you can see, the IEEE 802 standards form the basis for the physical and data link layers of the MAP and TOP specifications.

MAP AND TOP NETWORK STRUCTURE

The general network structure that both MAP and TOP assume is that of hierarchically interconnected networks. This structure is illustrated in Fig. 10.3.

At the lowest level are local area networks. These networks provide direct communication to end users at a single location, typically in a single building or even on one floor in a building. Individual LANs are then interconnected in various ways to provide for communication over wider distances.

A campus network typically connects networks over a wider range than one building but are physically close nevertheless. A metropolitan area network connects campus networks or more widely spread local area networks, operating in a range of 5 to 50 km. For distances greater than 50 km, a wide area network is required.

MAP AND TOP PROTOCOLS

Both the MAP and TOP specifications define protocols to be used at each of the layers of the OSI model (summarized in Fig. 10.2).

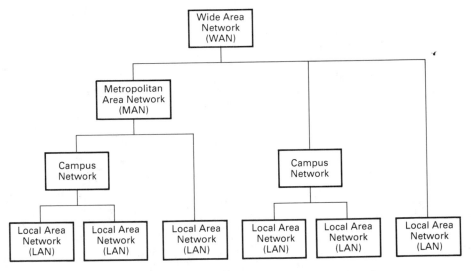

Figure 10.3   Example of a MAP or TOP network hierarchy

THE PHYSICAL AND DATA LINK LAYERS

At the physical and data link layers, both MAP and TOP use the IEEE 802 standards, although each of the two task forces has chosen different IEEE standards. Both specify the use of IEEE 802.2 logical link control protocols. Only Type 1, or connectionless service, is specified by the MAP and TOP specifications. As discussed in Chapter 5, with connectionless service, no sequence checking, message acknowledgment, flow control, or error recovery functions are performed at the data link level. These functions are left to higher-level layers. Optionally, a second type of service, known as acknowledged connectionless service, may also be used. With acknowledged connectionless service, a sending station transmits a frame and the receiving station acknowledges it with a response. There is no sequence checking or flow control with this type of service, but the acknowledgment does allow for detection of nondelivery and for retransmission at the data link level.

ACCESS CONTROL METHODS

MAP has chosen the IEEE 802.4 token bus standard as its access control method; 48-bit addresses are used. At the physical layer level, two standards are supported. One is the broadband bus standard, which provides for broadband transmission using multilevel duobinary AM/PSK modulation with a data rate of 10 Mbps. The other transmission type supported is single-channel phase-coherent FSK. This standard specifies baseband or single-channel transmission using coaxial cable. The modulation technique is phase-coherent frequency modulation with a data rate of 5 Mbps.

TOP has chosen the IEEE 802.3 CSMA/CD standard as its access control method; 48-bit addressing is used. For the physical layer, baseband transmission over coaxial cable at the rate of 10 Mbps with 500-m segments (10BASE5) has been specified.

NETWORK LAYER

The primary responsibility of the network layer in the OSI architecture is to relay and route messages between network nodes, whether within a single network or across interconnected networks. Additional services provided at the network level include message segmentation and reassembly if a message must travel across a network where it exceeds the maximum data unit size. The network layer may also be responsible for adjusting the services provided when subnetworks are being interconnected. The protocols defined in the MAP and TOP specifications are intended to be used primarily for local area networks. Provision is made, however, for the use of wide area network services to interconnect with individual local area networks. For WAN services, the use of an X.25 packet-switching function is specified. (See *Data Communication Technology* or *Principles of Data Com-*

munication by James Martin and The ARBEN Group, Inc., for discussions of packet switching and X.25.) The X.25 protocols specify the use of a connection-oriented class of service. When a connectionless service network, as defined by MAP or TOP, is interconnected with a connection-oriented network such as X.25, the network layer provides for the mapping of one network service to the other.

Addressing

Both MAP and TOP use an OSI approach to the format of addresses used at the network level. The general format used for addresses is shown in Fig. 10.4. The first byte of the address is a value that identifies the particular format used for the address. The network ID portion identifies a domain or area, which may consist of a collection of networks. The primary subnet ID, when combined with the network ID, identifies a particular network. The end system address portion identifies a particular station within the designated network. For a network that implements the IEEE 802.2 logical link control standard, this part of the address consists of a MAC address, a link station identifier, and a network user identifier. (MAP allows several network-level users to share a single LLC-level connection.)

Routing

A key function of the network layer is routing a message from network to network and from node to node within a network. (Chapter 12 discusses network interconnection in detail.) Standard protocols and algorithms for routing are still evolving. In the interim, MAP and TOP have specified a similar approach to be used for routing.

MAP and TOP routing is based on the use of router nodes and distributed routing tables. The sending station determines whether the destination station is part of the same network. If so, the message is sent directly to the destination station. If not, the sending station uses a table lookup to determine the address of a router node that is part of the sending station's network to which to send the message. The router node then determines, using stored routing tables, the network and node address that the message should be sent to next. This may be either the message's final destination or another router node. The MAP specification also suggests a method by which router nodes can exchange information about the availability of resources along a route.

Authority and Format ID (AFI)	Network ID (NID)	Primary Subnet ID (PSI)	End System Address

Figure 10.4   MAP and TOP address format

Optional Functions

Other functions that are part of the connectionless-mode network service protocol are considered optional in the MAP and TOP specifications. Optional functions include security checking, complete or partial source routing, priorities, route recording, and quality of service maintenance.

A number of potential addressing and routing functions are currently under discussion and may be included in future versions of the specifications. Issues being considered include global and local routing, static and dynamic routing, and hierarchical addressing.

TRANSPORT LAYER

The role of the OSI transport layer is to provide a requested class of service quality for the transfer of data. As part of this, the transport layer is concerned with optimizing the use of the services provided by the lower layers. The OSI definitions provide for five different classes of service. In the MAP and TOP specifications, one class, Class 4, is specified. This class provides for the following activities:

- Getting and releasing transport connections and transferring data over them
- Flow control
- Multiplexing of several transport connections onto a single network connection, to provide lower-cost transport
- Error detection and recovery

The services provided by the transport layer are divided into two categories: *data transfer* and *connection management*. Data transfer services provide for *normal* data transfer and *expedited* data transfer, where a limited amount of data is allowed to travel outside the normal data stream. Connection management services include establishing a connection, terminating a connection, and providing status and attribute information about a connection.

Error Detection and Correction

Two techniques are used to provide error detection and recovery services. The first involves *checksums*. A checksum is calculated by putting the various header and information fields used at this level through an arithmetic algorithm. The checksum is included in the data transmitted. The destination station recalculates the checksum, using an identical algorithm, and compares the recalculated value to the received value. If they do not agree, the message received is considered to be in error and is discarded.

The second technique involves the use of *sequence numbers*. Each message sent is assigned a sequence number. The destination station checks the sequence numbers on messages received to detect missing, out-of-sequence, or duplicate messages. Periodically, the destination station sends back an acknowledgment that indicates the sequence numbers of messages it has received correctly. If a message is not acknowledged in an appropriate period of time, it is retransmitted.

Flow Control

Sequence numbers are also used for flow control. As part of connection establishment, a window size is agreed on that represents the maximum number of messages that can be sent before an acknowledgment is received. By controlling the rate at which it sends acknowledgments, the destination station is able to control the rate at which it receives messages.

SESSION LAYER   The session layer provides ways to organize and synchronize conversations and to manage data exchange. The OSI protocols allow for full-duplex, half-duplex, or simplex interactions between end users. With full-duplex interaction, both end users are allowed to send messages at the same time. With half-duplex, the end users alternate sending. With simplex, only one end user is allowed to send.

The MAP and TOP specifications support only full-duplex communication. Functions included are connection establishment, data transfer, and connection termination. Functions that have been defined as optional in the MAP and TOP specifications are expedited data transfer and exception reporting.

PRESENTATION   The presentation layer is concerned with data repre-
LAYER   sentation. This includes representations used for data being transferred, representations of data structures used by the application layer, and representations of the set of actions that can be performed on the data structure. Currently, no presentation protocols are included in the MAP and TOP specifications. The specifications currently specify the use of either ASCII or binary data at the presentation layer.

APPLICATION   The application layer defines the interface through
LAYER   which an end user, either a person or an application program, accesses and uses network services. This is done through a collection of network utilities and procedure libraries.

The MAP specification supports the use of the file transfer, access, and management (FTAM) protocol, the common application service elements

(CASE) protocol, the manufacturing message format standard (MMFS), and the directory services protocol. The TOP specification supports only FTAM but has CASE and several other protocols and services under consideration.

File Transfer, Access, and Management (FTAM)

As its name suggests, the *file transfer, access, and management* (FTAM) protocol provides for two types of services: *file transfer* and *file access and management*. File transfer services allow a file to be transferred easily from one network station to another and supports functions that allow individual files to be created, deleted, read, and written. The file access and management services include protection functions and the use of file attributes. The MAP and TOP specifications describe the file attributes to be used, which include file name, access structure type, presentation context name, current file size, requested access, current access structure, current presentation context, future file size, and date and time of creation.

Common Application Service Elements (CASE)

The *common application service elements* (CASE) protocol provides services that will be used by most applications, regardless of their nature. These services are defined so that they can be provided in a uniform manner to all applications. Services currently specified in the MAP version of CASE include these:

- Establishing an association between two application entities
- Terminating an association between two application entities
- Allowing either of the two application entities to abort an association
- Allowing a lower network layer to abort an association
- Transferring data over an association between two application entities

Manufacturing Message Format Standard (MMFS)

The *manufacturing message format standard* (MMFS) is designed to facilitate communication between devices on the network, particularly between manufacturing-type devices such as numeric controllers, programmable controllers, and industrial robots. It is intended to provide a machine-independent method of information exchange between processes.

The standard defines both the form and the meaning of messages and their components, including the syntax and grammar of the messages and the semantics, or meanings, of standard fields. Standard formats ensure that messages sent by one device can be processed by another device. Standard semantics ensure that messages are processed properly and produce the intended result.

Directory Services

The *directory services* protocol provides information about objects, either in the local network or in another interconnected network. A general protocol allows a network user to request and receive information from a directory information base that is located on the network. One specific service defined as part of directory services is address resolution. A network name is provided as part of a request, and directory services, using information in the directory information base, returns the network address that corresponds to that name.

SUMMARY   The MAP and TOP specifications are based on existing OSI and IEEE standards. They employ selected options from these standards to provide an architecture for specific users. At the data link and physical levels, MAP specifies the use of the 802.4 token bus standard with either single-channel phase-coherent FSK transmission or broadband transmission with multilevel duobinary AM/PSK modulation. TOP specifies the use of the 802.3 CSMA/CD standard with baseband transmission at a data rate of 10 Mbps (10BASE5). Both specify Type 1 (connectionless) service for logical link control.

The network layer provides for hierarchical addresses that contain a network identifier as well as a destination station address. Routing is performed by means of stored routing tables. The transport layer provides for error detection and recovery based on checksums and sequence numbers; it also performs flow control. At the session layer, full-duplex transmission is specified.

The application layer for MAP includes several protocols: file transfer, access, and management (FTAM), common application service elements (CASE), manufacturing message format standard (MMFS), and directory services. TOP supports FTAM and has CASE and several other protocols under consideration.

11 PBX NETWORKS

With most local area networks, stations on the networks are considered to be peers, and no central station handles network control functions. In most implementations, the medium access control function is distributed among the many devices that are attached to the network. A node can gain access to the network on a *controlled* basis, using a technique such as token passing, or on *demand,* if an access control method such as CSMA/CD is used. But in either case, no central device determines when a node is given access. A LAN that uses private branch exchange (PBX) techniques, as introduced in Chapter 3, uses centralized control and is based on conventional telephone switching technology.

In common terminology, the term *local area network* is used to describe the types of networks discussed in the preceding chapters and not PBX networks. Much literature distinguishes between the use of LANs and PBXs for wiring up buildings. LANs with one cable linking many stations tend to be lower in cost than networks that link each station to a centralized PBX. The centralized PBX will remain in use for voice transmission. Many office buildings have both LAN cabling and PBX cabling, the LAN being used as a low-cost way of interconnecting computing devices and the PBX being used for voice and some data.

PRIVATE BRANCH EXCHANGES   In the early days of telephone systems, every telephone was connected to a central exchange by its own physical twisted-wire pair, as shown in Fig. 11.1. Residential telephones are still normally connected to the central exchange in this way. As the number of telephones in use in an organization grew, this method became physically unwieldy. Also, if someone in the building wished to call another person in the same building, the call had to be routed to the

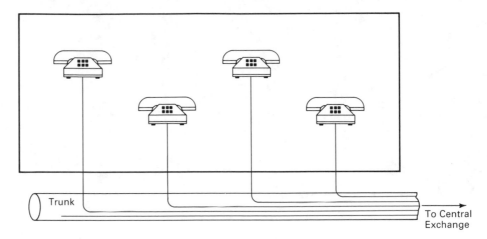

Figure 11.1   Central exchange switching

central exchange and back, since the central exchange performed all switching functions needed to connect and disconnect calls.

The *private branch exchange* (PBX) was developed to address these problems. With a PBX, some of the switching functions are performed on the organization's own premises. Each telephone in the organization is connected to the PBX, as shown in Fig. 11.2. When a user places an outside call, the PBX

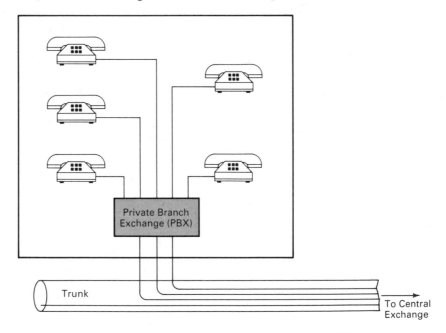

Figure 11.2   Using a private branch exchange (PBX)

connects the user's telephone with an available line that goes to the central exchange. The PBX also connects an outside line to a user's telephone when an incoming call is received from the central exchange. Typically, there will need to be fewer outside lines connected to the PBX than there are telephones connected to it, since only a fraction of the telephones will be making a call at a given time.

In addition to handling switching for the use of outside lines, the PBX also handles all the switching involved in internal calls. If a telephone is used to call another person in the same organization, the PBX provides all the support needed to connect and disconnect the call. Outside lines and the central exchange are not involved at all in such calls.

TELEPHONE NETWORK TOPOLOGY
The basic topology of a telephone network is that of a star, featuring a central controller to which all nodes are connected directly. All transmissions from one node to another pass through the central controller, which is responsible for managing and controlling all communication. With the telephone system, there are levels in the star configuration, as illustrated in Fig. 11.3. Here a PBX, which is a node in the basic star configuration, is a star itself, with additional nodes attached to it. This is sometimes known as a *snowflake* configuration.

Access to the telephone network is provided by a technique called *circuit*

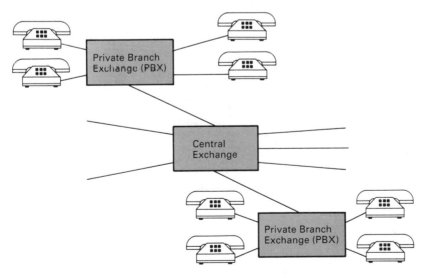

Figure 11.3   Telephone system network topology

switching, which involves *centralized control* and *demand access.* In the earliest days, switching was performed by a human operator, who physically inserted plugs into a switchboard *(centralized control).* Later technology employed electromechanical switches. Electromechanical switches are now being replaced by computerized devices. The improvements in switching technology have allowed both for a larger number of connections to be handled by a given switch and for switching to be done much faster. With circuit switching, the calling node requests the establishment of a connection with another node *(demand access).* The central controller, or *circuit switch,* determines if the connection can be made. If so, the nodes are connected. They stay connected throughout the duration of the conversation, and the path or circuit they are using remains dedicated to their use. At the end of the conversation, they are disconnected and the circuit is released.

Figure 11.4 illustrates circuit switching. At the top of the figure, a connection is established between two nodes within an organization, with the PBX providing the switching functions. At the bottom of the figure, a connection is established between nodes in two different organizations. Here both a PBX and a central exchange are involved in the switching process.

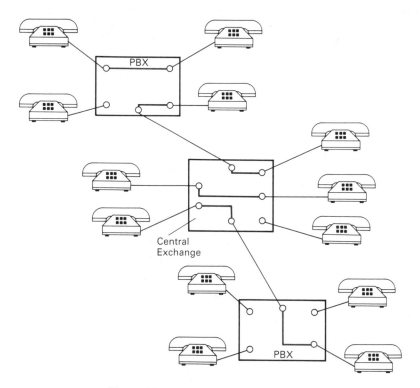

Figure 11.4 Telephone circuit switching

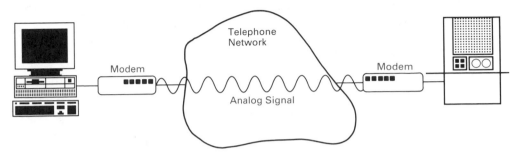

Figure 11.5   Data communication using the public telephone network

DATA COMMUNICATION USING THE TELEPHONE SYSTEM

The telephone system was originally designed to support only voice communication. However, it is now also widely used for data communication. Telephone lines are commonly used to allow terminals to communicate with a distant host computer.

Voice communication is analog, and telephone systems originally supported only analog transmission. When people began using the telephone system for data communication, which is digital, conversion devices were required. These devices are called *modems,* for *modulator-demodulator,* and their use is shown in Fig. 11.5. Data sent from a terminal passes through the modem, which converts it to an analog signal. The analog signal travels across the telephone network. When it reaches the host computer, another modem converts the analog signal back to the original digital signal. This same process operates in reverse for data traveling from the host computer back to the terminal.

DIGITAL PBXs

The development of digital PBXs has provided an alternative to the use of modems for communication over telephone circuits. Digital PBXs, which use electronic circuitry to control switching, offer a number of advantages. They provide faster switching and allow higher data rates to be supported. With digital PBXs, data rates of 64 kbps or higher can be used within an organization and 1.5 Mbps or higher outside the organization. They implement greater intelligence, which has led to the development of features such as automatic callback, call forwarding, least-cost routing, and data transmission from a touchpad. Also, they use digital rather than analog transmission. This allows the digital signals used in data communication to be sent directly, without the need for modems to perform conversion.

For voice communication passing through a digital PBX, conversion is performed in the opposite direction: Analog signals are converted to digital and back again. This is done using a device called a *codec,* short for *code-decoder.*

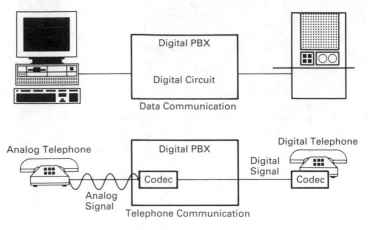

Digital PBX

Digital Circuit

Data Communication

Analog Telephone

Digital PBX

Digital Telephone

Codec

Digital
Signal

Codec

Analog
Signal

Telephone Communication

Figure 11.6 Digital PBXs

1   The signal is first "quantized" or made
    to occupy a discrete set of values

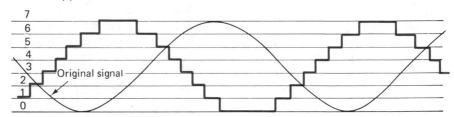

7
6
5
4
3
2
1
0

Original signal

2   It is then sampled at specific points. The
    PAM signal that results can be coded
    for pulse code transmission

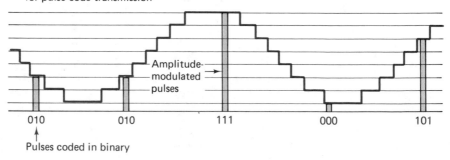

Amplitude-
modulated
pulses

010   010   111   000   101

Pulses coded in binary

3   The coded pulse is transmitted
    in a binary form

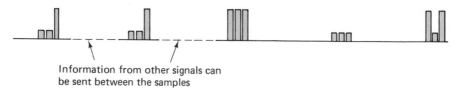

Information from other signals can
be sent between the samples

Figure 11.7   Pulse code modulation (PCM)

Figure 11.6 illustrates the use of a digital PBX, both for data and voice communication. The codec may be located in the digital PBX, or it may be built directly into the telephone instrument itself.

A technique commonly used to convert an analog voice signal to digital is *pulse code modulation*. With pulse code modulation, the analog signal is sampled at regular intervals. This is shown in Fig. 11.7, where the stairstep lines represent samples. The value obtained with each sample is converted into an 8-bit binary number, which is then transmitted digitally. The binary numbers are then used on the receiving side to reconstruct the analog waveform.

To reproduce speech with acceptable quality, samples are taken 8000 times a second. Eight bits are required to transmit the binary number that represents the sample, so 8×8000, or 64,000 bits per second (64 kbps), are required for voice transmission.

PBX NETWORKS

Many wide area networks, both public and private, make use of existing telephone systems for their transmission capabilities. Existing telephone systems offer direct access to almost all organizations, both large and small, nationally and internationally. For most companies, using these existing facilities is much more cost-effective than developing and installing their own transmission networks.

PBX-based transmission capabilities also offer another alternative for connecting computing devices in a building. Personal computers and other devices can be attached to a PBX, and communication between the devices can then take place using circuit switching controlled by the PBX.

One advantage the PBX approach offers is that wiring is often already installed, making it easy and inexpensive to attach the devices. PBX capabilities may already be in use for voice transmission, although typically additional PBX facilities are required to support data transmission.

Two considerations in using PBX technology as the basis for a computer network are the disruptive effect of the failure of the central controller (PBX) and the potential overhead involved in establishing connections, or circuits, between devices that are communicating.

NETWORK RELIABILITY

With local area networks based on distributed control, such as CSMA/CD, token bus, or token ring, the failure of a given device typically does not result in the failure of the entire network. With a PBX system, failure of the PBX would prevent any of the attached devices from communicating. However, developments in technology have increased the reliability of the various components in a telephone system, decreased their number by using denser chips, and decreased the cost. This has made it possible to use configurations where duplication of the vital equipment makes the risk of total system failure very small. The use of distributed intelligence in a PBX network has also lessened the impact of a failure of a particular component.

SWITCHING TECHNIQUES

Early manual and electromechanical switching devices used a switching technique known as *space-division switching*. With this technique, a connection was established using a switching element within the exchange. The caller had a dedicated electrical path for the duration of the conversation, and a continuous signal was carried along that physical circuit. When the conversation terminated, the two nodes were disconnected, and the switching element could be used to establish a different circuit.

Each exchange contained many switching elements, and the number of elements represented the maximum number of simultaneous connections that could be made through the exchange. If an exchange contains enough switching elements to handle every possible simultaneous connection of the nodes attached to it, it is known as a nonblocking switch. If it has fewer switching elements, it is a blocking switch. A nonblocking switch is usually not needed for voice-based systems, since it is rare that all users will try to use the system at the same time.

DIGITAL SWITCHING

With the development of digital PBXs, other switching techniques have come into use. Digital PBXs commonly employ a structure similar to that shown in Fig. 11.8. The PBX contains one or more data buses, each having a high-bandwidth transmission capability. Bus interfaces are used to connect devices to the data bus. Each device is attached through a port in the bus interface, usually using a single twisted-wire pair. The data bus has a higher transmission rate than the individual links to the devices. It is used to concentrate data prior to switching.

A switching technique is used to control access of the different devices to the data bus bandwidth, which provides another switching function within the network. A technique commonly used is called *time-division multiplexing*. With time-division multiplexing, transmission on the bus is divided into frames. Each frame contains some number of time slots, and a certain number of bits can be transmitted in one time slot.

For example, there may be 8000 frames per second, 500 time slots per frame, and 8 bits transmitted in parallel per time slot. This implies a capacity of 8000 frames per second $\times$ 500 slots per frame $\times$ 8 bits per slot = 32 Mbps. A particular connection between two devices is assigned to a particular slot and communicates during that time slot in each frame. Thus a given connection uses

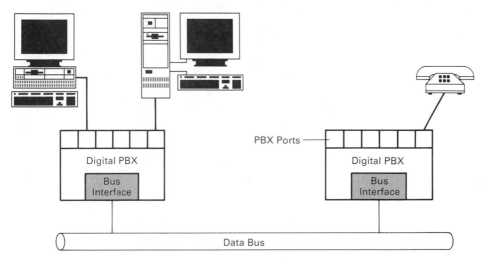

Figure 11.8 Digital PBX data bus structure

8 bits × 8000 frames per second = 64 kbps, and 500 different connections can communicate concurrently by sharing the bandwidth across time.

Another switching technique that increases interconnection capability is *time-multiplexed space-division switching*. This technique is based on the use of semiconductor switches that operate at high speed, up to one million times faster than electromechanical switches, and can allow switching elements to be shared among a number of simultaneous connections. With time-multiplexed space-division switching, an array of switch elements is used to set up a new set of connections in each time slot. For example, a switch might be able to handle ten unique connections per time slot. If there are 500 time slots per frame, the switch can handle the equivalent of 5000 connections. The different connections are handled by multiplexing the use of the physical connection paths in time.

DISTRIBUTED NETWORK STRUCTURES

As mentioned previously, distributed intelligence can be used as a way of distributing functions in a network, thereby reducing the impact of the failure of a particular component. With a distributed system, the switching function is distributed among several switching nodes. Two possible distributed network structures are shown in Fig. 11.9.

In both cases, connections between two users attached to the same switching node are handled entirely by that switching node. In the top part of the diagram, a hierarchical structure is used. End users connect directly to switching nodes. Switching nodes, in turn, connect to a higher-level node called a tandem switching node. All internode connections are made through the tandem switching node. The bottom part of the figure shows an interconnected architecture.

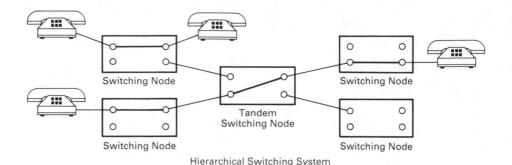

Figure 11.9   Distributed switching architectures

Here each switching node is connected directly to the other switching nodes. For internode connections, the two switching nodes communicate directly. It is also possible to have an architecture where not all switching nodes are directly connected, and an intermediate switching node is used to connect them. This can be done where the number of connections required for full interconnection would make the network unduly expensive and complex.

PACKET SWITCHING ON PBX NETWORKS

A PBX network can be used to provide a packet-switching type of service, which is more similar than circuit switching to the access control methods used with other types of local area networks. With packet switching, long messages are sliced up into smaller units, called *packets,* for transmission from one network node to another. A group of bus interfaces attached to the same data bus are configured to recognize a common bus address. The data bus then becomes a broadcast bus, and a number of bus interfaces can simultaneously receive data sent by one user.

A broadcast bus can increase the bandwidth used for broadcast mode by assigning a group of time slots to be used for broadcast mode. Dedicating several time slots to the same connection is called supermultiplexing. Supermultiplexing can also be used to provide a higher bandwidth for circuit-switched connections.

To implement packet switching, either the bus interfaces or their attached devices must be able to recognize the destination addresses contained in the packets being sent. Packets are then routed and received on the basis of these addresses.

An alternative to the broadcast capability is fast-connect circuit switching. With fast-connect circuit switching, the bus interfaces interact to establish a point-to-point connection between the sending and receiving devices with a minimum of access delay, typically in a few milliseconds. With either broadcast capability or fast-connect circuit switching, a PBX network is able to support both packet switching and circuit switching on a common switching bus. Separate buses can also be used to optimize each type of transmission.

FUTURE OF PBX LOCAL AREA NETWORKS

PBX networks are able to supply high-bandwidth communications to end users in an easy-to-install and reliable manner. The primary limit with PBX networks is their use of unshielded, twisted-wire-pair cable, which often supports fairly low data rates with reasonable transmission quality.

One feature being offered by PBX vendors is to provide interfaces with other types of local area networks, such as those using the CSMA/CD or token ring access control methods. This allows extended networks to be developed, encompassing various types of technology. PBX technology is particularly well suited to providing an integrated voice and data service. Such integrated services can be used for applications such as voice messaging and voice annotation of text. As facilities such as image processing, speech synthesis, and speech recognition are incorporated into future PBX systems, additional applications will become possible.

SUMMARY

PBX networks are based on the technology of circuit switching. The calling node requests establishment of a physical connection with another node. The central controller, or switch, makes the connection, and the connection is then used for data transmission. With digital PBXs used to support local area networks, time-division multiplexing and time-multiplexed space-division switching can be used to increase the number of circuits supported by a single switch. Distributed architectures can be used to increase reliability. Packet switching can also be provided on PBX networks using broadcast buses and supermultiplexing, or fast-connect circuit-switching techniques.

12 INTER-LAN CONNECTIONS

Local area networks allow a group of computer users to communicate with one another and to share data and peripheral devices. The users of a particular LAN will typically be located relatively close to one another, possibly in the same building, on the same floor, or in the same office. LANs are commonly used to allow members of the same work group or department to work cooperatively and to share resources, especially information.

LANs have proved to be very effective in improving the sharing of information within a work group or department. But work groups also need to communicate and share information outside their own area—with other work groups, with other departments within their own enterprise, with other enterprises, or with general sources of public information. Using separate networks or communication facilities for each of these needs is possible and is the approach used in many cases. However, *interconnecting* networks can provide a quicker, less expensive, and easier-to-use solution to this problem.

INTERCONNECTED NETWORK CONFIGURATIONS

Networks can be interconnected in a number of ways, some of which are shown in Fig. 12.1. Two or more LANs can be connected directly, as in the diagram at the top of the figure. A LAN can be connected to a wide area network, as shown in the middle diagram. The diagram at the bottom of the figure shows a wide area network being used as an intermediary to interconnect two separate LANs. Common carrier network facilities are often used to implement the WAN connection in situations like this.

Interconnected networks can also be structured hierarchically, as shown in Fig. 12.2. Here a WAN is used to interconnect geographically dispersed subnetworks, some of which are LANs and others of which are metropolitan area networks. The MANs can in turn be used to interconnect groups of LANs.

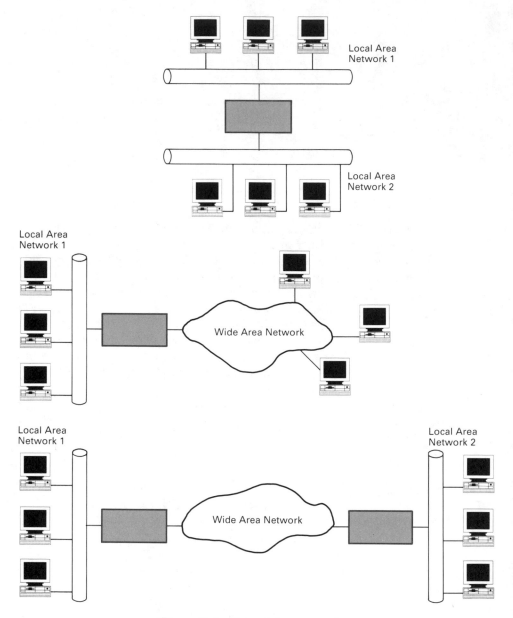

Figure 12.1 Network interconnection

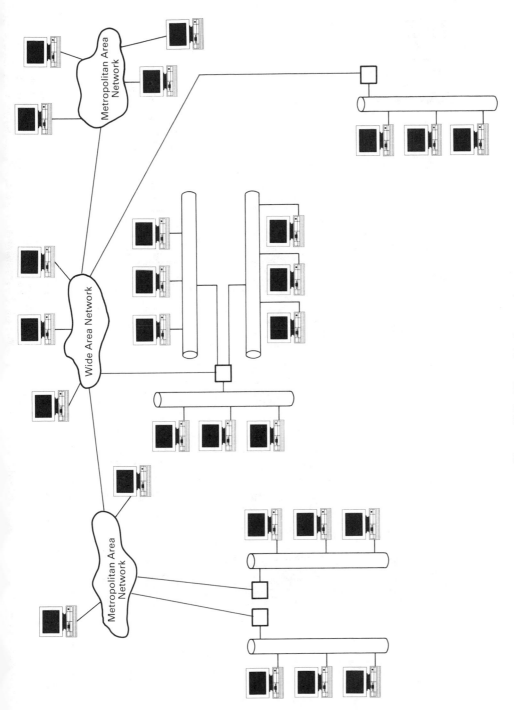

Figure 12.2 Hierarchical network structure

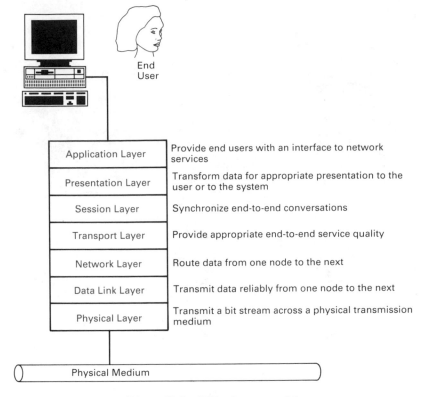

End
User

Application Layer	Provide end users with an interface to network services
Presentation Layer	Transform data for appropriate presentation to the user or to the system
Session Layer	Synchronize end-to-end conversations
Transport Layer	Provide appropriate end-to-end service quality
Network Layer	Route data from one node to the next
Data Link Layer	Transmit data reliably from one node to the next
Physical Layer	Transmit a bit stream across a physical transmission medium

Physical Medium

Figure 12.3 OSI reference model

LANs can be interconnected directly or through higher-level MANs or WANs.

  Network interconnection facilities can be used to construct complex network structures. Individual networks can be designed to meet specific local needs, yet provision can be made for information to be passed from one network to another. In this way, a variety of communication needs can be met. However, network interconnection is not always easy to accomplish.

  Networks, or network segments, can be interconnected in several ways. In

Interconnection Facility	Protocols		
	Physical Layer	Data Link Layer	Network Layer and Higher
Repeater	Same	Same	Same
Bridge	Different	Same	Same
Router	Different	Different	Same
Gateway	Different	Different	Different

Figure 12.4 Network interconnection methods

discussing these methods, we will use the layers of the OSI model, shown in Fig. 12.3. The methods are differentiated by which layer protocols must be the same for interconnection to take place. This is summarized in Fig. 12.4.

REPEATERS

The simplest facility used for network interconnection is the *repeater*. Repeaters are used not to interconnect dissimilar networks but to connect individual network segments to form a larger extended network. Figure 12.5 illustrates the use of a repeater. The function of a repeater is to receive a message and then to retransmit it, regenerating the signal at its original strength.

A LAN will usually have a limit on the physical size of any single network segment. This limit is based on the physical medium and transmission technique used. Repeaters allow a network to be constructed that exceeds the size limit of a single physical segment by allowing additional cable segments to be connected to form an extended network. The number of repeaters that can be used in tandem is generally also limited by the network architecture.

Repeaters are commonly used with LANs that use a bus topology. For those with a ring topology, each station typically acts as a repeater, receiving a message and retransmitting it with the signal restored to full strength.

For a repeater to be used, both network segments must be of the same type. They must use the same network protocols for all layers, including using the same media access control method and the same physical transmission technique. So, for example, a repeater could be used to interconnect two network segments that use CSMA/CD with broadband transmission. Stations on different segments are not allowed to have the same station address—all individual addresses in the extended network must be unique.

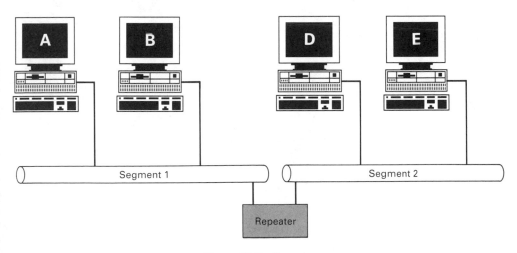

Figure 12.5 Repeater

BRIDGES   A second type of facility that can be used to connect network segments is called a *bridge*. A bridge is able to interconnect physically distinct networks, as shown in Fig. 12.6. A bridge may be a separate device but is typically a station that belongs to two or more networks simultaneously. The bridge receives all messages on each network of which it is a part. It checks the destination address, and when it recognizes that a message is intended for a station in a different network, it transmits the message on that network. So if, for example, station B sends a message to station N, station C receives the message as part of network 1 and then retransmits it on network 2. This type of connection implements a *store-and-forward* function, since messages are stored temporarily in the bridge and then forwarded to another network.

Figure 12.7 shows that a bridge operates at the data link level. A bridge interconnection can be used for networks that use different protocols at the physical layer level, as long as they use a common protocol at the data link layer. For example, a network using CSMA/CD with broadband transmission over coaxial cable could use a bridge to connect with a CSMA/CD network using

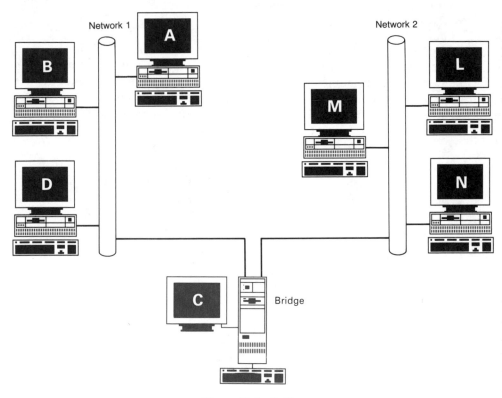

Figure 12.6   Bridge

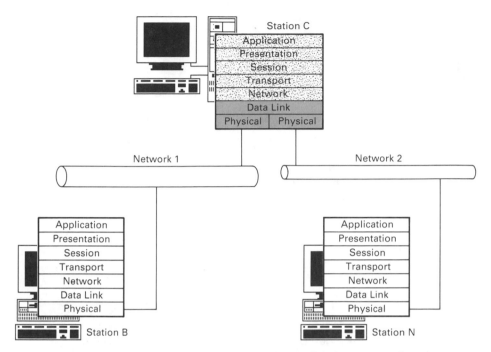

Figure 12.7   Bridge using the physical and data link layers to perform its function

baseband transmission over twisted-wire-pair cable. It is also possible for a bridge to implement an interconnection between LANs using different MAC methods—for example, a CSMA/CD network with a token ring network. Here both networks must have compatible implementations of the logical link control sublayer, and the bridge station must be able to forward messages at the LLC level. The bridge must also be capable of resolving any frame format or other differences between the two MAC methods.

Again, all addresses on the interconnected networks must be unique and must use the same format (16-bit or 48-bit). They must also use frame formats and sizes that are similar enough that any differences can be handled in the data link layer.

To pass on messages appropriately, a station operating as a bridge must know which stations belong to the different networks that it is interconnecting. In the example we looked at in Fig. 12.7, station C must know that station N belongs to network 2. Different approaches can be used for this. The bridge can be provided with this information from an external source, such as a network administrator. The bridge station may also be programmed to "learn" this information, for example, by sending out a broadcast message on one of the networks and soliciting responses from all the stations on that network. A bridge may also learn a station's location by observing transmissions. When station C

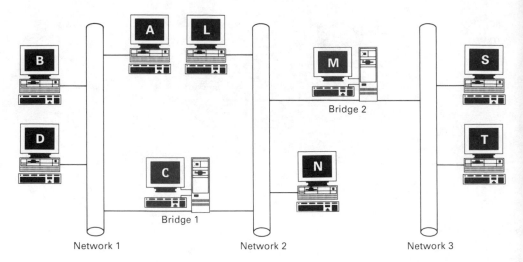

Figure 12.8   Multiple bridges

detects a transmission on network 1 with A as the source address, it records station A as being located on network 1. When it observes a transmission on network 2 with N as the source address, it records station N as being on network 2. The bridge then uses this stored information to determine when to forward a message.

Multiple bridges can also be used, as illustrated in Fig. 12.8. With multiple bridges, a station functioning as a bridge must be aware of all stations that it can reach, not only the stations on the networks to which it is connected directly. For example, to send a message from station B to station T, bridge station C must recognize that it should forward to Network 2 any messages that are destined for station T. If multiple bridges are used, the overall combined network structure is usually restricted to a branching tree, so that there is only one path connecting any two networks. If more than one path were used, dupli cate messages might be created or messages might arrive out of sequence.

ROUTERS

A more capable form of network interconnection uses a facility called a *router* or *intermediate system*. The use of a router is based on a concept that does not ordinarily apply within a single local area network—routing a message through intermediate nodes. In a LAN, when a message is transmitted, it is sent to all nodes in that network. A receiving node determines from the destination address in the message whether or not it should receive and process the message. However, when a LAN is interconnected with other networks, either WANs or other LANs, routing becomes a critical issue.

With other types of networks, particularly WANs, a message is ordinarily sent from one node to one other specific node in the network, and the message may pass through a series of intermediate nodes before it reaches the destination node. There may be more than one sequence of nodes (more than one *route*) that a message can take to get from the source node to the destination node. This is shown in Fig. 12.9; a message sent from node A to node E could either pass through node B (route 1) or through nodes C and D (route 2).

When a message is routed through intermediate nodes, two addresses must accompany it. The first is the address of the message's final destination node; this address remains constant as the message traverses the network. The second is the address of the next node along the route; this address changes as the message moves from node to node along the route it takes through the network.

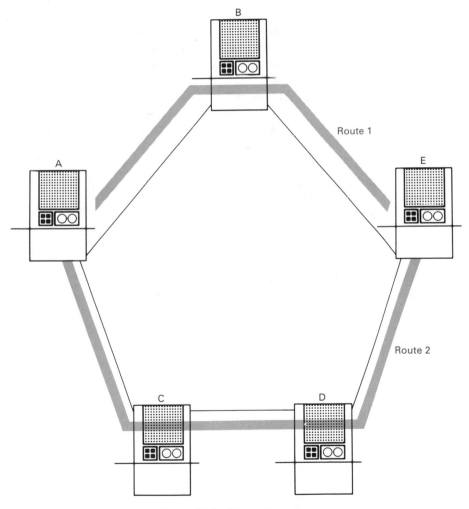

Figure 12.9   Network routing

Figure 12.10 shows, conceptually, how these two addresses are used. When the message leaves node A, the address of the next node is C. Node C determines that the next node along the route is D and passes the message on to node D. Node D determines that the next node is the destination node, E, and sees that the message is transmitted there. This routing function is performed by the network layer in the OSI architecture. Since LAN standards and architectures do not ordinarily address the network layer, they consequently do not ordinarily address the issue of routing.

When a router is used to interconnect networks, it functions much like an intermediate node. Figure 12.11 shows a router interconnecting two local area networks. With a router, a message is explicitly addressed to the router node. So here, for example, if station B wanted to send a message to station M, it would first send it to station E. Information embedded in the message, which would be processed by layers of software higher than the data link layer, would identify the final destination of the message as station M. Based on this information, the network layer in station E would determine that the message should be sent to network 2 and addressed to station M.

For a router to be used, the networks being interconnected must share the same network protocols and must be compatible at higher network layers. The networks may differ, however, at the data link and physical layers. Thus, for

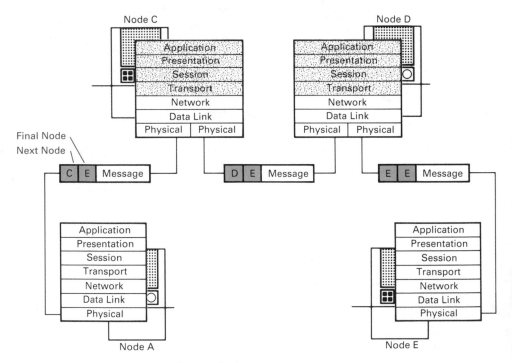

Figure 12.10　Intermediate nodes

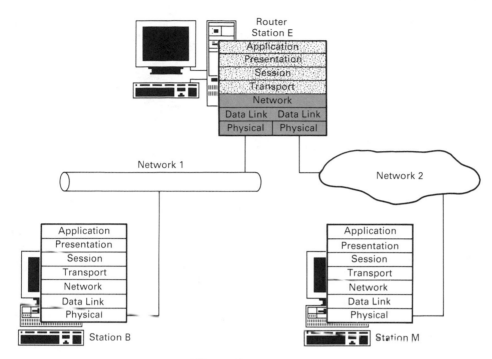

Figure 12.11   Router

example, a router could be used to interconnect a LAN using the IEEE token bus standard and IEEE logical link control with a WAN that uses packet-switching techniques and the X.25 protocols at the data link layer, as long as both have implemented compatible protocols at the network layer and higher.

Multiple routers can be used, and they can be connected in ways that allow for multiple paths between any two networks, as shown in Fig. 12.12. If a message is being sent from node B to node M, it is sent first to router node C, which sends it to either node G or node H. Since messages are sent to a specific router node, the presence of multiple paths will not cause a message to be duplicated. The possibility may exist, however, that different related message units will take different paths and may arrive out of sequence. If this is possible, the higher network layers must be prepared to resequence related message units.

A key function of a router is determining the next node to which a message is sent. Several methods can be used to do this. Routing information can be predefined as part of the network design and administration function and stored in the form of routing tables. Routers can develop a map of the network topology by exchanging information on active nodes and links and then select a route based on the current network map. With source routing, the source or sending station specifies the route to be used. This can be based on predefined informa-

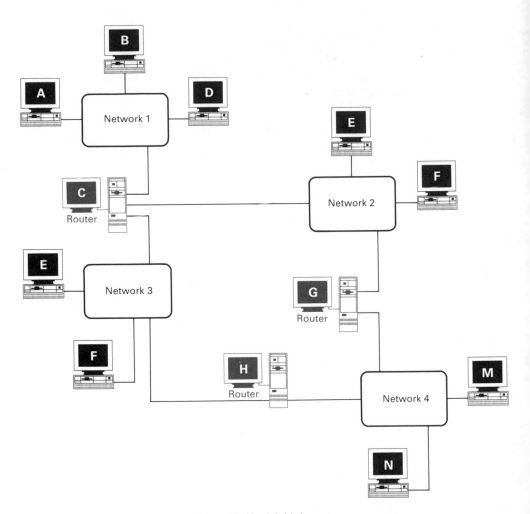

Figure 12.12   Multiple routers

tion or on information gathered as a result of a broadcast message. Some of the commonly used routing protocols are discussed further in Chapter 19. Standards for routing equivalent to the IEEE 802 standards for the lower layers have not yet emerged. This lack of defined standards has resulted in the diversity of routing algorithms and approaches that we see in the later chapters on network implementations. Routers are most commonly used when interconnecting networks from a single vendor or based on the same network architecture.

      Figure 12.12 also illustrates that node addresses do not always have to be unique throughout the interconnected networks. The addressing structure used by the network and higher layers often allows for a multipart address, which consists of a network identifier and a node address within that network. In this case, the node address must be unique within its network but not necessarily within the entire set of interconnected networks.

GATEWAYS

The last, and most complex, method of network interconnection is a *gateway*. A gateway is used to interconnect networks that may have entirely different architectures. A gateway, for example, could be used to interconnect an SNA network with an X.25 packet-switching network that conforms to the OSI model.

Figure 12.13 illustrates the use of a gateway. Since different architectures

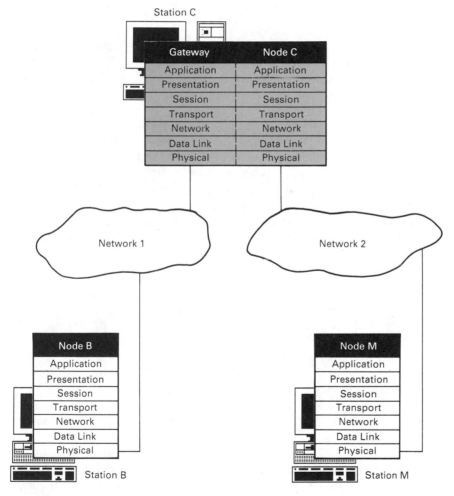

Figure 12.13   Gateway

are used, different protocols may be used at any or all of the network layers. The gateway handles any conversions that are necessary to go from one set of protocols to the other, including these:

- **Message Format Conversion.** The networks may employ different message formats, maximum message sizes, and character codes. The gateway must be able to convert messages to an appropriate format, size, and coding for the network the message is entering.

- **Address Translation.** The networks may use different addressing structures. The gateway must be able to translate all the addresses associated with a message to the address structure required by the destination network.

- **Protocol Conversion.** When a message is prepared for transmission through a network, each network layer adds control information that is used by the corresponding layer in the receiving node to determine what protocols are being used and how the message should be processed. A gateway must be able to replace the control information from one network with control information that is required to perform comparable functions in the other network. This conversion must allow for services such as message segmentation and reassembly, data flow control, and error detection and recovery to be performed in a consistent manner as a message travels across networks.

Gateways offer the greatest flexibility in network interconnection, since two completely different networks can be linked together. However, gateways are correspondingly more complex and more expensive to develop. They are typically constructed to interconnect networks that conform to two specific network architectures. Since conversion must be provided for protocols at every level, designing a generalized gateway becomes exceedingly complex. As we examine specific LAN implementations in later chapters, we will see some of the approaches taken to provide interconnectivity via gateways.

INTER-LAN NETWORKS

The interconnection of local area networks, forming what are called inter-LAN networks, has become a key issue in network planning and design for many enterprises. Inter-LAN networks can be built by directly interconnecting various LANs with bridges, routers, or gateways, depending on how similar the networks are at the various layers. For example, two token ring networks could be interconnected by a bridge that is a station in both networks, as shown in Fig. 12.14.

Another approach that can be used with inter-LAN networks is to employ a *backbone network*. A backbone network is a central network to which other networks connect. Users are not attached directly to the backbone network; they are connected to the *access networks,* which in turn connect to the backbone.

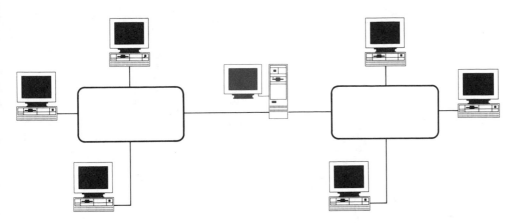

Figure 12.14   Simple inter-LAN network

An example of this is shown in Fig. 12.15. Here a central backbone token ring network is used to interconnect other token ring networks. The networks do not all have to be the same type to use a backbone network. A configuration using dissimilar networks is shown in Fig. 12.16. Here a Fiber Distributed Data Interface ring network, which runs throughout an entire building, is used to interconnect various LANs on a single floor or in a single department.

The use of a backbone network to tie together a number of small access networks offers several advantages over the construction of a single large LAN. The various LANs connected to the backbone are able to operate in parallel, providing greater processing efficiency. The multiple-network approach is also more reliable, since each individual LAN can continue operating if one of the other access networks, or even the backbone, fails. The backbone network typically filters traffic and forwards only messages destined for a different LAN. The different networks can also be optimized to meet different requirements. A backbone network normally requires a high bandwidth and the ability to transmit across long distances, since a backbone may be used to interconnect networks throughout a building or from one building to others. A backbone network must also be highly reliable, since the greater distances covered may make it difficult to locate and repair faults. The LANs that connect to the backbone must be flexible and low-cost in terms of installation and user connection.

Because of the requirement for high bandwidth and long transmission distances, optical fiber and microwave-based links are particularly suited for use in a backbone network. The fact that installation and connection costs are higher is less important, since the backbone network is less likely to require reconfiguration or a large number of connections. The FDDI standard discussed in Chapter 9 represents an important technology for backbone networks.

Connection to the backbone network may require a bridge, router, or gateway, depending on the architectures of the various LANs and the backbone

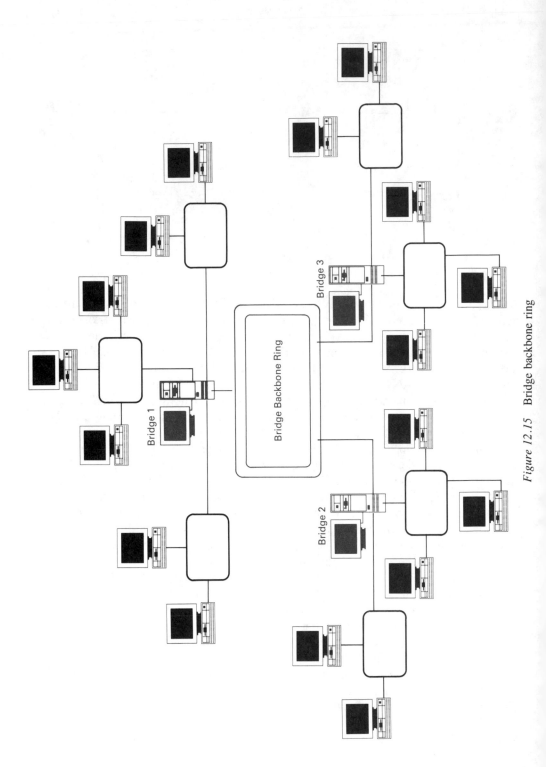

Figure 12.15   Bridge backbone ring

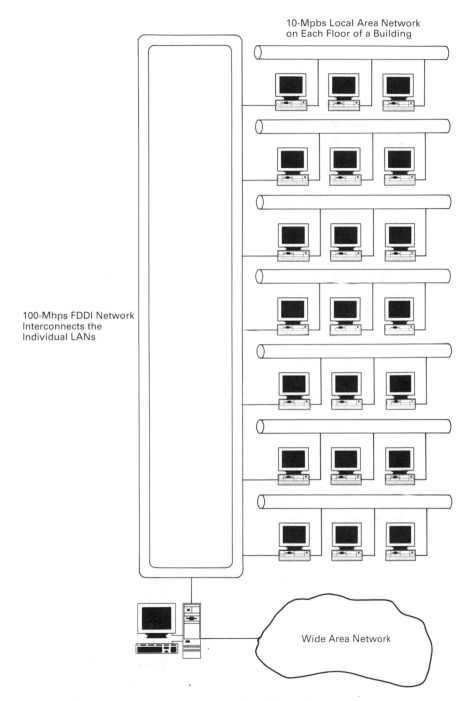

10-Mpbs Local Area Network
on Each Floor of a Building

100-Mhps FDDI Network
Interconnects the
Individual LANs

Wide Area Network

Figure 12.16   FDDI backbone network

179

itself. The backbone concept can also be used at the enterprise level, where a wide area network, possibly international in scope, is used to interconnect networks at individual locations.

DIGITAL EQUIPMENT CORPORATION: AN EXAMPLE OF CONNECTIVITY

Digital Equipment Corporation has been particularly supportive of network connectivity, for both networks built using DEC products and networks that use other vendors' products. Interconnection of DEC networks is based on DEC's proprietary network architecture, Digital Network Architecture (DNA), and on a family of products that implement that architecture, known as the DECnet product line. DECnet products all implement a standard set of protocols, as defined in DNA. The DECnet products support numerous protocols at the data link layer, including these:

- **Digital Data Communications Messenger Protocol (DDCMP).** DDCMP is the data link protocol defined as part of DNA. It supports transmission over leased lines, dial-up lines, and hard-wired connections. It is functionally similar to HDLC in the OSI reference model.

- **Ethernet.** Ethernet uses the CSMA/CD protocol defined in IEEE 802.3. DEC supports the use of Ethernet for building LANs.

- **CCITT X.25 Levels 2 and 3.** The CCITT X.25 standard has been defined as part of the OSI reference model. DEC supports the use of this protocol as a way of accessing public data networks and of interconnecting nodes via a packet-switched network.

Regardless of the data link protocol used and the underlying physical layer techniques, all DECnet products use the same protocols at the network layer and higher. This means that all networks built using DECnet products, LANs and WANs alike, can be interconnected using routers. Two DEC Ethernet LANs can be interconnected using a bridge.

DEC INTERVENDOR CONNECTIVITY

DEC also provides for networks that use products supplied by other vendors. For example, at the LAN level, VAX/VMS Services for MS-DOS, a member of the DECnet product line, allows IBM personal computers to be interconnected. Through various forms of gateway products, DEC networks and processors are able to communicate with networks and processors from IBM, Univac, CDC, and Wang and with systems running the UNIX operating system. A gateway can be used to allow DECnet hosts to use an X.25 packet-switching network to communicate with non-DEC hosts. Gateways also allow DECnet hosts to communicate with non-DEC systems using certain standards, such as the CCITT X.400 Recommendations for Message Handling Systems or the Manufacturing Automation Protocol (MAP) specifications described in Chapter 10.

In general, these gateway products provide specific ranges of functions and do not support the broad range of communication and distributed processing capabilities that are possible when interconnecting all DECnet-based networks. For example, it is possible to interconnect a DECnet network with an SNA network using the DECnet/SNA Gateway product. Using the appropriate sup-

BOX 12.1   DECnet/SNA Gateway functions

- **3270 Terminal Emulation.** This allows a VT200 terminal attached to a VAX processor to act as a 3270 terminal interacting with an IBM processor in the SNA network.

- **Remote Job Entry.** This allows VAX systems to function as SNA/RJE workstations, submitting batch jobs to an IBM host and receiving job output.

- **DECnet/SNA Data Transfer Facility.** This allows file interchange between a VAX/VMS system and an IBM MVS system for certain file and record formats.

- **DISOSS Document Exchange Facility.** This allows VAX systems to access document distribution and library services provided by an IBM host running DISOSS. Both final-form and revisable-form documents are supported.

- **Distributed Host Command Facility.** This allows 3270 terminals attached to an IBM host running the Host Command Facility to access VAX/VMS systems and perform functions such as executing VAX/VMS commands, editing files, and monitoring and controlling VAX/VMS processors.

- **Printer Emulator.** This allows VAX systems to receive printable data from IBM systems, typically consisting of output formatted for an IBM 3287 printer.

- **Programming Interfaces.** These interfaces allow VAX applications to communicate with IBM applications using LU 0 sessions, LU 2 sessions, or LU 6.2 sessions. (In an SNA network, each LU type is associated with a specific set of network protocols.)

- **Message Routing.** This allows for the transparent interchange of electronic mail, messages, revisable and final-form documents, and personal computer files between users of DEC office networks and IBM office networks.

plemental software, it is possible to perform the functions shown in Box 12.1. Separate products are required for each of the functions because of the complexity involved in converting protocols at all layers when interconnecting two unlike architectures.

DEC INTER-LAN CONNECTIVITY

DEC's DECnet-based connectivity, plus its support for intervendor connectivity, provides a broad base for inter-LAN connections. Individual LANs can be built using Ethernet at the data link level and the DECnet protocols for the higher layers. Either broadband or baseband transmission can be used for the physical layer.

Extended LANs can be created using repeaters, including fiber-optic repeaters that allow distances of up to 1000 m to be spanned. Baseband or broadband LANs can be interconnected using bridges. The bridges learn, by observing traffic, which nodes belong to which network and then perform a filtering function by forwarding only the messages intended for another network. LANs can be connected to DECnet-based WANs through the use of routers. LANs can also be interconnected with non-DEC networks and processors, using the various gateways that DEC provides. Through these various forms of interconnection, LANs can be constructed to provide efficient support for local processing while still providing access to resources spread throughout the organization or outside the organization.

SUMMARY

Repeaters provide interconnection of network segments of the same type. A bridge can be used to interconnect networks that use different physical transmission techniques but the same data link–level protocols. Routers can interconnect networks using different data link and physical protocols. Routers also provide a routing function and determine the next node to which a message should be sent on its path to the destination station. To use a router, the two networks must use common protocols at the network layer and higher. Gateways are used to interconnect two networks that use unlike protocols at all layers. The gateway handles all conversions necessary to go from one set of protocols to the other.

Inter-LAN networks are formed by interconnecting LANs with bridges, routers, or gateways. A backbone network is a central network to which other networks connect. A backbone network can be optimized to provide high-bandwidth, reliable transmission, while the LANs that attach to it are optimized for flexibility and low cost.

So far in this book, we have examined several LAN architectures, including those defined by the IEEE 802, FDDI, the MAP and TOP specifications, and PBX networks. We have also discussed various techniques for interconnecting similar and dissimilar networks. Parts IV and V of this book look at specific LAN implementations. Part IV examines implementations marketed by IBM, Part V several representative LAN implementations developed by other vendors.

PART **IV** LAN IMPLEMENTATIONS BY IBM

13 LOCAL AREA NETWORK IMPLEMENTATIONS

In this part of the book we examine representative local area networks that implement the various architectures and standards that we have been discussing. Chapters 14 through 18 examine LAN facilities marketed by IBM. In Part V, we look at products marketed by other vendors.

We have chosen the implementations discussed in this book to demonstrate the diversity of possible LAN implementations, without regard for their popularity or their suitability for a particular application. Because of the dynamic nature of the LAN marketplace, it would not be possible to discuss all of the most popular LAN products in use at a given time. An individual user's choice of a LAN product must ultimately be based on a study of the products that are currently available and the user's own particular requirements. In this chapter, we attempt to show how the concepts and architectures that we described earlier in the book can be applied in a variety of ways in creating actual LAN implementations.

BASIC LAN FUNCTIONS

As we have discussed throughout this book, the primary function of a local area network is to allow the stations that are attached to the network to exchange messages. From an architectural standpoint, LANs have been defined in terms of the services that are provided at the two lowest layers of the OSI reference model, the physical layer and data link layer. IEEE Project 802 has defined in detail services to be provided at these levels, and by and large, these services tend to be those that are actually offered by individual LAN implementations. However, as we will see, these services can be provided in a surprisingly wide variety of ways.

PHYSICAL COMPONENTS

LAN communication functions are typically performed by hardware and firmware that is specifically designed to implement them. The physical components used in a network that supports personal computers include the following:

- **Adapter Card.** A *network adapter circuit card,* purchased from the computer vendor or a LAN vendor, is typically installed in each personal computer that is to be a station on the network. The adapter card contains the hardware and firmware programming that implements the logical link control and media access control functions.

- **Cabling System.** The cabling system includes the *cable,* or wire, used to interconnect the network devices. The cabling system also typically includes *attachment units* that allow the devices to attach to the cable.

- **Concentrator.** Some LAN implementations use *concentrators,* or *access units,* that allow network devices to be interconnected through a central point. Attaching devices through a central concentrator typically simplifies the maintenance of the LAN.

The basic wiring alternatives used for most LAN implementations are twisted-wire-pair cable, various types of coaxial cable, and fiber-optic cable. In some instances, existing telephone wiring of adequate quality is already installed in appropriate locations to support the network. Thick, inflexible Ethernet coaxial cable has a reputation for being more difficult to install than twisted-wire-pair cable; sometimes it cannot be pulled through existing ducts. Often, shielded wire-pair cables are laid down, which give higher speeds than unshielded, lower-quality telephone wire pairs. However, newer forms of coaxial cable used with some network implementations are thinner and easier to handle for new installations than some types of twisted-wire-pair cable.

COMMON IMPLEMENTATIONS OF IEEE ARCHITECTURES

As we saw in Part II, IEEE 802 standards define three LAN architectures that provide a common set of communication functions (the logical link control sublayer) but use different access control methods. The IEEE standards have been widely adopted by vendors of LAN products, and many LANs based on CSMA/CD, token ring, and token bus are available. The use of standards has been successful from the standpoint of allowing different types of equipment to be attached to the same network. By choosing a LAN implementation that conforms to an accepted standard, it is more likely that the user will have a choice of vendors that offer compatible components for constructing the network and for attaching devices to it.

Networks that implement the various IEEE standards are not always known by the IEEE nomenclature but are instead referred to by the more common names. The following are descriptions of a few of the terms used to refer to networks that conform to the IEEE 802 standards.

- **Ethernet.** Ethernet is a LAN architecture that uses CSMA/CD for media access control. The Ethernet architecture was originally developed by Xerox Corporation, beginning around 1972. Many networks were installed using the Ethernet approach, and the early Ethernet specifications served as much of the basis for the definition of the IEEE 802.3 CSMA/CD standard. After the IEEE standard was agreed on, the Ethernet specifications were updated to bring them into complete agreement with the standard. The current, updated Ethernet specification is now published as a cooperative effort by Digital Equipment Corporation, Intel Corporation, and Xerox Corporation. Ethernet network components are manufactured and marketed by a number of vendors, and Ethernet is the most widely used version of the IEEE CSMA/CD standard.

- **IBM Token Ring.** IBM offers a wide variety of LAN products. Two of these, designed specifically for personal computers, are the *IBM PC Network,* which uses a CSMA/CD architecture, and the *IBM Token Ring Network,* which conforms to the IEEE token ring standard. The research performed by IBM in developing their Token Ring Network provided much of the groundwork for the IEEE 802.5 token ring standard, and IBM's network product is consistent with the standard. As is so often the case with IBM products, the IBM Token Ring Network quickly became the most widespread implementation of the token ring form of access control.

- **MAP.** As we pointed out in Chapter 10, the MAP task force has adopted the IEEE 802.4 token bus architecture as its standard for LANs. Vendors providing LAN products that conform to the MAP specification implement this standard. Vendors of products for this type of LAN will often refer to their network as a *MAP local area network* rather than as a *token bus* LAN. Many vendors provide products that conform to the MAP specification; this will make the MAP type of LAN a very widely used implementation of the token bus architecture.

NETWORK OPERATING SYSTEMS

The functions provided at the lowest two levels of the OSI model have become standardized, and most LAN implementations are in accord with one of the three IEEE LAN standards. Above the data link level, some commonality of function has developed. However, the same level of standardization does not exist for the network layer and above as does for the data link and physical layers.

LAN products can be, and have been, implemented using products that provide functions at only the two lowest layers. Such a network provides a generalized communication facility between stations on the network. However, to realize the full benefits of local area networking, additional functions, over and above a generalized communication facility, are considered desirable. These functions relate to the higher-level networking layers and are provided by what has come to be known as a *network operating system.*

While the lower layers are implemented in hardware and firmware, the network operating system is normally implemented in the form of software that runs in the devices attached to the network (for the purposes of this chapter, in a personal computer). Some network operating systems come in multiple versions, supporting different lower-level architectures. For example, one version may support Ethernet and another token ring.

Certain types of functions have now become commonplace in the generally available network operating systems:

- **Print Server Support.** One of the advantages of a LAN is the ability to share peripheral devices such as printers, especially expensive ones like laser printers or phototypesetters. A print server facility allows all stations of the network to use a printer owned by another station. Output can be sent to the printer exactly as if the printer were attached directly to the user's own station, and queueing facilities are generally provided so that output can be sent to the printer even when it is busy.

- **File Server Support.** High-capacity disk storage is another resource that is commonly shared on a LAN. A file server is typically a personal computer that manages a high-capacity hard disk drive. File server support allows other stations to access files stored on the file server. Sharing can be implemented in various ways. It can be done on a directory basis, whereby the station is allowed to access a particular directory and use any file in that directory. Sharing can also be at the file level, whereby the station is authorized to access only particular files. Shared access to disk storage is possible, but it may be the responsibility of the programs sharing the file or the directory to implement update integrity safeguards. Some network operating systems provide record-locking facilities, whereby a program can "lock" a specified string of bytes and prevent any other program from accessing them until the lock is released.

- **Electronic Mail.** Some network operating systems offer electronic mail applications, which allow end users to compose, send, receive, and store messages and documents easily. In this way users on the LAN can easily communicate with one another using the services of the LAN for transparent data transmission.

- **Network Name Service.** Network users and application programs that interface with the network operating system request services on the basis of *network names.* Network names are used to represent both network users and shared resources. A network name service translates a network name into a network address so that the messages needed to implement a service request can be addressed properly.

- **Connectivity.** Connectivity is a general term used to refer to communication outside the LAN. A network operating system can implement various types of connectivity, for example:

Allowing a personal computer that is not attached to the LAN to access the LAN over long-distance communication facilities such as a telephone line. This is known as *remote access*.

Allowing stations on the LAN to access a computer that is not part of the network, using a shared communication facility that is supported by one of the network stations. The station with the shared communication facility is sometimes referred to as a *communication server*. The computer being accessed can be attached to the local area network directly or through remote communication facilities.

Interconnecting two or more LANs. The networks may be of the same type or different types. Also, the networks may be interconnected directly or via a wide area network. Network interconnection facilities are discussed in Chapter 12.

- **Network Management.** Although lower-layer standards, such as the IEEE 802 standards, do address network management to some extent, they do not define it in detail, nor do they deal with the complex network management requirements of the higher layers. Network operating systems commonly offer management facilities aimed at maintaining network availability, reliability, and security, but the exact nature of these facilities may vary from one network to another. In some instances, network management deals only with a single LAN. In other cases, it may be part of a larger facility that deals with the management of a group of interconnected networks and transmission facilities.

RELATIONSHIP TO HIGHER LAYERS

The functions of a network operating system that we have just described relate to various layers of a network architecture. Figure 13.1 illustrates the basic relationships that exist between the functions and the layers of the OSI model.

Application Layer

The application layer provides a point of access to the local area network. It is responsible for performing *common application functions*, which are functions useful to many applications, and *specific application functions*, or functions that are unique to a particular application. The portion of a network operating system that implements the application layer typically provides general facilities, such as electronic mail, printer sharing, and file sharing, and may provide a network name service. These facilities may be accessible directly through an end-user interface, implemented in the form of menus, commands, or utility programs or through calls issued by an application program that interfaces with the network operating system.

Presentation Layer

The presentation layer is responsible for the presentation of information in a way that is meaningful to the application entity interfacing with the layer. This

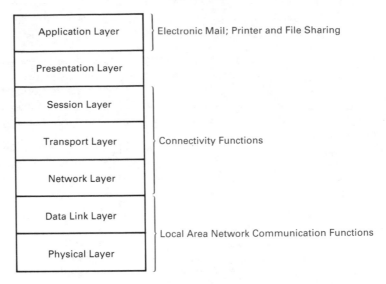

Figure 13.1   Network layers and network operating system functions

may involve translating from one encoding system to another, for example, from EBCDIC to ASCII. This type of function is not generally implemented as part of local area networking and is not included in the protocols of currently available network operating systems for local area networks. If this type of facility is required in a particular situation, it is more likely to be handled by an application program that interfaces with the network.

Session, Transport, and Network Layers

The session, transport, and network layers are heavily involved in implementing different forms of connectivity. Key issues related to connectivity include these:

- **Network Names.** With basic LAN communication, each station on the network knows its own addresses and accepts any message sent to one of its addresses. The sending station is responsible for specifying the appropriate address to use for the message. As discussed earlier, higher layers may provide a network name service, so that network users and application programs interfacing to the network can operate using network names rather than network addresses. A facility must then be provided that translates network names into network addresses. One approach is for each station to keep track of its own network names and to provide the address associated with one of its names when requested. A second approach is for a centralized facility to maintain a table of network names associated with different stations and the corresponding address for each name. Upon request, the central facility translates a name into the appropriate address using the table.

- **Routing and Addressing.** When a message travels outside a local area network, there may be more than one possible route that it can take to its destination. Two approaches can be used to determine the route. One, called source routing, has the sending station specify the route. The second approach involves routing information that is stored at different nodes in the network. The message is then routed according to destination network and station, using the stored routing information at each intermediate node. More information on routing in interconnected networks is presented in Chapters 12 and 19.

The data link and physical layers are responsible for providing communication in the local area network itself. They provide the basis on which the higher-layer functions are constructed.

STANDARDIZATION

The amount of standardization at different levels in a network architecture varies greatly from one LAN implementation to another. At the lower levels, standards have been formally defined, primarily through IEEE Project 802, and are now common. This has had the benefit of allowing greater flexibility in terms of connecting different vendors' products to the same LAN.

At the application layer level, de facto standards are emerging. They define an interface that allows personal computer software products to access printer and file servers and to provide record-locking facilities as part of file sharing. As is often the case, these standards are based on IBM protocols. For IBM LANs that support personal computers, these protocols are called the *Redirector* and *Server Message Block* (SMB) protocols (see Chapter 18). Other vendors are now offering network products that support these protocols, allowing a software product that has been modified to run on an IBM network to work on networks marketed by other vendors. Software vendors need not develop and provide multiple versions of their products to support different LANs.

The end-user interfaces at the application level are also moving toward standardization. Here, different LAN products tend to offer similar functions. However, in many cases, the interface used to invoke the functions, consisting of menus, commands, and utility programs, varies from one product to another. Some vendors offer an interface that is similar to, or a superset of, the interface used by IBM, but standardization at this level is not as advanced as for the application program interface. The greatest differences between network operating systems are in the types of connectivity offered and the way they have been implemented.

SUMMARY

The physical components of a LAN typically include adapter cards, a cabling system, and concentrators. Common implementations of the IEEE 802 architectures are Ethernet for the

IEEE 802.3 CSMA/CD standard, IBM Token Ring for the IEEE 802.5 token ring standard, and MAP for the IEEE 802.4 token bus standard. Network operating systems provide functions associated with the higher-level network layers, including print and file server support, electronic mail, network name service, connectivity, and network management. Formal standards, primarily IEEE 802, have been implemented at the physical and data link layer levels. A de facto standard emerging for the higher layers consists of the Redirector and Server Message Block protocols developed by IBM.

14 IBM LAN ARCHITECTURES AND PRODUCTS

IBM has established a set of goals that determine the desirable characteristics of a LAN. These goals are shown in Box 14.1. To meet these goals, IBM has developed numerous products and offers support for several architectures.

BOX 14.1 Local area network goals

- The network should permit transmission of data at a rapid rate.
- The network should be able to serve the entire establishment with many types of devices, unless the establishment crosses a public right-of-way. Because crossing a public right-of-way requires regulatory approval, existing public utilities such as telephone lines are ordinarily used in such cases.
- The network must be easily restructured to meet the rapidly changing communication needs within establishments.
- The network must be highly reliable.
- The network must have high availability.
- The network must be serviceable.
- The network should permit attachment by all devices that require access to the network.

IBM LAN PRODUCTS

IBM's local area network products offer several choices in terms of both architectures and interfaces. Figure 14.1 shows the basic LAN products and their

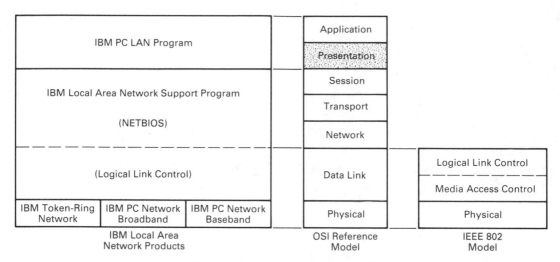

Figure 14.1   IBM local area network products

relationship to the layers of the OSI and IEEE network models. At the level defined by the IEEE media access control standards, there are three choices:

- **IBM Token Ring Network.** The IBM Token Ring Network implements the IEEE 802.5 token ring standard. It uses a baseband cabling system.
- **PC Network—Broadband.** The PC Network implements the IEEE 802.3 CSMA/CD standard. This version of the network uses broadband transmission.
- **PC Network—Baseband.** This version of the PC Network also implements the IEEE 802.3 CSMA/CD standard but uses baseband transmission.

These products, which implement the physical layer and the media access control sublayer of the data link layer, are implemented in hardware in the form of adapter cards that plug into IBM's various personal computer models.

The *IBM Local Area Network Support Program,* an IBM software product, offers a common interface, at the logical link control level, to all three hardware network products. This interface implements the IEEE 802.2 LLC standard. Originally, this interface was provided through a separate program called the *Adapter Support Interface.*

The IBM Local Area Network Support Program also supports a higher-level programming interface to the network, which IBM calls *NETBIOS.* This interface provides functions associated with the network, transport, and session layers. The NETBIOS interface offers two types of communication: *reliable data transfer* and *datagram service.* The reliable data service is based on the establishment of a session between the two communicating partners. With the datagram service, messages are sent without first establishing a session. NET-

BIOS also provides a naming facility. Through this facility, names can be associated with a station, and messages can be directed to a station by specifying a name rather than a network address. The NETBIOS interface was originally offered through a separate program, also called NETBIOS. The IBM Local Area Network Support Program now offers both interfaces, while providing compatibility with the earlier separate programs.

Another program product called the *IBM PC LAN Program* provides an application level interface to a LAN. It includes a messaging facility and implements print and file servers for printer and file sharing. These services can be accessed either by application programs or by end users using menus and commands. Many of the popular personal computer application software packages have been modified to use the IBM PC LAN Program interface. This allows the application package to run in a LAN environment and allows end users to take advantage of file and print servers when they use the application.

CONNECTIVITY

The products just discussed provide basic LAN services, including messaging and file and print server functions. Several products available also address the area of connectivity. These products, shown in Fig. 14.2, provide the following functions:

- Bridge-level connections between LANs of the same type
- Gateways that interconnect LANs of different types or that connect LANs with host computers and WANs
- A generalized facility for developing applications that communicate with each other.

These facilities are discussed in the sections that follow.

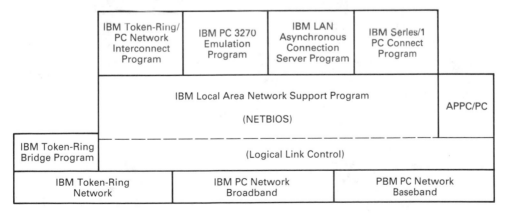

Figure 14.2　IBM connectivity products

IBM Token Ring Bridge Program

The *IBM Token Ring Bridge Program* allows rings to be interconnected to form a composite network. The rings are interconnected through a station, known as a *bridge,* that belongs to each ring. It contains two Token Ring adapter cards, one for each ring, and runs the IBM Token Ring Bridge Program. The primary function of the bridge is to transfer frames between rings. The Bridge Program also provides network functions and supervisory services, including the following:

- Providing ring numbers to stations as they are added to a ring
- Compiling, analyzing, and displaying error statistics
- Reporting error conditions to the operator
- Reporting configuration changes to the LAN manager
- Providing trace and self-test facilities

The IBM Token Ring Bridge Program interconnects only token ring networks. It does not use the NETBIOS or LLC interfaces. Figure 14.3 shows an example of interconnected rings. Station D is part of both rings and acts as the bridge. For frames where the destination station is on the same ring as the originating station, the bridge simply retransmits the frame to the next station on the ring. For example, if station B sends a frame to station F, when the message reaches bridge station D, the message is passed on to station E. When a frame is destined for a different ring, the bridge also copies the frame to that ring. For example, if station B sends a frame to station G, the bridge passes the frame from one ring to the other as well as to station E.

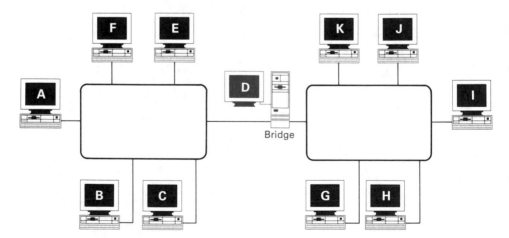

Figure 14.3   Token Ring bridge

GATEWAYS

In addition to the bridge product, IBM offers several gateway products that provide interconnection between unlike networks. As true gateways, these products are responsible for performing any protocol conversions that are necessary to allow for differences between the networks being interconnected. Each product provides for interconnection between two specific types of networks.

IBM Token Ring/PC Network Interconnect Program

The IBM Token Ring/PC Network Interconnect Program provides interconnection between an IBM Token Ring Network and an IBM PC Network that uses broadband transmission. The two networks are connected by a station that belongs to both networks and has an adapter card of each type installed in it. The station must be dedicated to the gateway function and cannot be used for any other processing. An example of the use of the Interconnect Program is shown in Fig. 14.4. Station D acts as the gateway between the two networks.

Because the Interconnect Program uses the NETBIOS interface, messaging can take place using names rather than specific station addresses. Any applications that wish to use the Interconnect Program for transmission from one network to the other must also use the NETBIOS interface.

When a session must be established between two stations in different networks, two sessions are set up. One is between the originating station and the gateway, and the other is between the gateway and the destination station. Messages are sent to the gateway, and the gateway then forwards them to the destination station in the other network. The gateway, rather than the receiving station, is responsible for returning acknowledgments. This makes it possible

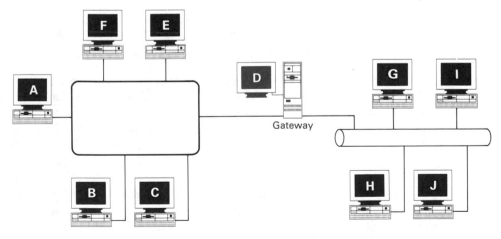

Figure 14.4   Token Ring/PC Network interconnection

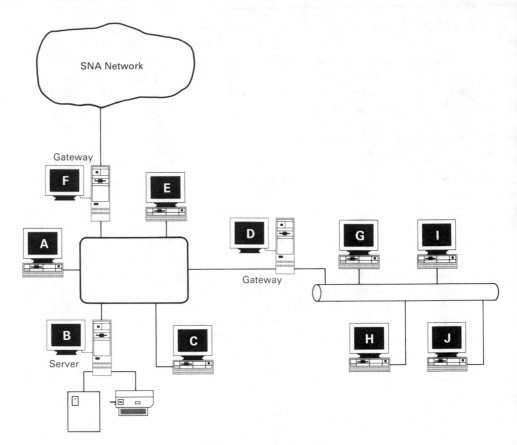

Figure 14.5 Using servers via the interconnect

that under certain conditions, a message will be acknowledged but will not actually reach the destination station. Applications that use this facility must take
this into account.

Through the use of the Interconnect Program, it is possible for a station in
one network to use servers in another network. This is illustrated in Fig. 14.5.
Here station B in the Token Ring Network is running the IBM PC LAN Program and is acting as a file and print server. A station on the IBM PC Network,
for example, station G, could also run the IBM PC LAN Program and then
access file and print services from station B. Similarly, station F in the ring is
a gateway to an SNA network. If station G had the appropriate program installed (e.g., the IBM PC 3270 Emulation Program, discussed next), it could
use station F's services as a communications server to access the SNA network.

It is possible to interconnect more than two networks. The interconnections
must be in a chain, with the type of network alternating between Token Ring
and PC Network, as shown in Fig. 14.6.

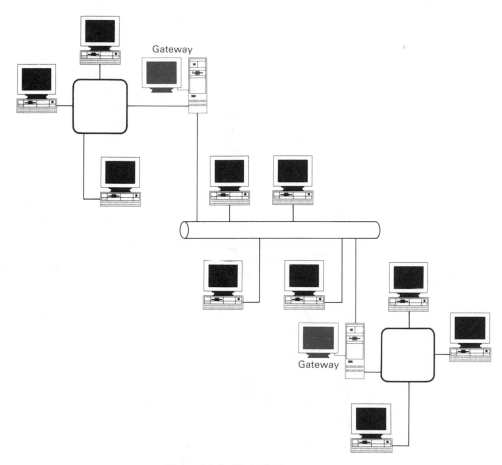

Figure 14.6   Multiple interconnects

IBM PC 3270 Emulation Program

The IBM PC 3270 Emulation Program can be used to construct a gateway between a LAN and an SNA network. A station that functions as a gateway uses the 3270 Emulation software to emulate a 3274 terminal controller. The LAN can be either a Token Ring Network or a PC Network. Figure 14.7 illustrates this using a Token Ring Network. Individual stations on the network can also use the 3270 Emulation program to emulate the functions of a 3270-type terminal. They then use the services of the gateway station to establish sessions with the SNA network. A network station may function as a 3278 or 3279 display device or as a 3287 printer. The gateway station provides the functions of a 3274 controller for establishing and supporting these sessions. It must contain an SDLC communication adapter to provide the communication link with the SNA network.

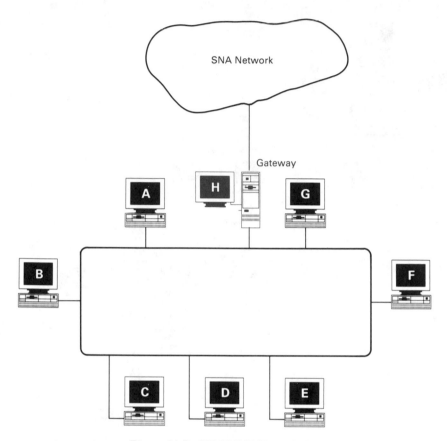

Figure 14.7 IBM PC 3270 emulation

A gateway can support up to 32 SNA sessions and can act as a network station as well as a gateway. There can be multiple 3270 Emulation gateways in a network. A network station can participate in one display session and one printer session at a time and can use only one gateway at a time.

The IBM PC 3270 Emulation Program also supports file transfers between LAN stations and a host computer. The host must be running VM/CMS, TSO, or CICS, plus the 3270-PC File Transfer Program. Additional functions provided include keyboard remapping, status displays, traces, and saving of display screens to disk.

IBM LAN Asynchronous Connection Server Program

The IBM LAN Asynchronous Connection Server Program provides interconnection between a LAN and an asynchronous device or host. This type of gateway can be used in a number of ways, as shown in Fig. 14.8. Network stations can

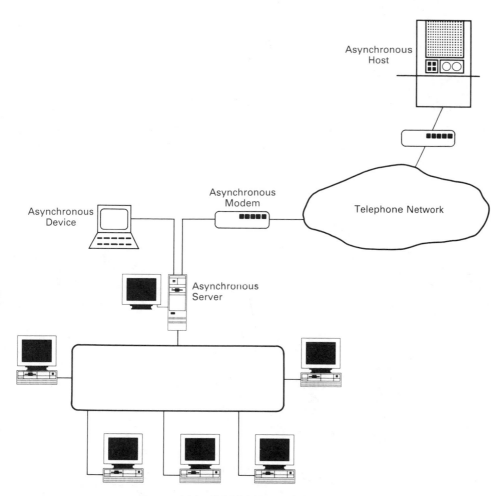

Figure 14.8   IBM LAN asynchronous server

use it to access an asynchronous host that is directly attached to the gateway. The host can be any type of computing system, including another IBM personal computer. A network station can access a remote asynchronous host, where the gateway uses a modem and telecommunications lines to effect the connection. Here the gateway acts as a communication server, allowing lines and modems to be shared by all network stations. Asynchronous terminals can be attached to the LAN through one gateway and then use another gateway to access asynchronous devices or hosts that are not part of the LAN.

The gateway must be dedicated as a communication server. The other network stations must run an application program that provides appropriate communication protocols for communicating with the particular asynchronous device it contacts. An earlier version of this program, called the IBM *Asynchron-*

ous Communication Server Program, allowed the communication server to run
in the background. However, this program supports only two communication
ports on the gateway and must be used with a baseband IBM PC Network. The
newer version supports up to 32 ports.

IBM Series/1 PC Connect Program

The IBM Series/1 PC Connect Program allows a Token Ring Network to be
connected to a Series/1 host. The Series/1 can be used as a file and print server
or as a communication server. As a communication server, it provides access to
a remote host, using either SNA 3270 protocols or 3270 binary-synchronous

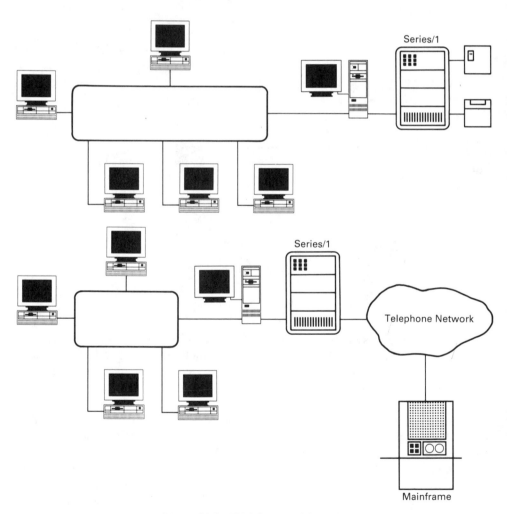

Figure 14.9   IBM Series/1 PC Connect

protocols. The Series/1 cannot act as both types of server at the same time. Possible configurations are shown in Fig. 14.9.

Advanced Program-to-Program Communications/PC

The various gateways that we have just discussed all use the NETBIOS interface as their way of gaining access to LAN communication facilities. The NETBIOS interface offers the following facilities:

- Reliable data transmission based on the establishment of a session between two partners

- Datagram service, which requires no session and does not provide acknowledgments to ensure that a message is delivered

- The use of names to identify senders and recipients

With NETBIOS, each station knows its own names and is responsible for recognizing them. Source routing is used to specify the route to an intended recipient. The source station determines the route to use by sending a broadcast message to all stations and then receiving a response from the intended recipient with the information needed to address and route transmissions directly to that station. In providing these services, NETBIOS essentially addresses the functions associated with the session, transport, and network layers of the OSI model. NETBIOS provides these functions in the context of a single LAN and does not itself attempt to provide support for generalized network interconnection.

The IBM program product called *Advanced Program-to-Program Communications/PC* (APPC/PC) can be viewed as providing an alternative to NETBIOS as an interface to LAN communication. APPC/PC is based on the Advanced Program-to-Program Communication (APPC) and LU 6.2 facilities defined as part of the SNA architecture. It uses the logical link control interface as its way of accessing the lower-level communication facilities. Any of the three LAN products can be used with APPC/PC.

APPC/PC is defined by IBM as "a data communication system that allows transaction programs to be written for the IBM Personal Computer that will communicate with transaction programs on other APPC systems." Just as programs have been written to use the NETBIOS interface to LAN communications, programs can and are written to use the APPC/PC interface. APPC/PC provides more than a way of using a LAN. It also provides a way of accessing SNA networks via SDLC and, through that, of communicating with programs on other hosts, including IBM mainframes that run CICS/VS, and System/36, System/38, and Series/1 minicomputers.

Figure 14.10 shows the different ways in which APPC/PC can be used to communicate. As shown at the top, two stations that are part of a Token Ring

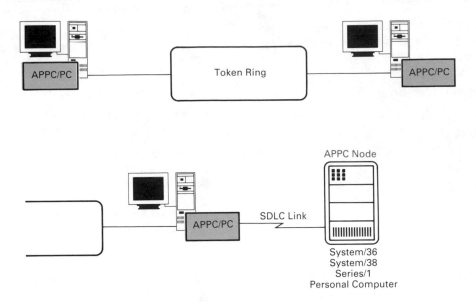

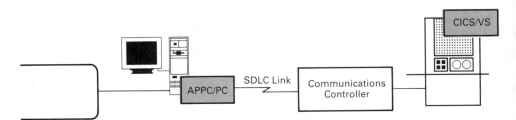

Figure 14.10 APPC configurations

Network can communicate using APPC/PC. A personal computer with an SDLC
communications adapter can use APPC/PC to communicate with directly attached hosts, including the System/36, System/38, Series/1, and another personal computer. The attached host must also be running an APPC program. A
personal computer with SDLC capabilities can also communicate with CICS/
VS, using intermediate nodes such as a 37X5 communications control if necessary to reach the host that runs the CICS/VS application. APPC/PC cannot be
used directly as a gateway, however. This means a station on a Token Ring
Network cannot use another station's SDLC link to reach an APPC node outside
the network unless an application program written to use APPC/PC provides the
necessary interconnection services.

APPC/PC uses different communication protocols than NETBIOS, since it
is based on the SNA network architecture. With APPC/PC, sessions are established between communicating partners, and the equivalent of datagram service
is not available. Also, partner names are predefined and are stored centrally,

where they are available to the originating partner. When routing involves the use of intermediate nodes, routing information is predefined and stored at each intermediate node.

We will examine both NETBIOS and APPC/PC in more detail in Chapter 17 and also look at other alternative architectures for these network layers.

SUMMARY

IBM supports a token ring LAN architecture with its IBM Token Ring Network product and a CSMA/CD architecture with its PC Network—Broadband and PC Network—Baseband products. The IBM Local Area Network Support Program provides logical link control and NETBIOS interfaces to its LAN products. The IBM PC LAN Program offers an application layer interface to the networks and provides messaging services, file and print servers, and a name service.

The IBM Token Ring Bridge Program allows multiple rings to be interconnected in a single network. The IBM Token Ring/PC Network Interconnect Program provides a way to interconnect Token Ring and PC Network networks. The IBM PC 3270 Emulation program allows network stations to access an SNA network, with the network station acting as a 3270 terminal. The IBM LAN Asynchronous Connection Server Program allows network stations to communicate with asynchronous devices and hosts that are connected to the network either directly or remotely. The IBM Series/1 PC Connect Program allows a Series/1 to be used as a file and print server or as a communication server to an SNA network. APPC/PC provides an alternative to NETBIOS and allows applications to be developed that can communicate over a LAN or over an SDLC link.

15   IBM TOKEN RING NETWORK

The IBM Token Ring Network uses a physical ring that is wired in a star-type configuration using a central access unit. The IBM token ring architecture is consistent with the IEEE 802.5 token ring standard. The system is designed to allow computers in the same building or group of buildings to be connected in a network and to exchange information over that network.

NETWORK COMPONENTS   The components that make up the IBM Token Ring Network product are the following:

- **IBM Token Ring Network Adapter Card.** The Token Ring adapter card provides the logic and control functions necessary to implement the MAC sublayer and physical layer of the network and enables the personal computer in which it is installed to send and receive messages across the network.

- **IBM Token Ring Network Multistation Access Unit.** The multistation access unit allows up to eight stations to be attached to form a star-wired subnetwork, as illustrated in Fig. 15.1. The cable used to connect a device to the access unit is called a *lobe*. The dotted line traces the logical ring that is formed with this type of attachment. Access units can be wired together to allow for a ring having more than eight network stations, as illustrated in Fig. 15.2. Again, the dotted line traces the ring that is formed. The use of the star-wired physical network structure makes it easier to maintain the network. When an attaching device is to be added or removed, this can be done at a central point. It is also easier to bypass a failing portion of the network while the problem is being repaired, since the bypass can be done at the central point. From the standpoint of logical message flow, however, the network implements a ring topology, since the multistation access unit does not contain the intelligence necessary to act as a station on the network.

- **Cabling System.** The IBM Token Ring Network uses baseband transmission

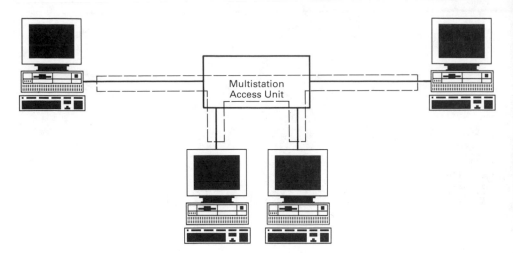

Figure 15.1   Star-wired network using IBM's multistation access unit

and a data rate of 4 Mbps over a cabling system that uses twisted-wire pairs. Data-grade or shielded, twisted-wire-pair cable is recommended for more reliable transmission. However, unshielded wire, which is the typical telephone wire already installed in many buildings, can be used with certain limitations on the length of the network, transmission speed, and the total number of devices attached to the network.

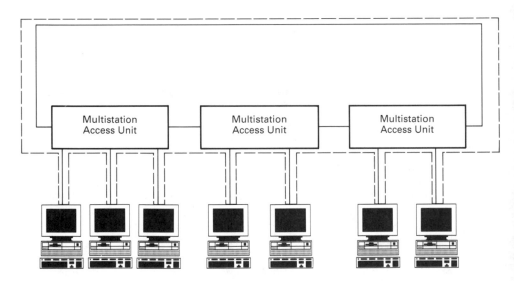

Figure 15.2   Multiple access units

Start Delimiter	Access Control	End Delimiter
1 Byte	1 Byte	1 Byte

Figure 15.3   Token format

MEDIA ACCESS MANAGEMENT

The basic method of media access management in the Token Ring Network is token passing. A special transmission frame, called the *token,* is passed from one device to the next around the ring. When a network station receives the token, that station is allowed to transmit. To transmit, the station changes the token to a frame containing control information and data. The frame is then passed around the ring, and each station checks the frame to see if it should accept and process the frame and then retransmits the frame to the next station on the ring. The frame continues around the ring until it reaches the station that originally sent the message. This station then changes the frame back to a token and transmits the token to the next station.

The format of a token is shown in Fig. 15.3. It begins with a 1-byte start delimiter field, contains a 1-byte access control field, and ends with a 1-byte end delimiter field. To change the token to a frame, the station changes one of the bits in the access control field and adds the necessary control information and data.

PRIORITY SCHEME

The IBM Token Ring Network supports the use of prioritization for station access, as defined in the IEEE 802.5 token ring standard. Three bits in the access control field are used to specify the priority of the token. Frames to be transmitted can also be assigned a priority value. When a station receives the token, it compares the token's priority to the priority of any frame it has ready to transmit. If the token's priority is equal to or lower than the frame's, the frame is transmitted. If the token's priority is higher than that of the frame, the frame is not transmitted.

The access control field also contains three bits called reservation bits. If a station has a frame to transmit that has a priority greater than zero, the station can put the frame's priority value in the reservation bits of a frame it is retransmitting, as long as the reservation bits are not already set to a higher value. When a station removes the frame from the ring and generates a new token, that station places the value from the reservation bits into the token's priority bits. The station that generates the token with the new priority value saves the previous priority value from the token. When the token eventually returns to this station, the station restores the token's priority bits to the original priority value. This process is illustrated in Fig. 15.4. The reservation process ensures

1. Station A transmits a frame with priority 2.

4. When the token reaches Station C, the station transmits its priority 1 frame.

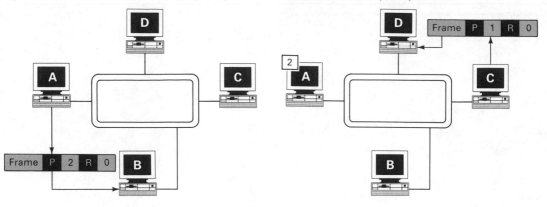

2. Station C has a frame with priority 1 ready to send, so it sets the reservation bits in the passing frame to 1.

5. When the frame returns to Station C, it transmits a token with priority 1.

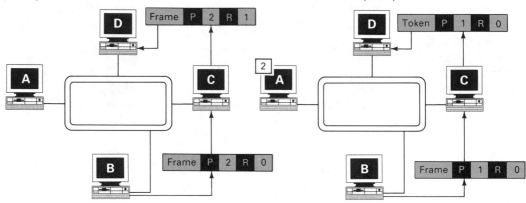

3. When Station A removes its frame from the ring and transmits a token, it sets the token's priority to 1 and saves the previous value of 2.

6. When the token reaches Station A, the station recognizes the priority value as one it set and changes it back to the stored value of 2.

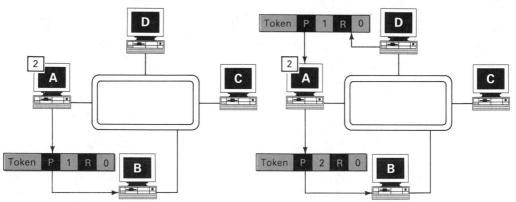

Figure 15.4 Priority and reservation

that the token will eventually be set to a lower priority value so that lower-priority frames can be sent.

**ERROR
CONDITIONS**

One of the stations on the network is designated the *active monitor*. This station is then responsible for detecting and correcting certain error conditions, such as these:

- **Lost Token or Frame.** The monitor maintains a timer that it starts each time it transmits a frame or token. If the timer expires before the monitor receives another frame or token, the monitor assumes that the frame or token was lost. It then purges the ring and originates a new token. Purging the ring involves sending a special frame around the ring that causes all stations to reset.

- **Persistently Busy Frame or Token.** The monitor also checks for a frame or a token with a nonzero priority that is not removed by the originating station after it has circled the ring once. When the monitor retransmits a frame or priority token, it sets a bit in the access control field, called the monitor bit, to 1. When a station generates a new frame or token, it sets the monitor bit to 0. If a frame or token returns to the monitor with the bit still set to 1, the monitor assumes that the originating station was unable to remove it, purges the ring, and originates a new token.

Other stations on the ring act as standby monitors. If the active monitor fails, the standby monitors go through a process called token claiming to determine which will assume the responsibilities of the active monitor.

**MEDIA ACCESS
CONTROL
SERVICES**

The interface to the Token Ring Network is defined in terms of three service primitives, which are consistent with the service primitives defined in the IEEE 802.5 token ring standard.

- **SEND_AC_DATA.** This primitive causes the transfer of one data unit to the MAC sublayer for transmission across the network. It corresponds to the IEEE **MA_DATA.request** primitive. Both use parameters to pass a frame control value, a destination address, a requested service class, and the data unit itself. **SEND_AC_DATA** also uses a parameter to provide routing information for network interconnection.

- **RECEIVE_AC_DATA.** This primitive causes a data unit that has been received from the network to be transferred from the MAC sublayer to the LLC sublayer. It corresponds to the IEEE primitive **MA_DATA.indication.** Its parameters include a frame control value, destination address, source address, reception status, and the data unit. **RECEIVE_AC_DATA** also defines a routing information parameter used for network interconnection.

- **CONFIRM_AC_DATA.** This primitive is a response to a **SEND_AC_DATA** primitive and signals whether or not the data unit was successfully transmitted. It corresponds to the IEEE **MA_DATA.indication.** Both support parameter values for transmission status and service class provided.

FRAME FORMAT

The basic frame format used in the IBM Token Ring Network is similar to that defined in the IEEE 802.5 token ring standard. Box 15.1 describes the format of the IBM Token Ring transmission frame and compares it to the format of the transmission frame used with the IEEE 802.5 standard.

There is a special frame format that is used if a station needs to abort a

BOX 15.1   Token Ring transmission frame

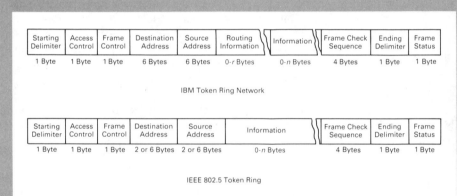

Starting Delimiter	Access Control	Frame Control	Destination Address	Source Address	Routing Information	Information	Frame Check Sequence	Ending Delimiter	Frame Status
1 Byte	1 Byte	1 Byte	6 Bytes	6 Bytes	0-r Bytes	0-n Bytes	4 Bytes	1 Byte	1 Byte

IBM Token Ring Network

Starting Delimiter	Access Control	Frame Control	Destination Address	Source Address	Information	Frame Check Sequence	Ending Delimiter	Frame Status
1 Byte	1 Byte	1 Byte	2 or 6 Bytes	2 or 6 Bytes	0-n Bytes	4 Bytes	1 Byte	1 Byte

IEEE 802.5 Token Ring

- **Starting Delimiter.** This field marks the beginning of a frame or a token. Its format includes signal combinations that allow it to be positively distinguished from data.

- **Access Control.** The access control field appears in both frames and tokens and has the bit format PPPTMRRR. The first three bits (PPP) are used to specify the priority of the frame or token. The next bit (T) identifies the data unit as either a frame or a token. The monitor bit (M) is used by the active monitor to detect a frame or token that is continuously circling the ring. The reservation bits (RRR) are used to request that a token be issued with a different priority.

- **Frame Control.** The frame control field is used to identify the purpose of the frame. Currently defined frame types are MAC (media access control) frames and LLC (logical link control) frames. For MAC frames, this field also specifies information about buffering.

BOX 15.1 *(Continued)*

- **Address Fields.** Addresses are 6 bytes long (48-bit addresses). The destination address identifies the station or stations that should receive the frame. The source address identifies the station sending the frame. The first bit of the first byte of the source address is used to identify whether or not routing information is present in the frame.

- **Routing Information.** The routing information field is a variable-length field used when a frame is to travel across a bridge to another ring in a multiring network. Since routing is not defined as part of the IEEE 802.5 token ring standard, this field represents an extension of the IEEE frame format.

- **Information.** The information field contains data that is being transmitted across the network. It is a variable-length field.

- **Frame Check Sequence.** The frame check sequence field contains a cyclic redundancy check value that is calculated on the basis of the contents of the frame control field, destination and source addresses, routing field, information field, and frame check sequence field. When the frame is received, the CRC value is recalculated, and the two values are compared. If they do not agree, the frame is assumed to have been received in error.

- **Ending Delimiter.** The ending delimiter identifies the end of the frame. As with the starting delimiter, it contains signal combinations that positively identify it as a delimiter. This field contains an intermediate frame bit, which provides for sending multiple frames using a single token. It also contains an error-detected bit. If a station detects an error when it retransmits a token or frame, it sets this bit to 1. This allows the sending station to know that the frame or token was sent in error. Types of errors that can be detected are the presence of a code violation that is not part of a delimiter, a frame that is not a multiple of 8 bits, and an error in the cyclic redundancy check value.

- **Frame Status.** This field is used by receiving stations to send status information back to the sending station. It has the bit format ACxxACxx. The address-recognized bits (A) are turned on when a receiving station recognizes the address in the frame as one of its addresses. The frame-copied bits (C) are turned on to indicate that the frame was copied onto the station's receive buffer. If both the A and C bits are turned on when a frame returns, the sending station knows it was recognized and copied. Other combinations indicate that the address was not recognized by any station or that a problem prevented the frame from being copied. Two copies of each bit are used to minimize the possibility of an error in this field, since this field is not included in the cyclic redundancy check.

frame that it is currently transmitting. Known as an abort delimiter, it consists of a starting delimiter field immediately followed by an ending delimiter field.

ADDRESSING   The IBM Token Ring Network supports three types of addressing: *individual, group,* and *functional.* An individual address identifies a particular station on a ring. An individual address can be either universal or locally administered. If it is universal, it will be unique across all networks. Each adapter card comes with a unique universal address already installed. However, an application program can assign a different individual address to the adapter and thus to the network station. If an alternate individual address is assigned, it must be locally administered.

A group address and a functional address can also be associated with each station. A group address identifies a group of stations on a ring. A functional address identifies a particular set of functions that a station is able to perform. Each bit in the functional address corresponds to a different function, and if the bit is on, the station implements that function. A functional address can be used to identify a station as an active monitor, an error monitor, a bridge, and so on.

The destination address in a frame contains bits that indicate which type of address is being used. Bit 0 of byte 0 in an address indicates whether the frame is being sent to an individual address or a group address. Bit 1 of byte 0 indicates whether the address is universal or locally administered. When a locally administered group address is specified, bit 0 of byte 2 specifies whether this is a functional address or a normal group address. Based on these bits in the destination address, a station uses its individual, group, or functional address to determine if it should process the frames that it receives.

Two special destination addresses act as all-stations broadcast addresses. The address X'C000 FFFF FFFF' specifies that the frame should be received by all stations on the sending station's ring. The address X'FFFF FFFF FFFF' specifies that the frame should be received by all stations on all rings on a multiring network.

ROUTING   An IBM Token Ring Network can consist of several interconnected Token Ring Networks, as illustrated in Fig. 15.5. The rings are interconnected by a station that is part of each ring. This type of station is known as a bridge. A bridge station must contain two Token Ring adapter cards, one for each ring. It must also have a copy of the IBM Token Ring Network Bridge Program.

A bridge copies frames from one ring to another and retransmits them to the next station on the same ring. A route is the path a frame travels through a network from the originating station to the destination station. Depending on how rings are interconnected, there may be more than one possible route for a

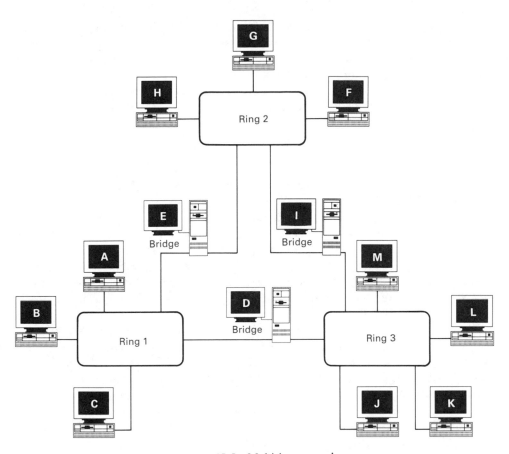

Figure 15.5   Multiring network

frame to use. For example, in Fig. 15.5, a frame going from station B to station J could travel across bridge D or across bridges E and I.

SOURCE ROUTING   The sending station specifies the route to use, using the routing information field of the frame. To determine the route, the originating station begins by sending either a TEST or XID command around its own ring addressed to the intended destination station. If the originating station receives a response, it knows that the destination station is on its own ring and does not need to use routing information for the subsequent data frames it sends it. If the sending station does not receive a response, it sends a TEST or XID command to all rings. As the command passes through interconnected rings, routing information is stored in its routing information field. If there is more than one route, more than one command will eventually reach the destination station, each containing different routing information. For each command it receives, the destination station sends back a response containing the routing information for one possible route. The responses travel their routes in the reverse direction. After receiving the responses, the originating station chooses one of the routes to use. It then sends data frames containing the routing information for that route, and the destination station uses that route in reverse if it has responses to return to the originating station.

ROUTING
INFORMATION

Figure 15.6 shows the format of the routing information field. If a frame contains routing information, a bit in the source address field is set to 1. The routing information begins with 2 bytes of control information and is followed by a series of segment numbers. Each separate ring in the total network is assigned a unique ring number, and each bridge is assigned a bridge number, which may or may not be unique. The combination of a ring number and a bridge number forms a segment number. These segment numbers then define the route a frame travels.

When a frame is being transmitted as part of an all-rings broadcast, each bridge that forwards the frame to a different ring adds a segment number to the routing information in the frame. Returning to Fig. 15.5, suppose that station B sends an all-rings broadcast frame. When the frame reaches bridge station D, it is copied to ring 3, and a segment number, based on bridge D's bridge number and ring 3's ring number, is added to the frame. The frame also continues around the ring to bridge E. Bridge E copies it to ring 2, adding a segment number for bridge E/ring 2. When that frame reaches bridge I, another segment number is added for bridge I/ring 3. When a bridge receives a broadcast frame, it checks all segment numbers. If no segment number matches its segment number, it adds the new segment number and copies the frame to the other ring. If there is a match, it discards the frame because it has already circled the ring.

With a nonbroadcast frame, the segment numbers in the routing information field are used to route the frame from the originating station to the destination station. When a bridge receives a nonbroadcast frame, it checks the segment numbers. If there is a match, it copies the new frame to the indicated ring. If there is no match, the frame is not copied to the other ring.

Figure 15.7 illustrates the contents of the routing control bytes in the rout-

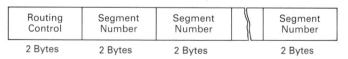

Figure 15.6   Routing information field

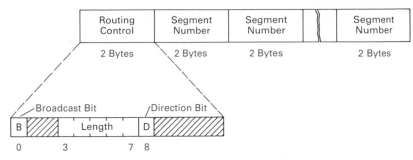

Figure 15.7   Routing control information

ing information field. The broadcast bit identifies the frame as either a broadcast frame or a nonbroadcast frame. This bit affects the way a bridge treats the routing information—whether it adds a segment number and forwards the frame or uses the existing information to determine whether to forward it. The length bits contain the length of the routing information field, which enables stations to separate the segment numbers from the information field that follows. When a bridge adds a segment number as part of forwarding a broadcast frame, the length value indicates where to add it. After adding it, the bridge updates the length value to reflect the new segment number. The direction bit indicates whether a frame is traveling from the station that originated the routing process or back to that station. Depending on this value, the segment numbers are used either left to right or right to left.

DIRECT INTERFACE

A program may interface with the IBM Token Ring Network in a number of ways. Programs can be written at the application level, using the interface defined by the IBM PC LAN Program. They can also use APPC/PC, NETBIOS, or LLC interfaces supported by the IBM Local Area Network Support Program. A program can also interface directly with the media access control sublayer, using what is called the direct interface.

The direct interface is based on the use of a control block known as a *command control block* (CCB). This control block provides the information necessary to execute a particular command. The CCB contains a command code that identifies the particular function to perform. It may also specify work areas and parameters that are used as part of the function. The CCB includes a completion code area for returning a code after the command is completed, which indicates whether or not the command was executed successfully. The CCB can also specify the address of a user routine that is to receive control after the command is completed.

BOX 15.2 Direct interface commands

Command	Function
Transmit.Dir.Frame	Transmit a frame of data
Receive	Receive data from a specified station
Receive.Cancel	Stop receiving data from a specified station
Dir.Cancel.Timer.Group	Cancel a group of timer commands
Dir.Close.Adapter	Close the adapter and terminate communication
Dir.Define.MIF.Environment	Define the environment required for a NETBIOS emulation program to use this interface
Dir.Interrupt	Force an adapter interrupt
Dir.Initialize	Initialize interface table, buffers, and areas
Dir.Modify.Open.Parms	Modify parameters associated with the adapter
Dir.Open.Adapter	Make the adapter ready for communication
Dir.Read.Log	Read log data and reset the log
Dir.Restore.Open.Parms	Restore parameters associated with the adapter to their original values
Dir.Set.Functional.Address	Set the addresses for which the adapter will receive messages
Dir.Set.Group.Address	Set the group address for which the adapter will receive messages
Dir.Set.User.Appendage	Change the addresses of user routines that are given control when commands complete processing
Dir.Status	Read general status information
Dir.Timer.Cancel	Cancel a timer
Dir.Timer.Set	Set a timer to expire in a specified time
PDT.Trace.On	Provide an interrupt trace for all adapter traffic
PDT.Trace.Off	Terminate a trace

Box 15.2 lists the commands that are available as part of the direct interface. These commands are used to perform the following operations:

- Open and close the adapter
- Set and modify adapter and execution environment values
- Obtain error status information

- Set addresses
- Transmit frames

PHYSICAL LAYER   The physical layer is responsible for providing attachment to the transmission medium and for encoding, transmitting, and recognizing signals. It accepts 0 and 1 bits and code violations from the MAC sublayer and transmits them across the transmission medium. It recognizes 0 and 1 bits and signal violations on the transmission medium and passes them to the MAC sublayer on the receiving side. It also recognizes signal losses.

The differential Manchester encoding scheme is used with the IBM Token Ring Network. With the differential Manchester code, there is always a transition in the midpoint of a bit signal when 0 and 1 bits are being transmitted. This allows the data stream to serve for synchronization also. (See Chapter 2 for a discussion of differential Manchester encoding.)

If there is no transition at the midpoint of a bit signal, this is considered a code violation. There are two types of code violations, known as J and K. If

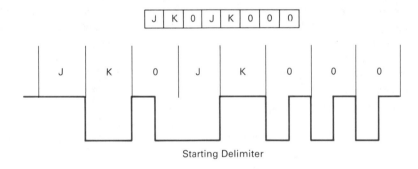

Starting Delimiter

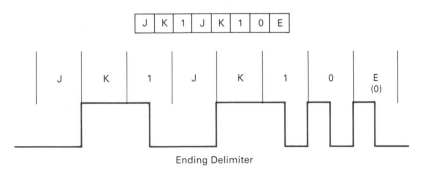

Ending Delimiter

Figure 15.8 Starting and ending delimiters

there is no transition at the start of the bit time and no transition at the midpoint, it is a J violation. If there is a transition at the start but none in the middle, it is a K violation. J and K code violations are used as part of the starting and ending delimiter values. This ensures that no combination of 0 and 1 bits in the data stream will be mistaken for a delimiter, thus allowing the start and end of a frame to be identified. Figure 15.8 shows the formats of the starting and ending delimiter fields and how they might be encoded. The encoding of the starting delimiter shown assumes that the signal begins at a high level. The ending delimiter encoding shown assumes that the signal is at a low level when the delimiter starts. It also assumes that the error bit has a value of 0.

As discussed earlier, the physical medium used with the IBM Token Ring Network consists of twisted-wire pairs. Data transmission is baseband, at a data rate of 4 Mbps.

SUMMARY

The IBM Token Ring Network uses a star-structured token ring architecture, based on the IEEE 802.5 token ring standard. A token that passes from station to station around the ring confers the right to transmit. The token and frames to transmit can be assigned priorities, allowing higher-priority frames to be transmitted sooner. Reservation bits can be used to request a change in priority for the token. The active monitor checks and corrects for a lost token or frame or a persistently busy token or frame. The frame format contains a starting delimiter, access control, frame control, destination address, source address, routing information, data frame check sequence, ending delimiter, and frame status fields. Individual, group, or functional addresses can be used. Individual addresses can be locally or universally administered.

Routing across a multiring network is based on segment numbers, consisting of a ring number and a bridge number. A broadcast message is used to collect routing information as the message travels across the network. The routing information is returned in a set of responses. The sending station selects the route from the responses received and includes the selected routing information in the data frames it transmits. Physical transmission uses twisted-wire pairs, baseband transmission, a data rate of 4 Mbps, and differential Manchester encoding.

16 IBM PC NETWORK

IBM offers two products that implement the IEEE 802.3 CSMA/CD standard. *PC Network—Broadband* supports it using broadband transmission, and *PC Network—Baseband* supports it using baseband transmission.

**NETWORK
INTERFACES**
Both the NETBIOS and logical link control interfaces are supported for the two PC Network products. The baseband version of PC Network supports both the NETBIOS and LLC interfaces through the use of the IBM Local Area Network Support Program. For the broadband version of PC Network, original versions of the adapter came with the NETBIOS logic incorporated on the adapter card. With newer adapters, the IBM Local Area Network Support Program provides the NETBIOS interface as well as the LLC interface. When new and old adapters are used in the same network, the *IBM PC Network Protocol Driver Program,* rather than the IBM Local Area Network Support Program, is used with the new adapters to provide the NETBIOS interface. This is to maintain compatibility with the version of NETBIOS on the older adapter cards.

**MEDIA ACCESS
MANAGEMENT**
A key responsibility of PC Network is medium access management, which is responsible for managing the sharing of the transmission medium among the different stations on the network. PC Network implements the methods defined in the IEEE 802.3 CSMA/CD standard. The media access management function takes a frame that has necessary control information added, as defined in the CSMA/CD frame format, and is responsible for seeing that it is transmitted. The approach used involves listening to the transmission medium before transmitting, or carrier sensing. Box 16.1 shows the PC Network frame format.

BOX 16.1   PC Network frame format

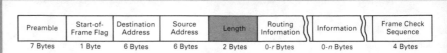

Preamble	Start-of-Frame Flag	Destination Address	Source Address	Length	Routing Information	Information	Frame Check Sequence
7 Bytes	1 Byte	6 Bytes	6 Bytes	2 Bytes	0-r Bytes	0-n Bytes	4 Bytes

- **Preamble.** The frame begins with a *preamble* consisting of 56 bits of alternating 1 and 0 bits to allow receiving stations to synchronize with the signal.

- **Start-of-Frame Flag.** The beginning of the frame is identified by the *start-of-frame flag,* which consists of the bit sequence 10101011.

- **Address Fields.** The *destination address* and *source address* identify the receiving and sending stations, respectively. PC Network employs 6-byte addresses, allowing for both locally administered and universal addresses. The destination address can specify either an individual station or a group of stations. Both multicast and broadcast group addresses are supported.

- **Length Field.** The PC Network frame format includes a *length field,* to be consistent with the IEEE 802.3 format, but this field is not used.

- **Routing Information.** Following the length field is an optional field for routing information. If the high-order bit in the source address field is 1, routing information is present; if it is 0, the routing information field is not present.

- **Information Field.** The information field contains the LLC data unit being transmitted. This contains the usual LLC fields, including DSAP, SSAP, control field, and information.

- **Frame Check Sequence.** The frame check sequence field contains a CRC value for the frame. This field is used by the receiving station to check for transmission errors.

Media access management determines, via the physical layer, whether or not the transmission medium, or carrier, is currently being used. If the carrier is free, media access management initiates transmission of the frame. If the carrier is busy, media access management continues monitoring the carrier until the carrier is free. Media access management then waits a specified time, to allow the network to clear, and begins transmission.

COLLISION DETECTION   Media access management continues to monitor the carrier after frame transmission begins. If two stations have begun transmitting at the same time, their signals will collide, causing their transmissions to become garbled. When the transmitting station detects the garbled signal, the station stops transmitting data and sends a jamming signal to ensure that all other stations detect the collision. All stations that have been transmitting stop their transmissions, wait a period of time, and, if the carrier is free, attempt retransmission of the frame.

Two methods are used to detect a collision. One is to monitor the incoming signal to see if any code violations are detected. A code violation is a bit time that does not fit the encoding rules and has a signal transition in an invalid place. The second method is based on that fact that data sent out is received by every station on the network, including the station that sent it. The sending station conducts a comparison of the data it sent with the data it receives. This comparison is done by calculating a cyclical redundancy check (CRC) value for a specified number of bits for the data being sent. The CRC value is saved. When the data is received, a CRC value is again calculated on the specified number of bits, and the two CRC values are compared. If they are not equal, the station assumes that a collision has occurred.

While transmitting, a station must listen long enough to ensure that a collision has not occurred. The length of time this takes varies, depending on whether baseband or broadband transmission is being used.

BACKOFF AFTER COLLISION

When a collision occurs, all transmitting stations stop sending, wait a calculated length of time, and then, if the carrier is free, start transmitting again. Each station generates from a predetermined range a random number that determines the length of time it waits before testing the carrier; this time interval is called the station's *backoff delay*. Backoff delay is calculated in terms of multiples of slot time.

Each station selects a random number from a range of numbers. It then waits that number of slot times before attempting retransmission. The range of numbers is determined by a method called *binary exponential backoff*, in which the range of numbers is defined as $0 \leq r < 2^n$, where n reflects the number of attempts made at retransmission. For the first ten attempts, n ranges from 1 to 10. For subsequent attempts, n continues to have a value of 10. If a station is unsuccessful in transmitting after 16 attempts, the station reports an error condition. Binary exponential backoff results in minimum delays before retransmission when traffic on the network is light. When traffic is high, repeated collisions will cause the range of numbers to increase, thus lessening the chance of further collisions.

IBM PC NETWORK— BROADBAND

The basic components of the broadband version of the IBM PC Network include the following:

- **Adapter Card.** The adapter card is installed in a personal computer and contains the logic required to implement the basic LAN communication functions, using the CSMA/CD media access control method.
- **Translator Unit.** The translator unit is responsible for receiving any signal transmitted by a station on the network and retransmitting it at a different frequency. The translator unit also comes with an eight-way splitter that allows the attachment of eight network stations.

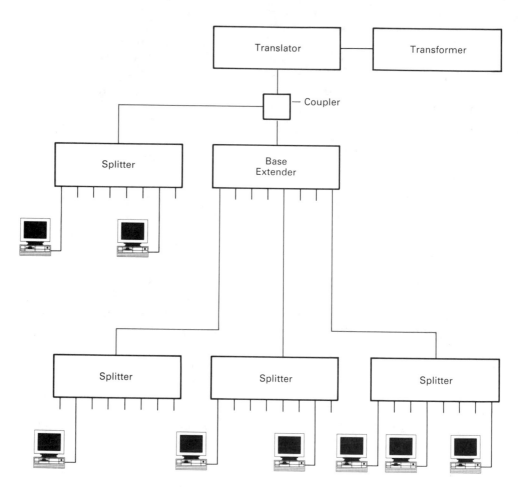

Figure 16.1   Broadband topology

- **Cabling Components.** The cabling components include a base extender, splitters, and the cable required to add stations to the network.

Network Topology

The components are used to construct a network that has a tree topology, as shown in Fig. 16.1. The translator forms the root of the tree. A transformer is used to supply power to the translator. One eight-way splitter attaches to the translator through a directional coupler, and up to eight personal computers can be attached to that. The base extender can be used to attach another eight splitters, which in turn attach additional personal computers. Up to 72 stations can be attached to a given broadband network, using the IBM components, with a maximum length of 1000 ft from any station to the translator. Larger networks, of up to 1000 stations located up to 5 km from the translator, can be constructed using non-IBM translators and cable. However, a specialist is required to balance these larger networks when they are installed or modified.

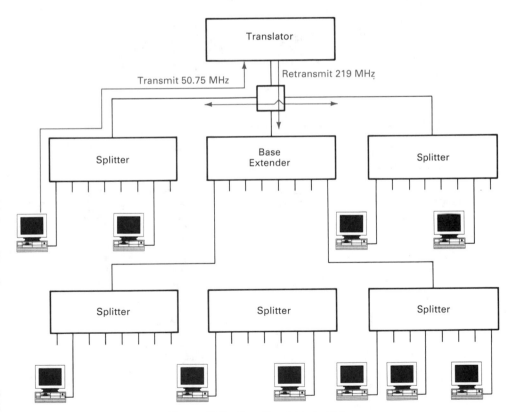

Figure 16.2   Broadband transmission

Transmission Characteristics

A 75-ohm, CATV-type coaxial cable is used as the transmission medium for the broadband PC Network. Transmission on the cable is frequency modulated, using continuous-phase frequency-shift keying with a transmission rate of 2 Mbps. Two channels are used, each with a 6-MHz bandwidth. When a station transmits, it sends out the data at a frequency of 50.75 MHz. When the transmission reaches the translator, the translator retransmits it on the same cable at a frequency of 219 MHz, as shown in Fig. 16.2. Every station on the network "listens" to the network at a frequency of 219 MHz, so when the retransmission arrives, it is received by all the stations on the network. Having the translator retransmit ensures that the signal will be of sufficient strength throughout the network.

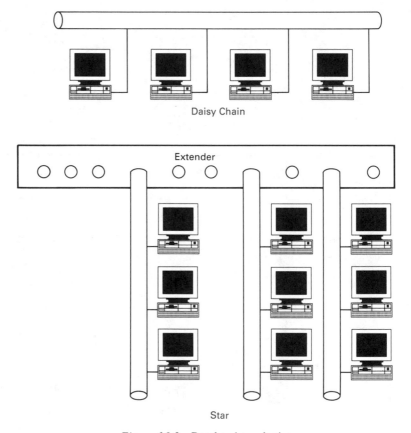

Daisy Chain

Extender

Star

Figure 16.3 Baseband topologies

IBM PC NETWORK— BASEBAND

The basic components of the baseband version of the IBM PC Network are as follows:

- **Adapter Card.** The adapter card is installed in each personal computer that is a network station and provides the logic required to implement CSMA/CD-based LAN communications.
- **Extender.** The extender is used to create larger, star-wired networks.
- **Cabling System.** The cabling used for the baseband version of the PC Network is twisted-wire-pair cable. The use of twisted-wire pairs allows networks to be constructed using installed telephone wire, where telephone wire of appropriate quality is already installed and accessible in the required locations.

Network Topologies

The baseband version of the PC Network can use one of two topologies, shown in Fig. 16.3. Up to eight stations can be connected serially, in a topology known as a daisy chain. An extender unit can be used to connect up to ten daisy chains in a star configuration, providing for up to 80 stations to be attached to a single network.

Transmission Characteristics

Transmission rate is 2 Mbps. Inverted differential Manchester format is used for transmission of data across the network.

SUMMARY

The IBM PC Network product uses the CSMA/CD method of medium access management. Carrier sensing determines if the transmission medium is free. If it is free, transmission starts; if not, medium access management waits. If two stations transmit at the same time, a collision occurs. When a collision is detected, the station stops transmitting, sends a jamming signal, waits a calculated period of time, and attempts retransmission. Backoff after a collision is based on the binary exponential backoff method. The broadband version of PC Network uses a tree topology, frequency modulated transmission using continuous-phase, frequency-shift keying, and a transmission rate of 2 Mbps. The baseband version uses either a daisy chain or star topology, inverted differential Manchester encoding, and a transmission rate of 2 Mbps.

17 IBM LLC, NETBIOS, AND APPC INTERFACES

The IBM LAN products offer interfaces to the network at several levels. The key interfaces are shown in Fig. 17.1. Direct interfaces to the different adapter cards, which are defined at the level of the MAC sublayer, have been covered in the earlier chapters in this part. In this chapter and the next, we will look at the interfaces used at other levels.

The IBM Local Area Network Support Program provides a logical link control (LLC) interface, consistent with the IEEE 802.2 LLC standard. Programs written to this interface will run with any of the three types of networks. In OSI terms, the LLC interface is at the level of the data link layer.

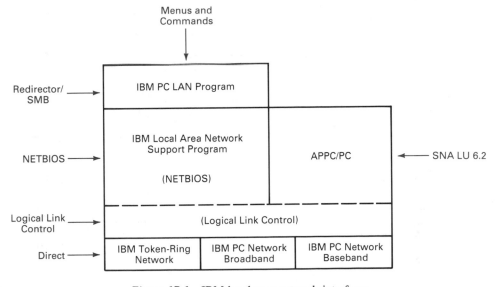

Figure 17.1 IBM local area network interfaces

The IBM Local Area Network Support Program also provides a NETBIOS interface. This interface takes place at the level of the session layer. APPC/PC offers an alternative interface at the session level. This interface implements the LU 6.2 facilities defined as part of the SNA architecture.

The IBM PC LAN Program, which we will discuss in detail in Chapter 18, provides two interfaces at the level of the application layer. One interface, available to application programs, uses the *DOS Redirector* facility and *server message blocks* (SMBs), also discussed in Chapter 18. The other interface uses menus and commands and is available to end users.

LOGICAL LINK CONTROL

The LLC interface provides two types of service. Type 1 operation, or connectionless service, provides transmission between stations with no guarantee of delivery. Type 2 operation, or connection-oriented service, is based on a session being established between two stations and provides reliable communication with acknowledgment of message receipt.

SAPS AND LINK STATIONS

LLC communication is based on the use of *service access points* (SAPs) and *link stations*. For two stations to communicate, each must set up a SAP in its adapter. SAPs can be used for Type 1 operation. For Type 2 operation, a link station must be set up within each SAP, and a session is established between two link stations. There can be multiple SAPs for one station and multiple link

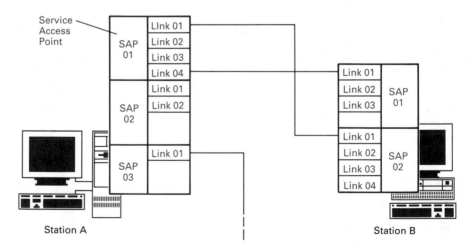

Figure 17.2   Service access points and link stations

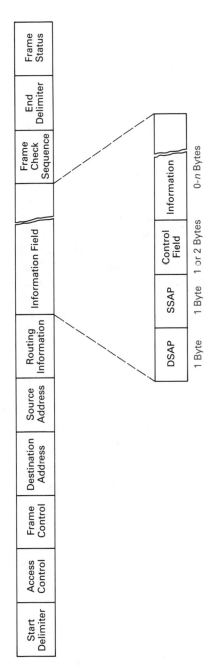

Figure 17.3 Logical link control data unit. DSAP = Destination Service Access Point; SSAP = Source Service Access Point.

stations for each SAP. This is illustrated in Fig. 17.2. The SAPs for a particular station are assigned one-byte identification values. Link stations for a particular SAP are also assigned 1-byte identifiers. A SAP can have more than one session established at one time. However, a given pair of SAPs can have only one session established between them. Given this restriction, the station addresses and SAP values for the two SAPs are sufficient to identify the session.

LLC DATA UNIT

The information passed from the LLC sublayer to the MAC sublayer, which becomes the information field in a MAC frame, contains LLC header information as well as data. To the MAC sublayer, the LLC header is simply data, but to the LLC sublayer, the fields in the header have specific meanings. This is illustrated in Fig. 17.3. The LLC header information contains a destination SAP value (DSAP), a source SAP value (SSAP), and a control field. The destination and source address fields in the MAC header contain the station addresses for the sending and receiving stations. These values are passed from the LLC sublayer to the MAC sublayer as parameters. The combination of station addresses in the MAC header and SAP values in the LLC header serve to identify the session being used for transmission. The format of the control field depends on the type of service and type of command the data unit contains.

LLC INTERFACE

The interface to the LLC sublayer is implemented in the form of *command control blocks* (CCBs). A program using the LLC interface creates a CCB containing the appropriate information and then uses a 5CH interrupt to pass it to the LLC sublayer. The information in the CCB identifies the particular command to be executed and provides any information needed to execute it, such as the addresses of work and data areas. Certain commands also use parameter lists to provide additional information.

Some of the commands that are part of the LLC interface are used to prepare or modify the general environment. These are shown in Box 17.1.

Box 17.2 lists the commands that are used to prepare for and accomplish data transmission. The STATION commands are used only with Type 2 service, when establishing and terminating connections between link stations. Both use the SAP commands to prepare SAPs for communication and to end communication on the SAP. Both use the RECEIVE commands to control the receipt of data. For sending data, Type 1 operation uses the TRANSMIT.UI.FRAME; Type 2 operation uses the TRANSMIT.I.FRAME.

BOX 17.1   General commands

Command	Function
Dir.Initialize	Initialize work areas, tables, and buffers associated with the adapter
Dir.Open.Adapter	Prepare the adapter for network communication
Dir.Close.Adapter	Terminate network communication for the adapter
Transmit.Dir.Frame	Transmit data using the direct interface
Buffer.Free	Return one or more buffers to the buffer pool
Buffer.Get	Acquire one or more buffers
DLC.Modify	Modify values associated with a link station or SAP
DLC.Reset	Return link station or SAP values to their original setting
DLC.Statistics	Read and reset log information
Transmit.XID.Cmd	Transmit an XID command
Transmit.XID.Resp.Final	Transmit an XID response with the final bit on
Transmit.XID.Resp.Not.Final	Transmit an XID response with the final bit off
Transmit.TEST.Cmd	Transmit a TEST command

BOX 17.2   Transmission commands

Command	Function
DLC.Open.SAP	Activate a SAP and reserve a number of link stations for it
DLC.Close.SAP	Deactivate a SAP
DLC.Open.Station	Reserve resources for a link station
DLC.Connect.Station	Send the command/response sequence needed to establish a connection between two link stations
DLC.Close.Station	Deactivate a link station
Receive	Receive data from a specified link station
Receive.Cancel	Stop receiving data from a particular station
Receive.Modify	Receive data and put some of the data in a buffer other than the SAP buffer
Transmit.UI.Frame	Transmit an unnumbered information frame
Transmit.I.Frame	Transmit an information frame

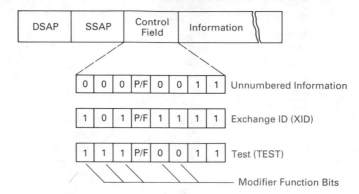

Figure 17.4 U-frame control field. DSAP = Destination Service Access Point; SSAP = Source Service Access Point; P/F = Poll/Final bit.

TYPE 1 OPERATION

With Type 1 operation (connectionless service), frames are sent from one SAP to another, without acknowledgment, using unnumbered, or U-format, frames. These frames use the control field format shown in Fig. 17.4. An unnumbered information frame is used for data transmission. With this type of frame, data can be lost if a problem occurs during transmission since no acknowledgment is sent.

An XID frame can be used to exchange information between two stations, including the types of service each station supports. The TEST frame can be used to test the transmission path between two stations.

TYPE 2 OPERATION

With Type 2 operation (connection-oriented service), a sequence-numbering scheme is used, and acknowledgments are sent. An information, or I-format, frame is employed for data transfer with Type 2 operation, using the control field format shown in Fig. 17.5. The sequence numbers shown in the control field are used both for sequence checking and for message acknowledgment.

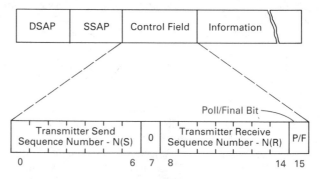

Figure 17.5 I-frame control field. DSAP = Destination Service Access Point; SSAP = Source Service Access Point; P/F = Poll/Final bit.

ACKNOWLEDGMENT AND SEQUENCE CHECKING

The sending station assigns a sequence number to each information data unit it sends. When a receiving station receives each data unit, it checks the sequence number in the frame to ensure that data units have arrived in the correct sequence. Periodically, the receiving station sends an acknowledgment so that the sending station knows the information data units have arrived successfully. If problems occur and information data units are not acknowledged, the sending station is able to retransmit them or take other actions.

Once a session is established between two link stations, each side maintains a send counter and a receive counter. When an information data unit is sent, it is sent in the form of an I-format frame. The control field contains the

BOX 17.3   Updating send and receive counters

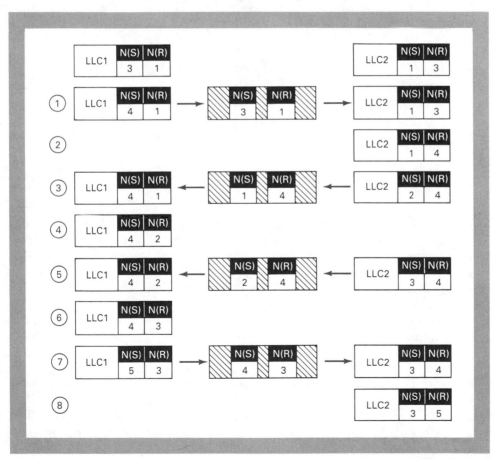

(Continued)

Box 17.3 *(Continued)*

1. LS1 sends an I-format command containing the current values of its send counter and receive counter. LS1 adds 1 to the current value of its send counter, making the new counter value 4.

2. LS2 then receives the I-format command, checks that the N(S) value in the received command matches its N(R) value, and updates its receive counter. The value of 1 in the N(R) counter in the data unit indicates that LS1 expects the next data unit it receives to have a sequence number of 1. This data unit acknowledges receipt of the data unit having the sequence number value of 0.

3. LS2 sends a data unit with a send sequence number value of 1 and receive sequence number value of 4; LS2 then adds 1 to its send counter.

4. LS1 receives the data unit, sequence-checks it, and adds 1 to its receive counter. This data unit acknowledges receipt of data unit 3 sent by LS1.

5. LS2 sends a data unit with a send sequence number value of 2 and updates its send counter.

6. LS1 receives the data unit, sequence-checks it, and updates its receive counter.

7. LS1 sends data unit 4 and updates its send counter.

8. LS2 receives the data unit, sequence-checks it, and updates its receive counter. This data unit acknowledges receipt of data units 1 and 2 sent by LS2.

current value of the transmitter's send and receive counters. The send counter contains the sequence number of the message currently being sent, and the receive counter contains the sequence number it expects to find in the next message it receives. After the link station sends an information frame, it updates its send counter; after a link station receives an information frame, if the frame has the correct sequence number, it updates its receive counter.

Box 17.3 demonstrates the use of send and receive counters when information frames are being sent in both directions. N(S) indicates a send counter and N(R) a receive counter.

S-FORMAT FRAMES

In the example in Box 17.3, information frames were being sent in both directions and were used to acknowledge receipt of messages. There may be times when a link station needs to send an acknowledgment but does not have an information data unit to send. In such situations, the receiving station uses su-

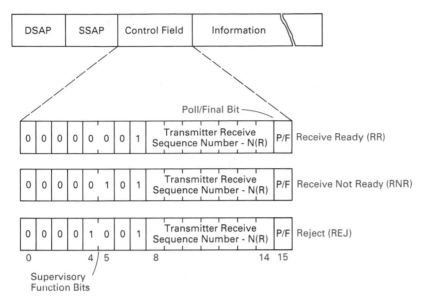

Figure 17.6 S-frame control field. DSAP = Destination Service Access Point; SSAP = Source Service Access Point; P/F = Poll/Final bit.

pervisory, or S-format, frames for acknowledgment and also for performing certain control functions. These frames have a 2-byte control field and contain an N(R) value. Figure 17.6 shows the format of the control field for an S-format frame.

The supervisory bits indicate the type of command this S-frame represents. A Receive Ready (RR) command can be used to acknowledge messages received and also indicates that the link station is able to receive additional messages.

A Receive Not Ready (RNR) command acknowledges messages received and indicates that the link station is temporarily unable to receive more messages, perhaps due to an internal constraint, such as lack of buffer space. When the busy condition clears, the link station can send one of several commands, including RR, to indicate it is able to receive again.

A Reject (REJ) command is used to request retransmission of I-format frames. It requests retransmission starting from the N(R) value specified in the REJ command. Messages prior to that value are considered to be acknowledged.

SENDING
ACKNOWLEDGMENTS

Several factors determine when an acknowledgment is sent. One is the poll/final bit in the control field. When an I-format frame is sent with the poll/final bit set to 1, this requests that an acknowledgment be sent back immediately. If the receiving station does not have an information data unit ready to send when it receives the frame, it responds with an S-format command.

When a station starts sending messages, it also starts a timer. If no acknowledgment is received before the timer runs out, it requests an acknowledgment by sending a supervisory message with the poll/final bit set to 1. Depending on the response received, the link station may resume sending, retransmit some messages, or perform a reset procedure.

There is also a limit to the number of messages a station can send before it stops and waits for an acknowledgment. This value, known as the *window size,* has a maximum value of 127, based on the size of the N(S) and N(R) fields in command control fields. Window size values, in each direction, can be set to smaller than 127; XID commands are used to exchange window size values prior to establishing a session. When a link station sends the number of messages specified by the window size without receiving an acknowledgment, it stops sending until it receives an acknowledgment.

When a link station receives an I-format frame, if the poll/final bit is set to 1, it sends an acknowledgment immediately. If not, the station may wait a period of time before sending an acknowledgment, waiting either until it has an I-format frame to send or until additional messages arrive. The length of time the station waits is based on the value used for the acknowledgment timer and on the window size.

PACING

The window size also serves as a pacing, or flow control, mechanism. The window size acts as a limit on the number of messages the receiving station receives before it sends an acknowledgment. The receiving station is thus able to control the flow of messages by controlling the rate at which it sends acknowledgments.

An additional flow control mechanism modifies the window size in response to congestion. When messages must travel across a bridge to another network segment, limits on buffer space may cause bottlenecks in message flow. If congestion is detected, the window size for the sending station is set to 1 so that the station waits for a response after every message. As congestion decreases, the window size is gradually increased until it reaches its original value.

U-FORMAT FRAMES

Type 2 operation also uses unnumbered, or U-format, frames. These frames are used primarily to control the establishment and termination of connections. The control field format for these frames is shown in Fig. 17.7.

The set asynchronous balanced mode extended (SABME) frame is used to request establishment of a connection. An unnumbered acknowledgment (UA) response accepts the request and establishes the connection. A disconnected mode (DM) response rejects the request and the connection is not established. A disconnect (DISC) frame is sent to terminate a connection. Either a UA or

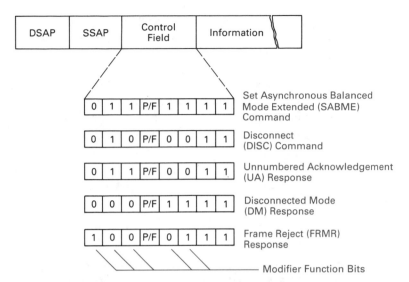

Figure 17.7 U-frame control field. DSAP = Destination Service Access Point; SSAP = Source Service Access Point; P/F = Poll/Final bit.

DM response acknowledges that the connection is terminated. The frame reject (FRMR) response is sent when the receiving station detects an error condition that cannot be corrected simply by retransmitting frames.

NETBIOS

The second interface we will look at here is the NET-BIOS interface, which operates at the level of the session layer and provides functions associated with the session, transport, and network layers.

The primary responsibility of the session layer is the management and structure of data transfer. This includes determining when session partners are allowed to send and receive. The three most common transmission protocols are these:

- **Full Duplex.** Both session partners are allowed to send simultaneously.

- **Half Duplex.** The session partners alternate sending, with only one allowed to send at a time.

- **Simplex.** Only one session partner is allowed to send, so transmission occurs in one direction only.

NETBIOS implements full-duplex transmission.

The transport layer is responsible for providing reliable and efficient data transfer. Possible functions of the transport layer include flow control, error detection and recovery using sequence numbers and checksums, and multiplexing of multiple sessions on one connection. NETBIOS implements a reliable form of data transfer using a virtual circuit. It also offers datagram service, where acknowledgments are not used.

The network layer is responsible for routing a message, which involves determining the path a message travels from sending node to receiving node, both within an individual network and across interconnected networks. NET-BIOS uses a source routing approach to determining the path that a message takes.

NETBIOS INTERFACE

The NETBIOS interface is based on the use of a message control block (MCB). A program using the NETBIOS interface formats an MCB with the appropriate information and then issues a 5CH interrupt. Based on the information in the MCB, including a command code that specifies a particular command to execute, the NETBIOS program performs the necessary operations. The interrupt used for the NETBIOS interface is the same as that used for the LLC interface. The initial byte in the control block indicates which of the two interfaces is being invoked.

NETBIOS FUNCTIONS

NETBIOS provides the following functions:

- **Status and Control.** Commands are available that provide for status reporting and control related to sessions and to the NETBIOS interface as a whole.
- **Name Service.** Names can be assigned dynamically to represent different logical entities in a single station. Transmission services are then invoked using names rather than addresses.
- **Session Service.** Sessions are established between two names. Information can be interchanged reliably using the session.
- **Datagram Service.** With datagram service, information is sent and received without first establishing a session. Receipt of the information is not guaranteed.

NETBIOS NAME SERVICE

The name service provides for multiple users in a single node. Names can be added and deleted dynamically, so at one time a name may be associated with one station and at a later time with another. This allows, for example, an end user to use different stations at different times and have the same services available. There is no permanent link between a name and a particular adapter, and there is no central directory of names that needs to be updated. Group names

BOX 17.4   Name service commands

Command	Function
Msg.Add.Name	Add a unique name to the station's table of names
Msg.Add.Group.Name	Add a group name to the station's table of names
Msg.Delete.Name	Remove a name from the station's table of names
Msg.Find.Name	Determine the location or locations of a specified name. Station addresses and routing information are returned in responses.

are also supported so that several logical entities, on the same or different stations, can all be addressed using a single name. Names are used both to establish sessions and to send datagrams. Box 17.4 lists the commands used in connection with the name service.

NETBIOS ROUTING   NETBIOS uses source routing. With source routing, the sending station is responsible for providing routing information for messages that cross multiple network segments. The sending station acquires routing information by means of the MSG.FIND.NAME command, which is used to determine the location or locations of a particular name. Responses to this command provide station addresses and, if necessary, routing information for reaching stations that have this name defined.

NETBIOS SESSION SERVICE   The NETBIOS session service provides reliable data transfer based on the establishment of a session, or virtual circuit, between two names. A given name can be involved in multiple sessions. When a session is established for a given name, a 1-byte session identifier is assigned to it. The identifier is then used to differentiate among the different sessions a name has active. Box 17.5 lists the commands used with session service. Data transfer as part of a session involves the use of sequence numbers and acknowledgments so that the service is reliable. If an acknowledgment is not received, the message is retransmitted. A single message can be up to 64K bytes in size.

NETBIOS also supports flow control. At open time, a window size is specified that indicates the maximum number of unacknowledged messages that can be outstanding. If congestion occurs on the network, this number is set to 1 and then gradually increases back to its original value as congestion decreases.

BOX 17.5   Session service commands

Command	Function
Msg.Call	Open a session with another name
Msg.Listen	Enable a session to be opened with a name specified in the command
Msg.Hang.Up	Close a session with another name
Msg.Send	Send data to the session partner
Msg.Chain.Send	Send data to the session partner using two buffers that are chained together
Msg.Receive	Receive data from a specified session partner
Msg.Receive.Any	Receive data from any session partner
Msg.Session.Status	Obtain status information about one or all sessions for a given name

NETBIOS DATAGRAM SERVICE

The NETBIOS datagram service allows messages to be sent without first establishing a session. A message can be sent to an individual name, to a group name, or as a broadcast message to all names. There are no acknowledgments for datagrams, so the datagram service is not considered to be reliable. Datagram messages can be up to 512 bytes long. Box 17.6 shows the commands used with datagram service.

BOX 17.6   Datagram service commands

Command	Function
Msg.Send.Datagram	Send a message using the datagram service
Msg.Send.Broadcast.Datagram	Send a message using the datagram service to all stations
Msg.Receive.Datagram	Receive a datagram message sent to this station
Msg.Receive.Broadcast.Datagram	Receive a broadcast message

BOX 17.7   **General commands**

Command	Function
Msg.Reset	Reset the NETBIOS interface
Msg.Cancel	Cancel a command
Msg.Status	Determine the status of the NETBIOS interface
Msg.Unlink	Provided for NETBIOS compatibility with an earlier version
Msg.Trace	Activate a trace of all commands issued to the NETBIOS interface and NETBIOS transmits and receives

GENERAL NETBIOS COMMANDS

In addition to the specific services, NETBIOS provides services that are part of general support and control. The commands used for these purposes are shown in Box 17.7.

NETBIOS AS A DE FACTO STANDARD

The NETBIOS interface does not conform to a published standard, as does the logical link control interface, which conforms to the IEEE 802.2 standard. However, the NETBIOS interface has developed into a de facto standard. The NETBIOS interface defines functions that are performed when services are invoked using a certain interrupt and control block format. Applications that are written using that interface can be run using the IBM Local Area Network Support Program to provide these functions. Other vendors have developed network operating systems that emulate the NETBIOS functions. These network operating systems also support the application programs that have been written using the NETBIOS interface. The interface, then, has become a standardized way for application programs to access LAN communications without becoming enmeshed in the details of a particular implementation.

APPC/PC

APPC/PC provides an alternative session layer interface to IBM's LANs. This interface is based on the Advanced Program-to-Program Communication (APPC) facilities that have been defined as part of SNA, and it reflects a number of SNA concepts. In SNA, the term *physical unit* (PU) is used for the node component that manages and monitors the node resources. Each node in an SNA network contains a PU and is identified by that PU's type. The term *logical unit* (LU) is used for the set of logical services by which an end user accesses the SNA network. It is possible for a node to contain several LUs. LUs are also identified as being of a particular type, and the LU type defines a particular set of SNA services that the LU implements. An *end user* of an SNA network can be either a *person* or an *application program*. For two end users to communicate across an SNA network, a *session* must be established between their two LUs, and both LUs must be of the same type.

APPC is based on a specific LU type, known as *LU 6.2*, and provides a special PU type, known as *PU 2.1*. LU 6.2 is designed to provide a general facility for program-to-program communication where the two programs operate on a peer level. PU 2.1 provides for peer-to-peer communication between nodes having more limited capabilities than traditional SNA host processors.

APPC AND PU 2.1

Non-APPC SNA sessions typically involve a peripheral device, such as a terminal, communicating with a host computer, using intermediate communication controller nodes for routing messages across the network. The host node maintains control information required for session initialization and takes a greater share of the responsibility for error recovery. This type of session is illustrated in Fig. 17.8. In this situation, the peripheral node is typically a PU type 2.0, and the host is a PU type 5.

With APPC, a new PU type, PU 2.1, is defined. A PU 2.1 node has fewer

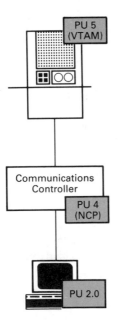

Figure 17.8   SNA session with PU 2.0 node

Figure 17.9   SNA session between two PU 2.1 nodes

capabilities than a PU type 5 host but is able to establish sessions with another PU 2.1 node without the intervention of a host node. This is shown in Fig. 17.9. With a PU 2.1-PU 2.1 session, the two nodes operate on a peer level and share recovery responsibilities. The nodes must be connected directly, however, and cannot use communications controllers as intermediate nodes.

APPC/PC supports a personal computer acting as either a PU 2.0 or a PU 2.1 node. The possibilities are shown in Fig. 17.10. Two personal computers that are connected by a LAN can establish a session, with both computers acting as PU 2.1 nodes. A personal computer with an SDLC adapter can communicate

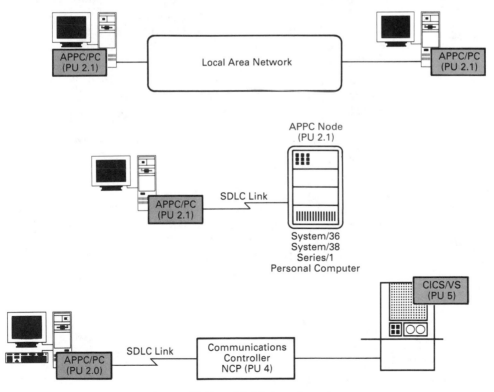

Figure 17.10   APPC/PC configuration

as a PU 2.1 node with another system acting as a PU 2.1 node and running an APPC program. The other system can be a System/36, System/38, Series/1, or another personal computer. A personal computer with an SDLC adapter can also communicate as a PU 2.0 node with a remote host, using intermediate communication controller nodes. APPC/PC by itself will not function as a gateway. For example, it is not possible to have one network station use APPC/PC to communicate through another network station with a computing system that is not part of the LAN. To provide this function, an application would have to be written that established one session across the LAN and another session from the network station to the off-network computing system.

Since we are viewing APPC/PC as a LAN interface, further descriptions of APPC/PC facilities will be based on its use with a LAN and as PU type 2.1 nodes.

APPC AND LU 6.2

Communication using LU 6.2 involves the concept of a *conversation*. A conversation is typically a short-term connection between two transaction programs, which is used to exchange data. For the two transaction programs to converse, a session must have been established between their respective LUs. A conversation then uses the underlying session as the basis for its communication. Conversations are assigned to a session serially; when one conversation ends, another conversation, involving the same or different transaction programs, can use the same session.

Two types of conversations are possible with LU 6.2: *basic* and *mapped*. In basic conversations, the application programs are responsible for managing the details of the data stream being used for transmission and take a greater responsibility for error recovery. In mapped conversations, programs can exchange data in logical form without being concerned about the format of the underlying data stream.

APPC CONVERSATION VERBS

LU 6.2 is defined in terms of *protocol verbs*. Some verbs are considered *conversation* verbs; others are *control* and *services* verbs. The verbs used for the two types of conversations are very similar. The conversation verbs are shown in Box 17.8. These verbs provide the following functions:

- Allocating and deallocating conversations
- Sending and receiving data
- Error notification
- Program-level synchronization
- Managing send/receive turnaround

BOX 17.8   Conversation verbs

Verb	Mapped Conversation
Allocate	yes
Deallocate	yes
Confirm	yes
Confirmed	yes
Flush	yes
Get_Attributes	yes
Get_Type	yes
Post_On_Receipt	no
Prepare_To_Receive	yes
Receive_and_Wait	yes
Receive_Immediate	yes
Request_To_Send	yes
Send_Data	yes
Send_Error	yes
Test	yes
Wait	no

Allocating a conversation establishes a conversation between two transaction programs and assigns it to a session. This allows the two transaction programs to use the SEND and RECEIVE verbs to communicate. Return codes associated with the verbs provide error notification. Deallocation ends the conversation and frees the session for use by another conversation.

APPC SYNCHRONIZATION

APPC/PC supports a process known as synchronization at the transaction program level. Different levels of synchronization are defined for LU 6.2; APPC/PC supports the *confirm* level. With confirm-level synchronization, a transaction program can request that its partner return an acknowledgment as to whether data sent has been received correctly. The sending program can request the confirmation either by issuing a CONFIRM verb or by specifying CONFIRM as a parameter on a DEALLOCATE verb. The receiving program responds with a CONFIRMED verb if it has received the data correctly and with a SEND_ERROR verb if it has not. The sending program waits for the response from the receiving program before continuing its processing. If a negative response is received, the sending program has the option of performing recovery processing.

| Transaction Program A | | Transaction Program B |

ALLOCATE
SYNC_LEVEL (CONFIRM)

1. Program A begins the conversation by allocating it and specifying that confirm-level synchronization can be used.

2. Program B issues a Receive and Wait, which puts it into the receive state and prepares it to receive data.

SEND_DATA

3. Program A sends data to Program B.

RECEIVE_AND_WAIT — Data

4. Program B issues another Receive and Wait.

RECEIVE_AND_WAIT

5. Program A issues a Receive and Wait, which prepares it to receive and sends permission for Program B to send.

RECEIVE_AND_WAIT — Send Indication

6. Program B receives the send indication and then sends data to Program A.

SEND_DATA

RECEIVE_AND_WAIT — Data

Confirmation Request

7. Program B sends a Confirmation Request to Program A.

CONFIRM

8. Program A receives the confirmation request via a Receive and Wait. Since it received the previous data without problem, it replies with a positive response by issuing a Confirmed, followed by another Receive and Wait.

CONFIRMED — Confirmation

9. Program B receives the confirmation and continues sending data to Program A.

RECEIVE_AND_WAIT — Data

SEND_DATA

RECEIVE_AND_WAIT — Send Indication

10. Program B finishes sending and issues a Receive and Wait, which gives permission for Program A to begin sending.

11. Program A receives the send indication and sends data to Program B.

SEND_DATA — RECEIVE_AND_WAIT — Data

12. Program B receives the data and issues a Receive and Wait.

RECEIVE_AND_WAIT

DEALLOCATE TYPE (SYNC_LEVEL) · · Deallocate with Confirm

13. Program A ends the conversation by issuing a Deallocate, which specifies the same type of synchronization that was specified in the Allocate.

14. Program B receives the deallocation request and responds with Confirmed. It then issues a Deallocate to terminate the conversation on its side.

Confirmation — CONFIRMED

DEALLOCATE

15. When Program A receives the confirmation, its Deallocate completes and the conversation terminates on its side.

Figure 17.11 Sample APPC conversation

CHANGE OF DIRECTION

APPC/PC implements half-duplex transmission, so that only one transaction program is allowed to send at a time. Specific verbs and verb parameters are used to control which program is allowed to send and to coordinate changes between send and receive state for the two programs. The PREPARE_TO_RE-CEIVE and RECEIVE_AND_WAIT verbs change a program from send state to receive state. RECEIVE_AND_WAIT also gives permission to the partner program to begin sending. A program can use a REQUEST_TO_SEND verb to send a request to its partner program, asking that program to enter the receive state and send permission to send.

Figure 17.11 shows a simplified view of an APPC conversation, using both confirmation processing and change of direction.

APPC CONTROL VERBS

A number of control verbs are used to define and manage the APPC/PC environment. These verbs are shown in Box 17.9. One that is particularly important is the ATTACH_LU verb. This verb is used to define a particular LU that will support APPC/PC conversations. The parameters for this verb define information about the LU, such as its network address and the maximum number of

BOX 17.9   Control verbs

Node Management

Access_LU_LU_PW
Activate_DLC
Attach_LU
Attach_PU
Change_LU
CNOS
Create_TP
Detach_LU
Detach_PU
Display
Get_Allocate
SYSLOG

TP_Ended
TP_Started
TP_Valid

Network Management

Transfer_MS_Data

APPC Services

Convert
Disable/Enable_APPC
Passthrough
Set_Passthrough
Trace

sessions it can support at one time. They also specify information about any partner LUs with which this LU will establish sessions. For each potential partner LU, the partner's network name and adapter address must be specified. This information is used when sessions are established. The ATTACH_LU verb can also be used to specify a pacing value to use to control the flow of data on the sessions established with this LU.

APPC/PC INTERFACE

In APPC/PC, each verb corresponds to a specific record format. A program that interfaces with APPC/PC must format an appropriate record and then issue a 68H interrupt. The APPC/PC program then performs the function specified by the information contained in the record.

APPC NETWORK PROTOCOLS

As with NETBIOS, APPC/PC provides functions associated with the session, transport, and network layers. However, APPC/PC uses a different set of protocols for providing these functions than NETBIOS.

At the session level, APPC/PC uses half-duplex transmission, allowing only one partner to send at a time. The LU 6.2 verbs used to send and receive include features that allow the transaction programs to control and coordinate changing between send and receive modes.

At the transport level, APPC/PC offers several mechanisms for ensuring reliable and efficient data transfer. The confirmation processing available at the verb level allows the transaction programs involved in the conversation to ensure that data is received correctly. APPC/PC also provides sequence numbering of messages sent and checks on the receiving side that all messages arrive and that they arrive in sequence. Acknowledgments are sent indicating the sequence numbers of messages that have been received correctly. Messages that are not acknowledged are retransmitted. This is handled automatically by APPC/PC and does not require any action on the part of the transaction programs.

Another transport-level service that APPC/PC offers is *session-level pacing*. Session-level pacing is used to control the rate at which messages flow across a session so that the receiving end does not receive more messages than it can handle. This mechanism works in much the same manner as LLC pacing, which uses send and receive counters. However, APPC/PC pacing controls the flow of messages between the two LUs involved in a session; LLC pacing controls the flow between two link stations. A pacing window size defines the number of messages that can be sent before receiving a response acknowledging the messages. The PACING_SIZE parameter of the ATTACH_LU verb can be used to specify a pacing window size and the use of session-level pacing.

At the network level, APPC/PC uses predefined information to determine the location of a partner LU and thus be able to establish a session and exchange data with it. An LU must be defined to APPC/PC through the ATTACH_LU verb prior to starting any transaction programs for the LU. As part of that definition, any partner LUs must be described, including the adapter address of the station in which the partner LU is located. Also, configuration data must be predefined for each station, specifying the adapter address to use for the station. If an application system and its LUs are moved to a different station, both the configuration data and all ATTACH_LUs that reference those LUs must be updated appropriately so that the adapter address in both locations remains consistent.

SUMMARY

The logical link control interface operates at the data link level and implements the IEEE 802.2 LLC standard. It provides two types of service. Type 1 operation, or connectionless service, provides no guarantee of delivery. Type 2 operation, or connection-oriented service, uses sequence numbers and acknowledgments to provide reliable data transfer and flow control. Communication involves the use of service access points and, for Type 2 operation, link stations. The LLC data unit contains the destination SAP, source SAP, control field, and information field. Type 1 operation uses unnumbered information and control frames. Type 2 operation uses information frames, supervisory frames, and unnumbered frames. The interface to logical link control is implemented using command control blocks (CCBs) and a 5CH interrupt.

NETBIOS provides a session-level interface and includes session, transport, and network layer functions. The NETBIOS interface provides full-duplex transmission and supports both reliable data transfer based on the establishment of a session and an unacknowledged datagram service. NETBIOS provides a name service that supports the establishment of a session on a name basis and supports the use of both individual and group names. Station addresses and routing information are acquired by the sending station through a NETBIOS command and are then used for source routing. Message control blocks (MCBs) and a 5CH interrupt are used to interface with NETBIOS.

APPC/PC provides a session-level interface and includes session, transport, and network functions. APPC/PC uses the LU 6.2 and PU 2.1 facilities of SNA. Data transfer takes place using a conversation between two transaction programs. APPC/PC uses half-duplex transmission and provides reliable data transfer and flow control. Routing is based on predefined information stored at the sending station. The interface to APPC/PC is defined in terms of specific record formats that correspond to different conversation verbs and uses a 68H interrupt.

18 THE IBM REDIRECTOR/SMB INTERFACE

A software package called the *IBM PC LAN Program* provides interfaces at the level of the application layer to IBM's local area network products. The role of the application layer is to provide services directly useful to application programs that access a LAN. Among these services are printer sharing, disk sharing, file transfer, and electronic mail. The IBM PC LAN Program provides interfaces to both end users and application programs that enable them to use IBM LAN services.

IBM PC LAN PROGRAM FUNCTIONS

The functions provided by the IBM PC LAN Program include the following:

- **Print Server.** The print server function allows printers to be shared across the network. Print jobs are queued, and separator pages can be printed between jobs. The status of a print job can be checked remotely, and the print queue can be modified by an operator.

- **File Server.** The file server provides facilities for disks and directories to be accessed remotely and shared across the network. Access to a disk or directory can be controlled by the way in which access rights are granted. DOS facilities can be used to control sharing at the file level and to lock records in a shared file. The file server also allows files to be transferred from one network station to another.

- **Message Server.** The message server allows messages to be sent to a station having a given name or to be broadcast to all stations. Messages can be saved in a file and later retrieved and can then be forwarded to a different station. When a message arrives, a currently executing program can be interrupted to display the message, allowing the operator to respond.

The IBM PC LAN Program offers multiple interfaces to these functions. An end user can invoke the functions directly, either through a series of menus or by entering commands on the DOS command line. An application program can invoke the functions by executing commands or by using a program interface based on interrupts and a set of control blocks known as *server message blocks* (SMBs).

STATION CONFIGURATIONS

Stations that run the IBM PC LAN Program can be configured in various ways, the configurations corresponding to various sets of functions that are available. The configurations are as follows:

- **Redirector.** A station configured as a *redirector* has the most limited set of functions. A station that is a redirector is able to use disks and printers belonging to a station that is acting as a server. This is done by redirecting I/O requests for these disks and printers from the redirector station to the server station. A redirector is also able to send messages.

- **Receiver.** A *receiver* station is able to perform the same functions as a redirector in terms of using shared disks and printers and sending messages. In addition, a receiver is able to receive messages and route them to the display screen, a printer, or a file.

- **Messenger.** A *messenger* station can perform the same functions as a receiver. It can also receive messages sent to names assigned to another station and can forward those messages to that station. It has a full-screen editor for editing messages and can switch back and forth between an application and the full-screen editor.

- **Server.** A *server* station performs all the functions of a messenger. In addition, it is able to share its disks and printers with other stations on the network. When an I/O request is redirected, the server actually processes the I/O request using its devices and returns the results of the operation to the station that originally issued the request.

NAMING

Access to the various network functions is on the basis of names. Names known as *network names* are assigned to users, to stations, to the redirector and server functions in a station, and to resources that are to be shared. When a user wishes to access a shared resource, that user specifies the server name and resource name. Users can also send messages by specifying the *user name* of the user to which the message is destined; a user name is associated with a particular station. If the user wishes messages to be forwarded to another station, that user name can be added to the other station as a *forwarded name*.

DISK AND DIRECTORY SHARING

When a disk or directory is made available for sharing, all files that are on that disk or in that directory become sharable. At the time the disk or directory is specified as sharable (through a NET SHARE command), certain access rights are granted; these access rights control the way in which stations other than the server are allowed to access the files. Possible access rights are as follows:

- **Read-Only.** Remote users are allowed only to read information contained in the files.

- **Write-Only.** Remote users are allowed to make changes to the information in existing files but are not allowed to view the information already in them. For example, a remote user might be able to add records to an existing file using this acess right.

- **Read/Write.** Remote users are allowed both to read and to make changes to existing files but cannot create new files or delete files.

- **Read/Write/Create.** Remote users are allowed to read and change existing files, create new files, and delete files. This is the type of access that the server itself normally has and is the default access if none is specified.

- **Write/Create.** Remote users are allowed to change existing files, create new files, and delete files. However, they are not allowed to view the information in existing files.

It is possible to give different access rights to each remote user. This is done by using multiple NET SHARE commands for the same disk or directory, specifying different network names or passwords in each command. The network name or password the remote user specifies then determines the access rights granted.

MENU AND COMMAND INTERFACE

As mentioned earlier, the functions of the IBM PC LAN Program can be accessed directly by end users either through selections made from a series of menus or through commands entered on the DOS command line. Application programs can also execute the commands by using the DOS EXEC function call. Box 18.1 lists the various server-related tasks that can be performed using either menus or commands and shows the names of the commands used to perform the various tasks.

REDIRECTOR/SMB INTERFACE

Application programs are also able to access IBM PC LAN Program functions through a program interface. This interface consists of a set of interrupts with their

BOX 18.1　Server tasks

Message Tasks	Command
Send messages	NET SEND
View received messages	—
Start or stop saving messages	NET LOG
Start or stop receiving for another name	NET NAME
Start or stop forwarding messages	NET FORWARD
Pause or continue receiving messages	NET PAUSE, NET CONTINUE

Printer Tasks	
Start or stop sharing your printer	NET SHARE
Start or stop using a network printer	NET USE
Print a file	NET PRINT
Change the print size on a network printer	MODE
Start or stop printing a separator page	NET SEPARATOR
Pause or continue using a network printer	NET PAUSE, NET CONTINUE
Pause or continue sharing your printer	NET PAUSE, NET CONTINUE
Pause or continue printing a file	NET PAUSE, NET CONTINUE

Disk or Directory Tasks	
Start or stop sharing your disk or directory	NET SHARE, PERMIT
Start or stop using a network disk or directory	NET USE
Pause or continue sharing your disk or directory	NET PAUSE, NET CONTINUE
Pause or continue sharing a network disk or directory	NET PAUSE, NET CONTINUE

associated function calls and a set of data structures called *server message blocks* (SMBs). Figure 18.1 shows how this interface operates. The shaded portions of the diagram represent functions that are performed by the IBM PC LAN Program.

The 21H interrupt represents a class of interrupts an application program can issue that are associated with I/O requests. The *redirector* function checks these interrupts to see if they apply to a server device or file rather than to a

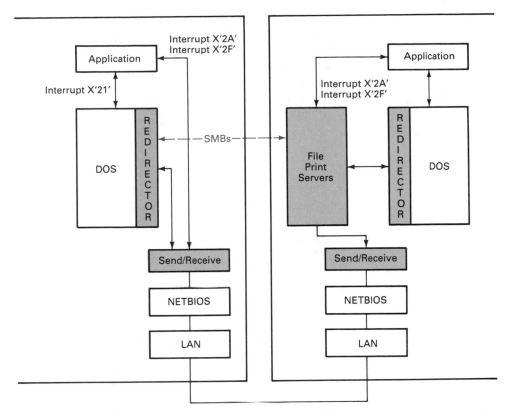

Figure 18.1   Server operation

local resource. If the interrupt is associated with a server resource, the redirector redirects the request across the network to the appropriate server. This is done by creating a server message block and using NETBIOS facilities to send the SMB across the network. On the receiving side, the SMB is passed up to the appropriate server function. The server processes the request, using normal DOS facilities to handle the processing. The results of the request are then sent back to the original station using another SMB, and the results are returned to the application program. To the user at the network station and to the application program, it appears as if the request had been processed locally.

The 2AH and 2FH classes of interrupt are used to provide network control functions. These interrupts are sent directly to the server. Interrupt 2AH also provides an interface directly to NETBIOS, allowing the application program to invoke NETBIOS functions directly. Care must be taken when using this interface, however, to ensure that the application program's use of NETBIOS does not conflict with the IBM PC LAN Program's use of NETBIOS.

DOS FUNCTION CALLS

Various function calls are associated with a given interrupt. Beginning with DOS Version 3.10, certain function calls associated with interrupts 21H, 2AH, and 2FH were made available that are particularly useful in a LAN environment. Box 18.2 lists the function calls associated with interrupt 21H that provide facilities for working with redirected files and devices. The function calls associated with interrupts 2AH and 2FH that provide network control functions are shown in Box 18.3.

File Sharing

The interrupt 21H function calls are particularly useful in supporting file sharing. In a LAN environment, where stations and applications are able to share disks and directories, the possibility arises of a file being shared by multiple applications. File sharing can lead to problems unless measures are taken to preserve file integrity and to prevent updates processed by one application from interfering with some other application's use of the file. The access rights granted for a particular disk or directory provide one level of control over file sharing. However, access rights apply to all the files on a disk or in a directory.

BOX 18.2   Interrupt 21H function calls

Function Call	Description
Get Extended Error	Returns an extended error code
Create Temp	Creates a temporary file with a unique name
Create New	Creates a new file
IOCTL Retry	Changes sharing retry count
IOCTL Is Redirected Block	Determines if a logical device is associated with a network directory
IOCTL Is Redirected Handle	Determines if a handle is local or remote
Open	Opens a file with multiuser sharing rules enforced
Lock	Prevents access to the specified byte range in the file
Unlock	Releases a lock to a region of a file
Get Machine Name	Returns the name of the local computer
Redirect Device	Redirects a device over the network
Cancel Redirection	Cancels a previous redirection
Get Redirection List	Returns nonlocal network assignments
Set Printer Setup	Specifies an initial string for printer files
Get Printer Setup	Gets an initial string for printer files

BOX 18.3   Network control function calls

Function Call	Description
2A Installation Check	Checks to see if the 2A interface is installed
2A Check Direct I/O	Checks to see if an absolute disk access is allowed to the device
2A Execute NETBIOS	Executes a NETBIOS function call
2A Get Network Resource Information	Returns the network resource information available to an application
2F APPEND Installation Check	Checks to see if the APPEND command is installed
2F PC Network Program Installation Check	Checks to see if the network program is installed
2F Get Current Post Address	Returns the address that is posted on network events
2F Set New Post Address	Sets the address to post on network events

Several DOS facilities can be used to control the way in which individual files are shared. When an application opens a file, that application can specify an *access mode* for the file. Access mode specifies the way in which the application will access the file. Possible access modes are *read-only, write-only*, and *read-write*. The application can also specify a *sharing mode* at the time it opens a file. Sharing mode specifies what types of access other programs should be allowed to have for the file being opened. The sharing mode can be specified as *deny read, deny write, deny all, deny none,* or *compatibility*. Compatibility sharing mode is provided to maintain compatibility with earlier versions of DOS and the IBM PC LAN Program. Read-only sharing is allowed between applications that all open a file using the compatibility sharing mode. Sharing is not allowed if one application opens a file using the compatibility sharing mode and another application opens the file using some other sharing mode.

Suppose that application B opens a file that has already been opened by application A. The access mode specified by application B is compared with the sharing mode specified by application A, and the sharing mode specified by application B is compared against the access mode specified by application A. If there is any conflict, application B's open fails.

Record Locking

One approach to file sharing is to allow files to be shared for read-only access but not to allow sharing while the file is being used for write-only or read-write access. A less restrictive approach to sharing can be implemented by using record-locking facilities. Record locking permits a program to lock a particular string of bytes. While that string of bytes is locked, no other program sharing that file is allowed to access the string of bytes. In this way, a program can update a record without interfering with any other program that is accessing the same file, as long as no two programs attempt to update a given record at the same time.

Unique File Names

A program may need a file to use as a temporary or work file that should not be shared with other applications. Since many programs use the same names for work files each time they are invoked, it is possible for the same application running on two or more network stations to create work files with the same name. This problem can be avoided by using a DOS function call that generates a unique file name. The file can then be opened with a sharing mode of *deny all* to ensure that no other program will be allowed to access it.

Common Sharing Situations

Certain sharing situations arise frequently and have recommended ways of handling them. Data that will be shared but not updated, such as help text and program overlays, should ordinarily be opened with an access mode of *read-only* and a sharing mode of *deny write*. Files that will be shared and also updated, such as an application database, should be opened with an access mode of *read-write* and a sharing mode of either *deny all* or *deny none*. If record locking is used, *deny none* sharing should be specified, allowing other programs to access the file concurrently. If record locking is not used, *deny all* sharing should be specified, to preserve data integrity while an application is updating the file.

The various DOS facilities for managing file sharing—access mode, sharing mode, record locking, and unique file name generation—are available to users of the IBM PC LAN Program. However, the program does not use these facilities automatically whenever disks or directories are shared, and these facilities are not supported through the menu and command interfaces. It is up to individual applications to issue the appropriate DOS function calls and to open files with appropriate modes. The IBM PC LAN Program then supports the use of these facilities across the network. Since these function calls work in the same manner whether the file is local or remote, if an application uses these facilities for all its I/O requests, the application does not need to know where the file is located or whether it is being shared at the time it executes.

SERVER MESSAGE BLOCKS

Communication between the redirector and the server function takes place using server message blocks. Different SMBs perform different functions, and a

BOX 18.4　Session control SMBs

Command	Purpose
Verify Dialect	Establish the dialect to be used on a session
Start Connection	Establish a redirector/server connection
End Connection	Terminate a redirector/server connection

defined record format is associated with each. SMBs are sent across the network using NETBIOS and LAN communication facilities. The format of the SMBs is not meaningful to NETBIOS or the LAN; SMBs are treated as data. However, SMB formats are meaningful to the redirector and server functions of the IBM PC LAN Program.

Box 18.4 lists the SMBs used for session control. These SMBs perform two major functions: controlling connections between a redirector and a server resource and determining the particular set of SMBs being supported.

The SMBs related to file access are shown in Box 18.5. The **Open File**

BOX 18.5　File access SMBs

Directory Commands	Purpose
Create Directory	Implement the DOS MKDIR function
Remove a Directory	Implement the DOS RMDIR function
Check Directory	Determine if a directory exists at the server
File Creation/Deletion/ Maintenance Commands	
Create File	Create a new file or truncate an old file to zero length and establish a handle for the file for subsequent access
Create New File	Create a new file
Create Unique File	Create a unique file
Delete File	Delete a file
Rename File	Rename an existing file within a network resource
Get File Attributes	Obtain information about a file
Set File Attributes	Set a file's attributes for subsequent access

(Continued)

BOX 18.5 *(Continued)*

Get Disk Attributes	Get storage sizes and disk layout
Search Multiple Files	Implement the FCB and ASCIIZ search function

File Access Commands

Open File	Establish a handle to an existing file for subsequent access
Close File	Close a file
Commit File	Cause all buffers for a file to be written to the media
Read Byte Block	Read a block of data from a file
Write Byte Block	Write a block of data to a file
LSEEK	Move the file read/write pointer
End of Process	End all work within this connection that belongs to a given process

File Locking Commands

Lock Byte Block	Lock a region of bytes within a file
Unlock Byte Block	Unlock a region of bytes within a file

SMB supports file sharing and allows access mode and sharing mode to be specified in the **Open File** request. The **Lock Byte** and **Unlock Byte** SMBs are used by an application to implement record locking. The **Create New File** function guarantees that the file name of a file being created is unique. These SMBs allow the various DOS file sharing facilities to be implemented in applications using the IBM PC LAN Program.

Box 18.6 lists the SMBs used for print server and message delivery tasks. The print server SMBs can be used to queue files to a print queue, check the status of a print queue, and change queue status. The message SMBs can be used to send and receive a message as a single transmission, send and receive a message with several transmissions, broadcast a message to all stations, and forward messages to another station.

IBM PC LAN PROGRAM AS A DE FACTO STANDARD

The IBM PC LAN Program interfaces have become, to an even greater extent than the NETBIOS interface, a de facto standard. Several LAN vendors offer network operating systems that will run applications that use the commands and function calls that make

BOX 18.6   Print server and message SMBs

Print Server Commands	Purpose
Create Spool File	Mark a new print spool data stream
Spool Byte Block	Transfer a block of data to be spooled
Close Spool File	Mark the end of a print spool data stream
Return Print Queue	Get the contents of the server print queue

Message Commands	
Send Single Block Message	Send a message that is a single block
Send Broadcast Message	Send a single block message to all user names on the network
Send Start of Multi-Block Message	Signal the start of a message that consists of multiple blocks
Send Text of Multi-Block Message	Sent text of message that is multiple blocks
Send End of Multi-Block Message	Signal the end of a multiple block message
Forward User Name	Request that the server receive messages for the given user name
Cancel Forward	Request that the server no longer receive messages for the given forwarded user name
Get Machine Name	Obtain the machine name for a user name

up the interfaces to the IBM PC LAN Program. Since many popular applications have been modified to use these interfaces, providing this type of compatibility is an important factor in the commercial acceptance of a network operating system.

Two approaches can be taken to providing compatibility with the IBM PC LAN Program. One is to develop a network operating system that directly accepts the commands and function calls issued by the application programs and then provides the same processing functions as the IBM PC LAN Program. This approach is shown in Fig. 18.2. The communication between the redirector and the server can use SMB formats, but this is not required. Also, the LAN portion of the communication may use the NETBIOS interface or may choose to use a different method. As long as the IBM PC LAN Program functions are accurately emulated, the application program need not be concerned with how the functions are implemented.

The second approach uses a product available from Microsoft Corporation, known as the Microsoft Redirector. This product provides the same functions as

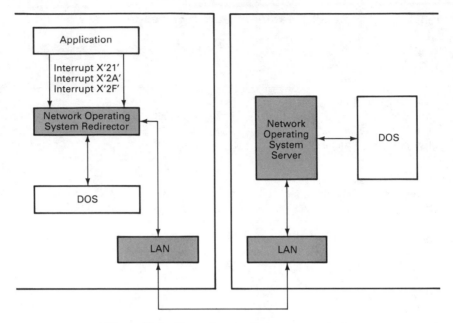

Figure 18.2 Network operating system emulation

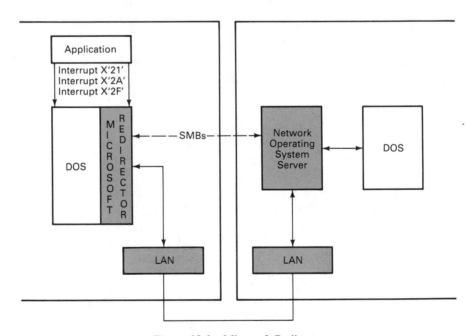

Figure 18.3 Microsoft Redirector

the redirector portion of the IBM PC LAN Program. It intercepts function calls and redirects them to a server, using SMBs for communication. The network operating system must then provide transmission across the network and the server functions. This is illustrated in Fig. 18.3. Here the server function must be able to handle the defined SMB functions and formats, since these will be used by the Microsoft Redirector.

SUMMARY   The IBM PC LAN Program provides interfaces at the application level through menus, commands, and the use of interrupts and server message blocks (SMBs). Services provided include printer sharing, file sharing, and message delivery services. Services are provided on a name basis. Applications have the option of using DOS function calls to control access rights for file sharing and to use record locking. Processing of DOS function calls associated with network I/O involves the use of a redirector function. LAN vendors providing emulation of the IBM PC LAN Program facilities can either emulate the redirector function directly or use the Microsoft Redirector. If the Microsoft Redirector is used, the SMB protocol must also be used.

PART **V** **LAN IMPLEMENTATIONS
BY OTHER VENDORS**

19 ROUTING PROTOCOL ALTERNATIVES

As we saw in Chapters 17 and 18, IBM supports a number of interfaces to its LANs, operating at different network layers. These interfaces also differ in the amount of standardization they reflect. At the lowest level, the data link layer, IBM supports both MAC and LLC interfaces. These interfaces conform quite closely to the IEEE-defined standards. At the highest level, the application layer, IBM supports the interfaces associated with the IBM PC LAN Program, described in Chapter 18. These interfaces do not correspond to any formally published standard. However, the vendors of many popular software packages have employed these interfaces to adapt their programs to a networking environment. Because of this, the IBM-defined application-level interface has become a de facto standard in the industry, and many LAN vendors provide networking products that support this interface.

For the middle layers, the session, transport, and network layers, the IBM-supplied interface is the NETBIOS interface. One of the key functions of these layers is routing. Routing is responsible for determining the route, or path, a message takes in traveling from the originating network node to the destination node. When both nodes are in the same LAN, routing is not an issue, since messages sent out on the network reach all stations on that network. Routing is an issue, however, for messages that must travel across interconnected networks. NETBIOS routing protocols are not designed for general transmission across interconnected networks. NETBIOS will support interconnected token ring networks, using the underlying LLC source routing facilities. But beyond that, gateway products that run above NETBIOS must ordinarily be used when LANs are interconnected. Many vendors provide network operating systems that support the NETBIOS interface to maintain compatibility with IBM and to support software products that have been modified to run in the IBM environment. But these vendors often use protocols other than those used in NETBIOS at the session, transport, and network layers to provide more robust internetworking capabilities along with IBM compatibility. In this chapter, we will look at some of the alternative protocols that are being used for routing, both by IBM and by other LAN vendors.

NETBIOS PROTOCOLS

We will begin by reviewing the protocols supported by NETBIOS. At the session level, NETBIOS supports full-duplex transmission. Both session partners are allowed to send messages at the same time.

At the transport level, NETBIOS supports two kinds of service. *Datagram service* can be used to send messages to individual, group, or broadcast addresses. Datagram service is not considered to be reliable, since no acknowledgments are sent, and it is possible for a message to be sent but never delivered. *Session service* provides reliable data transfer. A session, or virtual circuit, is established between two stations. Messages that are transmitted as part of the session are assigned sequence numbers; these sequence numbers are checked on the receiving side to identify lost, out-of-sequence, or duplicate messages. Acknowledgments are returned, identifying messages that have been received correctly. If messages are not acknowledged, they are retransmitted. Session service also provides a pacing mechanism, which defines a limit to the number of messages a session partner can send without receiving an acknowledgment.

At the network level, NETBIOS uses source routing for messages that travel across interconnected token ring networks. With source routing, the sending partner provides the routing information needed to deliver the message. NETBIOS uses the underlying LLC facilities to acquire routing information. A broadcast message is sent out and responses are returned that contain information on possible routes to the destination. One route is selected, and the routing information is then provided as part of the LLC header. There are no facilities at the NETBIOS level for routing messages across other types of network interconnections.

APPC/PC

The APPC/PC program is an alternative to NETBIOS. With APPC/PC, applications can be developed that are able to communicate, without change, either over a LAN or across an SDLC link to a directly connected or remote SNA node. However, a single session cannot be established that includes both LAN transmission and an SDLC link in its route.

APPC/PC uses half-duplex transmission at the session layer. Only one session partner is permitted to send at a time, and the partners exchange indicators to coordinate changing between send and receive mode.

At the transport layer, APPC/PC provides reliable data transfer based on the establishment of a session. Messages are sequence-numbered, acknowledgments are sent, and unacknowledged messages are retransmitted. There is also a confirmation facility that can be used at the application program level. APPC/ PC provides a pacing mechanism, whereby a window size determines the number of messages that can be sent before an acknowledgment is received. This window size is adjusted downward and upward in response to varying amounts of congestion along the route.

At the network layer, APPC/PC uses predefined routing information. For communication across a LAN, the station address of each potential partner is predefined and specified in the destination address. For communication to a remote SNA node, each intermediate node along the route contains predefined information that determines the next node the message should be sent to.

We will next examine some of the protocols that have been developed by vendors other than IBM to handle routing in the LAN environment.

XNS

The *Xerox Network Systems* (XNS) architecture was developed by Xerox Corporation as a way of providing communications between different Xerox products, including the interconnection of Ethernet LANs with each other or with public data networks. The XNS architecture has been published and made generally available by Xerox. It includes general protocols for the session, transport, and network layers, and several LAN vendors have adopted forms of its protocols to provide additional routing functions in their products. The XNS architecture for these layers consists of two pieces. The *Courier* protocol addresses the presentation and session layers, and the *Internet* protocol addresses the transport and network layers.

XNS COURIER PROTOCOL

The Courier protocol defines a method by which a request for a service or unit of work is sent and by which the results of the service or work are returned. The basic mechanism is a procedure call with arguments that specifies the service requested. The provider of the service returns either the results of the service request or an indication that an error has occurred. The Courier protocol is responsible for translating the call that is passed from the application layer into packets of information suitable for sending across the network using the services of the Internet protocol. This translation is primarily a presentation layer function.

XNS INTERNET TRANSPORT PROTOCOLS

The Internet portion of XNS is responsible both for routing messages and for providing data transmission with a specified level of quality. To do this, a set of protocols, known as the *Internet Transport Protocols,* is used. The Internet set of protocols is illustrated in Fig. 19.1. These protocols, on one side, interface with the session layer, which may be the Cour-

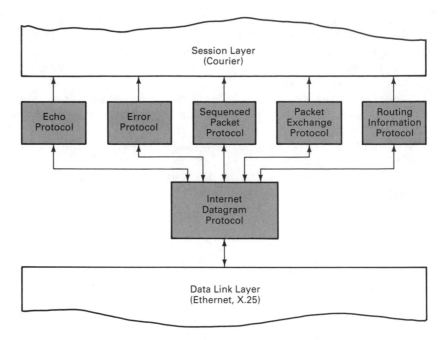

Figure 19.1   Internet transport protocols

ier protocol. On the other side, the interface is at the data link layer level, which could be an Ethernet LAN or an X.25 packet-switching network.

Internet Datagram Protocol

The *Internet Datagram Protocol* provides the basic data transmission service. It uses the packet format shown in Fig. 19.2. The checksum is used by the receiver to verify that the packet has been transmitted without error. The addressing scheme used in XNS is based on each network's having a unique 32-bit address and each station a unique 48-bit address. (Xerox uses the term *host* to refer to stations on the network; we will use the more conventional term *station*.) The network number is used for routing, so that routing information is kept on a network basis and not on an individual station basis. The socket number allows a station to have processes that are both sending and receiving data and permits these processes to be addressed separately. XNS addressing also allows for the use of group and broadcast addresses. The Internet Datagram Protocol does not provide reliable data transfer. Messages are sent on a best-effort basis, with no acknowledgments or retransmission. The Internet Datagram Protocol can be invoked directly if reliable data transfer is not required; one of the other protocols can be used if reliable service is required.

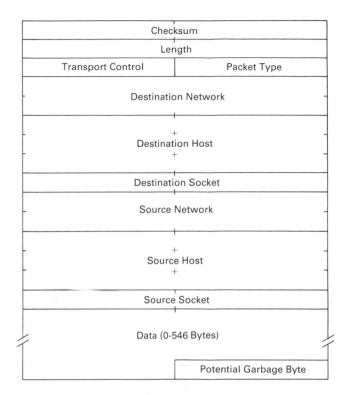

Figure 19.2   Internet packet

Sequenced Packet Protocol

The *Sequenced Packet Protocol* is used when reliable data transfer is required. With this protocol, additional information is added to the packet, as shown in Fig. 19.3. The protocol establishes a connection, or virtual circuit, between the sender and the receiver. Messages that flow across the connection are assigned sequence numbers that the receiver uses to check for missing, out-of-sequence, or duplicate messages. The receiver sends back acknowledgments, and if a message is not acknowledged, it is retransmitted.

Packet Exchange Protocol

The *Packet Exchange Protocol* is a simpler protocol that can be used when only a single message and response are to be exchanged. The packet format for this type of service is shown in Fig. 19.4. Sequence numbers are not used. If a response is not received, the message is retransmitted. This protocol does not

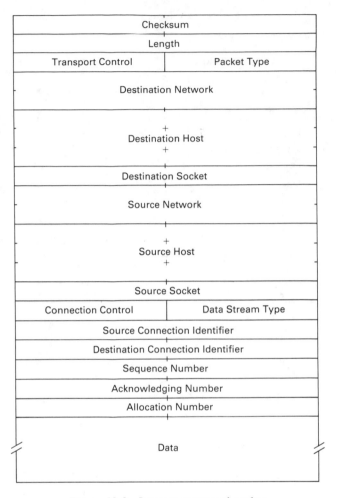

Figure 19.3   Internet sequenced packet

provide the reliability of the Sequenced Packet Protocol but is more reliable than the Internet Datagram Protocol.

Other Internet Protocols

The other protocols provide support to the ones just described. The *Error Protocol* standardizes the manner in which errors are reported. The *Echo Protocol* is used to verify the existence and correct operation of a station and the route to it. The *Routing Information Protocol* provides for the exchange of routing information between network nodes. Information is sent either on request or at periodic intervals.

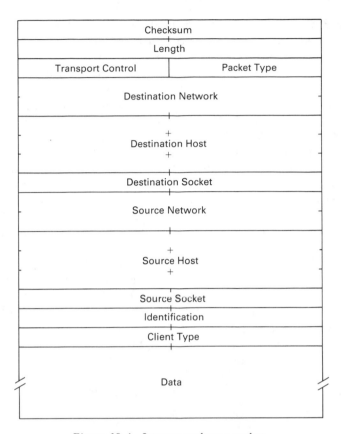

Figure 19.4 Internet exchange packet

XNS INTERNET ROUTING SERVICES

The XNS architecture provides for delivering messages across interconnected networks. The networks can be of different types, but all must use the XNS protocols for communication to take place. In XNS terminology, the individual networks are known as *subnetworks,* and the entire interconnected collection of subnetworks is called the *internet.* The routing function of Internet is based on the use of *routers* to pass a message from one subnetwork in the internet to another. The router is responsible for determining, from the destination network address, the next subnetwork the message should be sent to.

Each subnetwork must contain at least one node that is a router and is capable of providing the *Internet Routing Service* (IRS). The IRS is used in conjunction with routing services available in each station to route messages from their source to their destination. Each station must maintain routing tables that indicate, for different destination network addresses, the address of an IRS on the local subnetwork to be used for routing messages to those destination networks. For messages not destined for the local subnetwork, the station must determine the address of the local IRS to use and then send the message to that IRS. Each IRS maintains a complete map of the internet, in the form of routing information tables. For every remote subnetwork, these tables indicate the next subnetwork on the route and the distance from the destination subnetwork. The IRS uses this information to send a message across the next subnetwork, either to another IRS or to the destination station if this is the destination network.

This approach to routing assumes that routing information is predefined, at the station and in the IRS routers, and that the routing information can be updated as necessary to reflect changes in the internet. XNS does provide a mechanism for propagating changes to routing information. The Routing Information Protocols cause IRSs to exchange routing information periodically. This way, changes to the configuration gradually spread throughout the internet. Also, stations are able to use the protocol to update their routing information.

TCP/IP

Another widely used set of routing protocols is *Transmission Control Protocol/Internet Protocol* (TCP/IP), which was developed by the Department of Defense (DoD) as part of the work done on ARPANET, an early packet-switching network. The *Internet Protocol* (IP) is designed to provide a datagram service whereby packets can be sent and received across networks, although the data transfer cannot be considered reliable. The *Transmission Control Protocol* (TCP) provides reliable connection-oriented data transfer using the underlying Internet Protocol.

TCP PACKET FORMAT

Figure 19.5 shows the packet format used with TCP. The TCP header specifies a source port and a destination port. A *port* in TCP/IP corresponds to a *socket* in XNS or a *session partner* in NETBIOS. A port represents the process in a

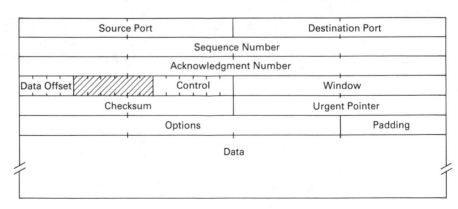

Figure 19.5   Transmission Control Protocol (TCP) packet format

network station that is doing the communicating. Use of ports allows a station to support multiple communications processes simultaneously. The connection-oriented communication provided by TCP is based on the establishment of a connection between two ports. Both ports are then able to send and receive over that connection, using full-duplex transmission. Source and destination addresses are carried in the IP header. TCP must pass these values to IP along with the TCP packet.

TCP RELIABLE DATA TRANSFER

Sequence numbers are used to ensure reliable data transfer. The receiving port checks the sequence numbers to identify missing, out-of-sequence, or duplicate packets. Acknowledgments are returned, and if a packet is not acknowledged, it is retransmitted. The checksum also provides a way of checking for damaged packets.

TCP FLOW CONTROL

TCP also includes a flow control mechanism. When a connection is established, a window size is agreed on for transmission in each direction. The window size specifies the number of bytes that the sender is allowed to transmit before receiving an acknowledgment. Each acknowledgment that is returned also contains a window value. This value determines the number of bytes that can be sent before the next acknowledgment. The window value in the acknowledgments can be adjusted upward or downward to respond to changing congestion conditions in the network.

TCP USER DATAGRAM PROTOCOL

In addition to TCP, which provides reliable connection-oriented data transfer, the *User Datagram Protocol* provides datagram service. Datagram service is a way of sending messages with a minimum of protocol mechanism. Delivery is not guaranteed. There is no checking for missing, out-of-sequence or duplicate packets, and no acknowledgments are sent. This protocol uses a much simpler packet format, shown in Fig. 19.6. The only error

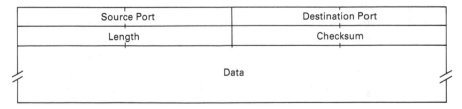

Figure 19.6   User Datagram Protocol (UDP) packet format

checking provided is via the checksum. If the checksum calculated by the receiving port does not agree with the checksum in the packet, the packet is discarded.

INTERNET PROTOCOL SERVICES

The *Internet Protocol* (IP) performs two primary functions. One is to route packets across an interconnected system of networks, known in TCP/IP terms as a *catanet*. The other is to segment a packet, if necessary, to accommodate a network that has a smaller maximum packet size and then to reassemble the packet when it reaches its destination.

Figure 19.7 shows the format of a packet as it is processed by IP. The identification, flags, and fragment offset fields are used to handle segmentation and reassembly, if it is required. The header checksum field is used to check the data in the IP header itself on a received packet, to be sure that the data was not damaged during transmission. The source and destination addresses are passed to IP along with the packet to be transmitted and are used by IP for routing. The options field may also contain information used for routing.

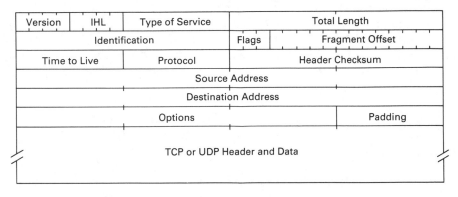

Figure 19.7 Internet Protocol (IP) packet format

IP ADDRESSING

To perform routing functions, IP must correctly interpret the destination address field. The addresses used are 32 bits in length and contain both a network address and a station address. The address field can be formatted in various ways, and the format used is indicated by the high-order bits. Possible formats are shown in Fig. 19.8.

High-Order Bits	Network Address Number of Bits	Host Address Number of Bits
0	7	24
10	14	16
110	21	8
111	Extended Addressing Mode	

Figure 19.8 Address formats

IP ROUTING

IP routing is conceptually similar to the approach used in XNS. The IP function in the sending station is responsible for determining if the destination address is part of the local network. If it is, the packet is sent there directly. If not, IP uses stored routing information and the destination address to determine the address of a gateway on this network to which the packet should be directed. The gateway is then responsible for determining the next step in the route.

Gateways maintain tables of routing information and are able to exchange such information so that changes are propagated throughout the catanet. The routing information maintained in the table consists of an entry for each network that can be reached via this gateway. The entry contains the network address of the destination network and the address of the next gateway along the shortest route to the destination network. The routing information that is sent from one gateway to another contains the destination network address, the gateway address, and the number of hops required to reach the destination network via this gateway. The number of hops reflects the number of intermediate networks that must be crossed to reach the destination network. The number of hops is used by the receiving gateway to determine if this is the shortest route to the destination network and to update the receiving gateway's routing table only if this is the shortest route. The messages that send routing information also contain sequence numbers that are used to ensure that the latest version of the routing information is used to update the routing table.

IP also supports the use of routing information provided by the source station. Routing information can be specified as a parameter when the packet is passed to IP and is then carried in the IP packet as an options field. The routing information consists of a series of network addresses. These addresses identify the networks and gateways that the packet should pass through as it travels to its destination.

The collection of routing information is useful, even when the source station provides routing information, because of the fact that gateways have multiple addresses, and the correct address to use depends on the direction in which a packet is traveling. This is illustrated in Fig. 19.9. When a packet travels from station A to station B, the routing addresses it uses are 00301 for the first gateway, 00503 for the second gateway, and 01007 for the destination. When a packet travels from station B back to station A, the route addresses are

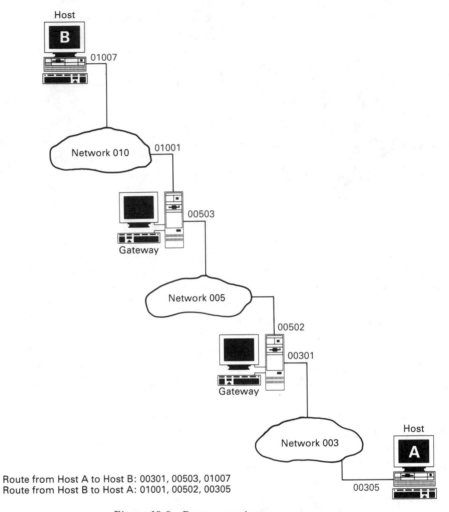

Route from Host A to Host B: 00301, 00503, 01007
Route from Host B to Host A: 01001, 00502, 00305

Figure 19.9   Reverse routing

01001, 00502, and 00305. As a packet travels through a gateway, it saves the gateway address associated with the network it is entering. So when a packet traveling from station A to station B passes through gateway 00301, it saves the address 00502, which is the address of the gateway in network 005.

MAP/OSI PROTOCOLS

The goal of the MAP specification is to provide a way for diverse devices to communicate. This includes providing for interconnection of multiple LANs and for connections between LANs and WANs. As we saw in Chapter 10, the MAP specification uses OSI protocols as the basis of its definition.

MAP SESSION AND TRANSPORT LAYER FUNCTIONS

MAP specifies full-duplex transmission for the session layer. At the transport layer, communication is connection-oriented and provides for the reliable and cost-effective transfer of data. Sequence numbers are assigned to messages as they are transmitted. The receiving partner checks the sequence numbers to identify missing, out-of-sequence, or duplicate messages. Acknowledgments are sent back, and unacknowledged messages are retransmitted. A checksum is used to check for damaged packets. Flow control is provided by the use of a window size that specifies the number of unacknowledged messages that can be outstanding at a given time.

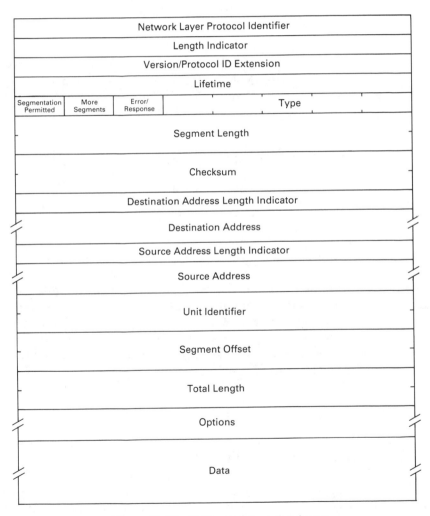

Figure 19.10 MAP network packet format

MAP NETWORK LAYER FUNCTIONS

The network layer in the MAP architecture is responsible for routing messages across interconnected networks and for delivering messages to their final destinations. The network layer is also responsible for segmenting a packet if its size exceeds the maximum packet size for a particular network along the route and for reassembling the packet, either when it reaches its destination or when it has passed all networks where it would be too large.

Figure 19.10 shows the packet format used in a MAP network at the network level. A number of fields are used in connection with the segmentation and reassembly functions. The checksum field is used to check for damaged packets. The destination address plays a key role in routing, and the options field may also contain information related to routing.

MAP ADDRESSING

Since a single universal addressing standard does not exist, MAP has adopted an approach to addressing whereby different address formats can be used. The structure of a MAP address is shown in Fig. 19.11. The first byte of the address is a value that identifies

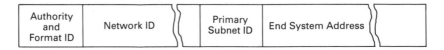

Figure 19.11   MAP addressing

the particular format used for the address. The network ID portion identifies a domain or area, which can consist of a collection of networks. The primary subnet ID, when combined with the network ID, identifies a particular network. The end system address portion identifies a particular process communicating at the network level on a particular device. For a network that implements the IEEE LLC 802.2 standard, this part of the address consists of a MAC address, a link station identifier, and a network user identifier. (MAP allows network-level users to share a single LLC-level connection.)

MAP ROUTING

MAP routing is based on the use of *router nodes* and *distributed routing tables*. The source node determines whether the destination is part of the local network. If not, the source node uses a table lookup procedure to determine the address of a router node on the local network to which to send the packet. Using stored routing tables, the router node determines the network and node address to which the packet should be sent next. This may be either the packet's final destination or another router node. The MAP specification also suggests a method by which router nodes can exchange information about the availability of resources along a route.

Recording of route information as a packet travels along its route is an option that can be specified in the options field. Routing based on information supplied by the source node is not defined in the MAP specification, but a MAP implementation is allowed to support this if it chooses.

ROUTING STANDARDIZATION ISSUES

Standards organizations, in particular IEEE Project 802, are working to develop standards for the routing of messages across interconnected LANs. Two methods of routing are under active consideration. One is known as *adaptive source routing*. With this method, used in the IBM Token Ring Network, the source station is responsible for providing all the routing information. A source station obtains routing information by sending out a broadcast message. The responses to the message describe the route each copy of the message traveled. The second method is called the *transparent* method. With this method, each bridge or router is responsible for maintaining and using a routing table that provides routing information based on the destination address.

Issues that must be considered for each method include performance, complexity, and the ability to respond to changes in network configuration and availability. IEEE Project 802 is currently working to standardize both routing methods in a way that will allow them to coexist and interoperate. The IEEE 802.1 committee is addressing transparent routing, and the 802.5 token ring committee is addressing adaptive source routing, with the proviso that it should be able to operate with 802.1 transparent routing.

Work is also being done to provide a standardized way for NETBIOS-compatible applications to send messages over interconnected networks using TCP/IP protocols. A number of products provide a NETBIOS-TCP/IP interface, but they are not compatible and cannot easily be interconnected. A group of vendors is developing a specification that standardizes the NETBIOS-TCP/IP interface. A key issue being addressed by the specification is formulating a method for NETBIOS-compatible applications to access a centralized TCP/IP name service. With NETBIOS, each station is responsible for knowing its own names. Addresses corresponding to a name are determined from the responses to a broadcast message. For larger, more complex collections of interconnected networks, this approach becomes impractical. TCP/IP uses a centralized table of names and addresses and a name service that returns the address or addresses associated with a name. The challenge is to integrate the two approaches and to do this in a standard manner so that products from different vendors can be easily interconnected.

SUMMARY NETBIOS supports full-duplex transmission at the level of the session layer. At the level of the transport layer, NETBIOS offers a datagram service, which uses no acknowledgments or error checking, and session service, which uses sequence numbers and acknowledgments to provide reliable data transfer and flow control. NETBIOS uses source routing, where the sending station is responsible for providing all routing information. Routing information is obtained through responses to a broadcast message.

APPC/PC supports half-duplex transmission at the level of the session layer. At the level of the transport layer, APPC/PC provides reliable data transfer, using sequence numbers and acknowledgments for reliability and flow control. Routing is based on predefined information. For routing on a LAN, the information is stored at the sending station. For routing across an SNA network, information is stored at each intermediate node.

XNS supports a procedure call at the level of the session layer, where a request is sent and the results are returned. At the level of the transport layer, XNS offers datagram service, reliable data transfer, and a single message and response protocol. Routing is based on the use of distributed routing tables that are stored at router nodes. The router is responsible for determining the next subnetwork the message should be sent across and the destination station within that subnetwork. The addressing structure provides for both a network number and a station address as part of the network address.

TCP/IP does not address the session layer. At the level of the transport layer, TCP provides for reliable data transfer, using sequence numbers and acknowledgments for reliability and flow control, and datagram service, which does not use acknowledgments. IP provides routing based on distributed routing tables, stored at gateway nodes. The gateway is responsible for determining the next network in the catanet that the message should be sent across and the destination station in that network. The addressing structure provides for both a network address and a station address as part of the destination address.

MAP/OSI supports full-duplex transmission at the level of the session layer. At the level of the transport layer, MAP/OSI offers reliable data transfer, using sequence numbers and acknowledgments for reliability and flow control. Routing is based on the use of distributed routing tables that are stored at router nodes. A router is responsible for determining the next network across which the message should travel and the destination station in that network. The addressing structure provides for both a network number and a station address as part of the overall address.

20 ETHERNET

Beginning in about 1972, the Palo Alto Research Center (PARC) of Xerox Corporation began developing a LAN system known as Experimental Ethernet. The design was very successful, and many Ethernet networks have now been installed. The early Ethernet specifications contributed substantially to the work done by the IEEE on the 802.3 standard defining the CSMA/CD access control method. Later, Digital Equipment Corporation, Intel Corporation, and Xerox Corporation jointly defined an Ethernet specification that is substantially compatible with the IEEE 802.3 standard. Many vendors now offer Ethernet network products that are compatible with various network operating systems. We will look at some of those network operating systems later in the book. The Ethernet specification itself does not define the types of functions found in a network operating system; as with other LAN standards, the specification is limited to defining the functions performed by the data link and physical layers.

ETHERNET GOALS   The goals of the Ethernet design are stated as part of the Ethernet specification, as listed in Box 20.1. These goals are consistent with the communication requirements that have driven the development and spreading use of LANs.

ETHERNET DEFINITIONS   In Ethernet terminology, Ethernet is an architecture that provides best-effort datagram service, with error detection but not error correction. It is a multiaccess, packet-switched network that uses a passive broadcast medium, with no central control. Data units transmitted over the network reach every station, and each station is responsible for recognizing the address contained in a data unit and

BOX 20.1 Ethernet goals

- **Simplicity.** Features that would complicate the design without substantially contributing to meeting the other goals have been excluded.

- **Low Cost.** Since technological improvements will continue to reduce the overall cost of stations wishing to connect to Ethernet, the cost of the connection itself should be minimized.

- **Compatibility.** All implementations of the Ethernet should be capable of exchanging data at the data link level. For this reason, the specification avoids optional features, to eliminate the possibility of incompatible variants of Ethernet.

- **Addressing Flexibility.** The addressing mechanisms should provide the capability to target frames to a single station, a group of stations, or all stations on the network.

- **Fairness.** All stations should have equal access to the network when averaged over time.

- **Progress.** No single station operating in accordance with the protocol should be able to prevent the progress of other stations.

- **High Speed.** The network should operate efficiently at a data rate of 10 megabits per second.

- **Low Delay.** At any given level of offered traffic, the network should introduce as little delay as possible in the transfer of a frame.

- **Stability.** The network should be stable under all load conditions, in the sense that the delivered traffic should be a monotonically nondecreasing function of the total offered traffic.

- **Maintainability.** The Ethernet design should allow for network maintenance, operation, and planning.

- **Layered Architecture.** The Ethernet design should be specified in layered terms to separate the logical aspects of the data link protocol from the physical details of the communication medium.

for accepting data units addressed to it from the transmission medium. Access to the transmission medium is governed by the individual stations, using a statistical arbitration scheme.

ETHERNET FUNCTIONAL MODEL

Figure 20.1 shows the functional model of Ethernet and compares it to the functional model documented in the IEEE 802.3 standard. In Ethernet terminology,

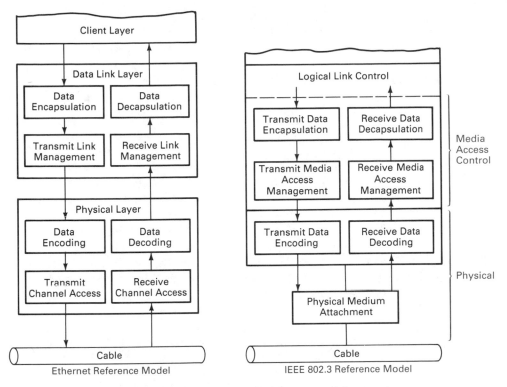

Figure 20.1   Ethernet/IEEE 802.3 reference model comparison

the software layer operating above the data link layer in called the *client* layer. The client layer works with data units called *packets*. The client layer passes packets to the Ethernet data link layer for transmission through the network. Although there are some differences in terminology, the same basic functions are defined for the data link and physical layers:

- **Data Encapsulation/Decapsulation.** When a packet is received from the client layer for transmission, it is encapsulated with the control information necessary for transmission, forming a *transmission frame,* or *frame.* When the frame is received, the control information is removed before the data unit is passed up to the client layer in the form of the original packet. The Ethernet frame format defines the control information that is added.

- **Link Management.** The link management function is responsible for *collision avoidance* and *collision handling.* Collision avoidance involves monitoring the carrier sense signal and deferring transmission if the channel is already in use. Collision handling involves transmitting a jam signal, to ensure that all stations are aware of the collision, and then scheduling a retransmission attempt, using a defined algorithm to determine the time to wait before retransmitting.

- **Data Encoding/Decoding.** Encoding involves adding bits needed for synchronization and converting a binary signal to phase-encoded form, using the Manchester encoding scheme. Decoding involves converting back from Manchester to binary and removing the synchronization bits.

- **Channel Access.** The channel access function transmits bits to and receives bits from the transmission medium, or cable. It also senses the carrier (the presence of data transmission on the medium) and detects collisions.

LAYER-TO-LAYER SERVICES

The two services that the data link layer provides to the client layer are *transmission* and *reception* of frames. These services are defined by the **TransmitFrame** and **ReceiveFrame** functions. These functions correspond to the **MA.DATA.request** and **MA.DATA.indicate** primitives defined by the IEEE 802.3 standard, although there are some differences in the parameter definitions. The **MA.DATA.confirm** primitive, which is used to report on the success or failure of a transmission, is implemented in Ethernet through a parameter that is part of the **TransmitFrame** function.

The physical layer provides the following services to the data link layer:

- **TransmitBit.** The **TransmitBit** procedure passes one bit of a frame to be transmitted from the data link layer to the physical layer. The variable **transmitting** is used to indicate the beginning and the end of the stream of bits that make up the frame. The variable **collisionDetect** is used by the physical layer to inform the data link layer that a collision has occurred on the transmission medium. The variable **carrierSense** is used by the physical layer to indicate that data is present on the transmission medium. The data link layer must check this variable and not start a transmission when the transmission medium is in use.

- **ReceiveBit.** The **ReceiveBit** function is used to pass a bit of a frame being received from the physical layer to the data link layer. The variable **carrierSense** is used to indicate when there are bits to be received and when the stream of bits that make up the frame ends.

- **Wait.** The **Wait** procedure allows the data link layer to measure a specified number of bit times. This is used to wait the proper amount of time after a collision before attempting retransmission.

These services match very closely the interface between the MAC sublayer and the physical layer defined in the IEEE 802.3 standard.

ETHERNET FRAME FORMAT

The data encapsulation/decapsulation functions performed by the data link layer are primarily concerned with producing a correctly formatted frame for transmission across the network and then processing a received frame to be sure it

BOX 20.2 Ethernet transmission frame

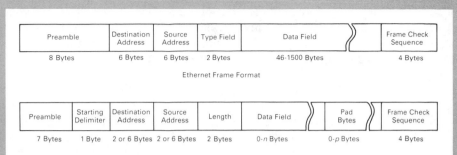

Ethernet Frame Format

IEEE 802.3 Frame Format

- **Preamble.** The *preamble* is used to provide synchronization and to mark the start of a frame. The same bit pattern is used for the Ethernet preamble field as in the IEEE 802.3 preamble and start frame delimiter fields. (The preamble is actually generated and removed as part of the data encoding/decoding function in the physical layer and is not always shown as part of the Ethernet frame format.)

- **Address Fields.** The frame includes both destination and source *address* fields. Ethernet specifies the use of 48-bit addresses, whereas IEEE 802.3 allows either 16-bit or 48-bit addresses.

- **Type Field.** Ethernet does not support the use of a length field and padding. Instead, the 2 bytes are used to contain a *type* field. The value specified in the type field is meaningful to the higher network layers and is not defined as part of the Ethernet specification.

- **Data Field.** The *data* portion of the frame is passed to the data link layer by the client layer. It must be a multiple of 8 bits. Ethernet defines a minimum frame size of 72 bytes and a maximum frame size of 1526 bytes, including the preamble. If the data to be sent is smaller or larger than these sizes, it is the responsibility of the higher layers to pad it or break it into individual packets. The reason for specifying a minimum frame size is to reduce problems in collision handling. (This issue is described in detail in Chapter 6.) The maximum packet size reflects practical considerations related to buffer sizes in the adapter card and a need for a limit on the length of time the transmission medium is tied up while transmitting a single frame.

- **Frame Check Sequence.** Ethernet uses a *frame check sequence* field as a way of providing error checking. The field contains a cyclic redundancy check (CRC) value that is calculated from the other fields in the frame. When the frame is received, the value is calculated again using the received data, and the calculated value is compared to the value in the frame. If the two do not match, an error has occurred, and this is reported to the client layer.

has arrived correctly before passing it on to the client layer. The processing performed is determined by the frame format that is defined as part of the Ethernet specification. Box 20.2 describes the Ethernet frame format and compares it to the frame format described by the IEEE 802.3 standard.

NETWORK ADDRESSES

Ethernet provides for using either universal or network-specific addresses. Xerox Corporation provides vendors of Ethernet products with blocks of addresses to use in assigning unique addresses to individual network devices. The address is assigned in the network adapter card and can be accessed by the device in which the adapter card is installed.

With *universal* addressing, all network devices have unique network addresses. With *network-specific* addressing, each station is assigned an address that is unique within the network but can be the same as a station on some other network. In this case, a unique network identifier must be used with the station address to provide a unique address when networks are interconnected. Since Ethernet does not define how the 48 bits of an address must be used, network-specific addressing is possible, but it is the responsibility of higher-level network layers to implement it.

Each station is associated with a physical address, which can be either universal or network-specific. The address can be set by the station itself as part of initialization. Any frame sent to this address is received and processed by the station. Ethernet also supports the use of multicast (group) and broadcast addresses. An address consisting of all 1 bits is defined as the broadcast address and is received by all stations. A multicast address is associated with a particular group of stations. A multicast address is identified by the value 1 in the first bit of the address. A station can have multicast mode either on or off. If it is on, the station accepts any frame with multicast addresses. Higher layers must then determine if the station is part of the group for a particular multicast address.

DATA ENCAPSULATION/ DECAPSULATION

The data encapsulation function is responsible for constructing a frame in the proper format. The destination address, source address, type, and information fields are passed to it by the client layer in the form of a packet. A CRC value for the frame check sequence field is calculated from them, and the frame is constructed.

Data decapsulation is responsible for checking incoming frames for errors. This can include a frame that is not a multiple of 8 bits or that exceeds the maximum packet length. It is also responsible for checking the address to see if the frame should be accepted and processed further. If it is, a CRC value is calculated and checked against the value in the frame check sequence field. If the values match, the destination address, source address, type and data fields are passed to the client layer.

LINK MANAGEMENT

The method used to control access to the transmission medium, known as *media access management* in IEEE terms, is named *link management* in Ethernet. Link management is responsible for the following functions:

- **Collision Avoidance.** Transmit link management monitors the transmission channel to see if there is currently traffic on the channel. This is known as carrier sense. If no carrier is detected (no traffic), a serial stream of bits is sent to the physical layer for transmission. If no collision is detected during the period of time known as the collision interval, the station is said to have acquired the channel and can complete the transmission without danger of collision. If carrier is detected (traffic is present), link management defers until the channel is clear.

- **Collision Handling.** If a collision occurs, the physical layer notifies link management, which transmits a bit sequence called the *jam*. This sequence ensures that every station on the network recognizes the collision. Transmit link management then terminates the transmission it started and schedules a retransmission attempt after a calculated amount of time. If there are repeated collisions, link management uses a process called backing off, which involves increasing the time waited before retransmission following each successive collision. The method used to determine the amount of time to wait is the binary exponential backoff method described for the IEEE 802.3 CSMA/CD standard (see Chapter 6). On the receiving side, link management is responsible for recognizing and filtering out fragments of frames that resulted from a transmission that was interrupted by a collision. Any frame that is less than the minimum size is assumed to be a collision fragment. These fragments are not reported to the client layer as errors.

ETHERNET PHYSICAL MODEL

Figure 20.2 illustrates the physical implementation model that is assumed in the Ethernet specification. In this model, the data link functions and the data encoding/decoding function of the physical layer are assumed to be packaged in a controller board, or card, that is installed in a network device, such as a personal computer. A device called a *transceiver,* containing a small amount of circuitry, implements the channel access function and is located close to, or directly on, the coaxial cable. A transceiver cable is used to connect the transceiver to the controller card, thus allowing the network station to be located a short distance away from the coaxial cable. In IEEE 802.3 terms, the trans-

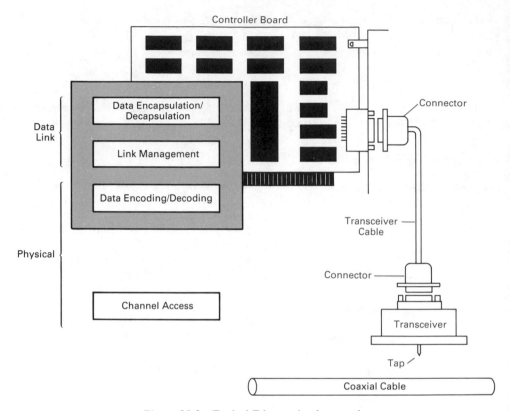

Figure 20.2   Typical Ethernet implementation

ceiver cable and connectors correspond to the *attachment unit interface* (AUI) and the transceiver to a *medium attachment unit* (MAU).

In Ethernet, the functions of the physical layer are referred to as the *physical channel,* or just the *channel*. This includes the logic in the controller board that does encoding and decoding, preamble generation and removal, and carrier sensing. The transceiver contains the logic required to send and receive bits over the coaxial cable and to detect collisions.

DATA ENCODING/   Ethernet uses the Manchester encoding scheme
DECODING   shown in Fig. 20.3. This is the encoding scheme de-
                           fined for the IEEE 802.3 CSMA/CD standard. With
Manchester encoding, there is a transition in every bit. A 1 bit signal goes from low to high, 0 bit from high to low. The transition in every bit allows clocking to be combined with data transmission. It also allows carrier to be detected by the presence of a transition on the transmission medium.

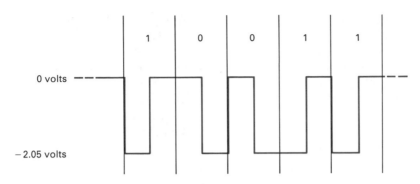

Figure 20.3   Manchester encoding

The data encoding function is also responsible for adding a preamble to every frame transmitted. Data decoding removes the preamble before the frame is passed to the data link layer. Carrier sensing is also performed at this level.

CHANNEL ACCESS   The channel access function is performed within the transceiver. The functions provided by the channel access function include these:

- Accepting encoded bits from the controller and putting them onto the coaxial cable.
- Taking bits from the coaxial cable and passing them to the controller
- Detecting collisions and passing an appropriate signal to the controller

PHYSICAL SPECIFICATIONS   The Ethernet specification defines electrical, mechanical, and other physical characteristics for the components of the physical channel. Requirements are detailed for the following:

- Physical configuration limits, such as coaxial cable segment length, number of repeaters, total path length, and transceiver cable length
- Coaxial cable component specifications, including the cable itself, connectors, and terminators
- Interface specifications for the transceiver cable and the transceiver
- Configuration requirements and environmental specifications

The most commonly used Ethernet implementation uses baseband transmission over coaxial cable at a data rate of 10 Mbps. The maximum cable length is 500 m, making this an implementation of 10BASE5 transmission. The initial Ethernet implementations used a relatively expensive coaxial cable, now called *thick Ethernet cable*. Ordinary CATV-type coaxial cable, called *thin Ethernet cable,* has since been used in many lower-cost Ethernet implementations. Most recently, a form of Ethernet has been developed that uses twisted-wire-pair cable to support a data rate of 10 Mbps.

Adherence to the physical specifications has allowed for the manufacture of network components from different vendors that can be combined to form a single functioning network. Many vendors today produce Ethernet network components to support Ethernet variations.

SUMMARY

Ethernet functions include data encapsulation/decapsulation, link management, data encoding/decoding, and channel access. The Ethernet frame format includes a preamble, address fields, type field, data field, and frame check sequence. Link management is responsible for avoiding collisions by listening for a free transmission medium before beginning transmission. Collisions are handled by stopping transmission and then waiting for a calculated period of time before attempting retransmission. Manchester encoding is used with Ethernet. Transmission is ordinarily baseband, at a data rate of 10 Mbps, with a maximum cable length of 500 m (10BASE5).

21 3COM: 3+

3Com Corporation (the name stands for *computers, communication,* and *compatibility*) is a major LAN vendor offering products for both the IBM and Apple lines of personal computers and for other computer vendors. 3Com's initial LAN products concentrated on providing affordable Ethernet network components; however, the company now offers both hardware and software products for many LAN architectures, including products compatible with IBM's token ring network. The hardware includes adapter cards, transceivers, and file servers for various types of LANs. In this chapter, we will focus on the software offered for the IBM personal computer LAN environment. The major components in 3Com's IBM PC software line are the following:

- **3 + Share.** *3 + Share* is 3Com's network operating system for the IBM environment.
- **3 + Mail.** *3 + Mail,* which runs under the control of 3 + Share, provides electronic mail services for stations on the network.
- **3 + Route.** *3 + Route* is one of many connectivity products offered and provides for the interconnection of remote 3 + networks.
- **3 + Remote.** *3 + Remote* allows remote access to a 3 + network via a modem and telephone lines.
- **3 + NetConnect.** *3 + NetConnect* enables physically close LANs to be interconnected.
- **3 + 3270.** *3 + 3270* allows personal computers on a 3 + network to access IBM SNA hosts, emulating a 3270 terminal.

3Com offers many other products as well that provide various operational enhancements to a 3 + network. However, we will restrict ourselves to the products listed, since they provide the key LAN functions.

3 + SHARE

3 + Share is the base component of a 3 + network. It acts as the network operating system and can be used, at the hardware level, with either an Ethernet or a token ring LAN. 3 + Share provides three major functions:

- Multiuser file sharing
- Spooled printer sharing
- A directory-based name service for identifying users and resources on the network

The user interface to 3 + Share has both menu-driven and programmable options.

3 + SHARE FILE SHARING

3 + Share file sharing operates at the directory level. A directory can be shared, and through it, all the files in the directory can be shared. When a directory is made available for sharing, access rights can be specified for the directory. Possible access rights are as follows:

- **Read-Only.** Users can only read information in existing files.
- **Write/Create.** Users can change an existing file, create a new file, or delete a file, but they cannot read existing files. For example, with this access right, a user might be allowed to add records to an existing file.
- **Read/Write.** Users can read and change existing files but cannot create a new file or delete a file.
- **Read/Write/Create.** Users can read and change existing files, create new files, and delete files.
- **Sharable.** Nonowners of the directory can assign share names to this directory or to any of its subdirectories.
- **Private.** Only one user can use the directory at a time.
- **Home Directory.** Only the owner has access to a home directory. However, subdirectories under it can be shared, under their own names.

These access rights can be assigned to a directory through the menu-level interface to 3 + Share. The program interface to 3 + Share is based on the use of a redirector and the DOS 21H interrupts. Through this interface, the DOS facilities are supported that control sharing at the file level and provide record locking.

3 + SHARE PRINTER SHARING

3 + Share allows users to share access to network printers. A network user prints output in the same manner as if the printer were attached to the user's own personal computer. When a print job is sent to a shared printer, a spool file is created and stored in a print queue. Users are able to display the status of print queues and can modify characteristics of a print job while its printed output is in the queue.

3 + SHARE NAME SERVICE

The name service that is part of 3 + Share provides a central directory of user and resource names. Each name consists of three parts: logical name, domain, and organization. The logical name portion corresponds to the logical name of a user or resource. The domain corresponds to a logical group that the user or resource belongs to, such as a department or physical location. The organization portion is typically used to represent an entire enterprise or company. The use of domain and organization provides support for network interconnection. For example, each network can be assigned a different domain or organization value. Then references can be made to other networks through logical names without concern for duplicate name values. Also, a domain value can be associated with a particular network number, which is useful for internetwork routing.

Profile information is maintained in the directory for each name. This includes an indication of whether the name belongs to a server or a user. For server names, there is also an address, consisting of network number, station number, and socket number. For user names, a password and other descriptive information can be specified. Aliases can be specified so that a name can be referenced using a shorter or more convenient form. A name can have more than one alias. Group names can also be defined; a group name specifies a collection of names that are addressed when the group name is referenced. Aliases and group names are stored in the directory, each with its own type of profile information. Domain names and their associated network numbers can be stored in the directory and can be used to provide a distributed directory organization. Each directory contains detailed information on names associated with its own domain or network. The domain or network number entry for other domains then indicates where information is stored for the names associated with those domains or networks.

The name service uses persistent naming. Once names are defined, they are permanently stored, typically on disk, and are retained even when the user is not logged onto the network. When the user logs on, the name and password in the directory are checked against the name and password the user enters. Persistent naming is important for the mail service provided as part of 3 + Mail, since a valid destination exists for a user even when that user is not logged on.

3 + MAIL   3 + Mail provides a message delivery service, which operates on a store-and-forward basis, with messages being passed from one mail server to another and distributed to local users served by a given mail server. There can be several servers on one network, or a server can represent interconnected networks. 3 + Mail includes automatic notification when mail arrives.

3 + NETWORK CONNECTIVITY PRODUCTS   Several products provide LAN-to-LAN or LAN-to-WAN interconnection. *3 + Route* allows two or more 3 + networks to be interconnected, using remote communication facilities (telephone lines) between the networks. The name service is used to provide the ability to address users or resources on another network without having to know the address or location of the user or resource. The following are descriptions of the major 3 + network connectivity products:

- **3 + Remote.** *3 + Remote* allows a remote personal computer to access a 3 + network and communicate with the network over telephone lines. The remote personal computer establishes a connection with a server on the network, which acts as a communication server as well as a file and print server. Once the connection is established, the remote personal computer is able to access network resources and services transparently in the same manner as a station that is directly connected to the network (although at the speed of the telephone connection).

- **3 + NetConnect.** *3 + NetConnect* provides for interconnection of 3 + networks that are physically close together and can be connected directly. The program can be used to connect two token ring networks, two Ethernet networks, or one of each. The interconnection is provided by a server that is considered to be a member of both networks. Users on one network can share resources that belong to the other network. Resources are accessed via names, so the user does not need to be aware of their locations.

- **3 + 3270.** *3 + 3270* allows stations on a 3 + network to access an IBM SNA host by emulating a 3270 terminal. The user may function as a 3278 or 3279 display using an LU 2 session or a 3287 printer using either an LU 1 or LU 3 session. Print output from the session can be spooled to any network printer or disk or to any network station. A dedicated 3270 server must be used. The 3270 server communicates with the SNA host using SDLC protocols.

3 + NETWORK PROTOCOLS AND INTERFACES   3Com, like IBM, offers choices in terms of protocols supported and interfaces that can be used with its LAN products. The principal protocols and interfaces supported are shown in Fig. 21.1. At the data link

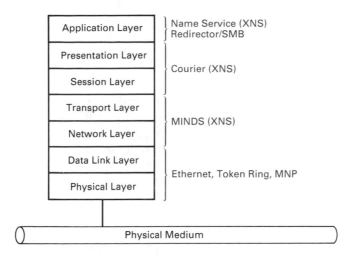

Figure 21.1   3Com protocols

level, three different protocols are supported: Ethernet, token ring, and the Microcom Network Protocol (MNP). MNP allows for reliable communication over telephone lines. At the higher-level network layers, adaptations of some of the Xerox Networking System (XNS) protocols are used. An interface is also provided that uses a Redirector and SMB formats (see Chapter 18) to provide compatibility with the IBM PC LAN Program.

Through the use of the Redirector/SMB protocols, 3Com provides compatibility with the IBM networking environment and with applications written or modified to run in that environment. The XNS-related protocols allow the 3Com products to offer additional functionality, particularly in the area of network interconnection.

ETHERNET AND TOKEN RING   3Com supports the use of Ethernet at the physical and data link levels. Transmission is at the rate of 10 Mbps, and packets can either be in Ethernet or in IEEE 802.3 CSMA/CD format. 3Com also supports the token ring protocol at the physical and data link levels, and 3Com software can be used with IBM Token Ring adapters or those manufactured by 3Com.

MICROCOM NETWORK PROTOCOL   The Microcom Network Protocol (MNP) is used to provide reliable data transfer over asynchronous communication facilities. It is used by 3Com for products where communication takes place over telephone lines, including 3+Route and 3+Remote. This protocol is supported by many communication services and information utilities, such as Telecom, The Source, and GEISCO. Checksums and sequence numbers are used to provide error detection and correction. The protocol is also able to handle blocking and deblocking.

MS-DOS INTERNAL NETWORK DRIVE SCHEME

3Com uses an implementation of the XNS protocols to provide network and transport layer functions of routing and reliable data transfer. Its implementation is called the *MS-DOS Internal Network Drive Scheme* (MINDS). The MINDS protocols are used to implement parts of 3 + Share, 3 + Route, 3 + Remote, and 3 + NetConnect.

INTERNET DATAGRAM PROTOCOL

At the level of the network layer, 3Com supports the XNS *internet datagram protocol* (IDP). This protocol provides basic data transfer capabilities and a routing service based on network numbers and distributed routing tables. Source and destination addresses consist of three parts: network number, host number, and socket number. When a packet is to be sent to a station whose network number is other than the local network number, IDP in the sending station uses a routing table to determine the local address of a router in the local network that can forward the packet. The packet is sent to the router, which uses a routing table to determine the network number and local address for the next station to which the packet should be sent. This next station may be a router in the next network, or it may be the destination station. The packet is sent from router to router until one is reached that is able to deliver the message to its final destination.

Routers periodically share information with one another by broadcasting a description of the connections they currently have established. Nonrouter nodes that are servers also listen to these broadcasts and use the information to update their routing tables. Nonrouter nodes, servers or not, can also request routing information from a router and use the response to update their routing tables.

Routing information includes the addresses of routers, the network numbers those routers can establish a connection with, and a *hop count*. The hop count is the number of routers a packet will pass through to reach its final destination. If the destination network is directly connected to the router, the hop count is 1. If the router can open a connection but hasn't yet done so, the count is 15. If the router is unable to open a connection, the count is 16. If more than one route can service a destination, the one with the lowest hop count is chosen.

SEQUENCED PACKET PROTOCOL

At the level of the transport layer, 3Com uses the XNS *Sequenced Packet Protocol* (SPP). SPP provides for reliable data transfer using a virtual circuit that is established between the sending and receiving processes. Messages are assigned sequence numbers, and, on the receiving side, the sequence numbers are used to check for out-of-sequence, missing, or duplicate messages. Acknowledgments are sent, and unacknowledged messages are retransmitted. Window sizes are used to control the number of unacknowledged messages that are allowed to be outstanding. Spe-

BOX 21.1   SSP message flow example

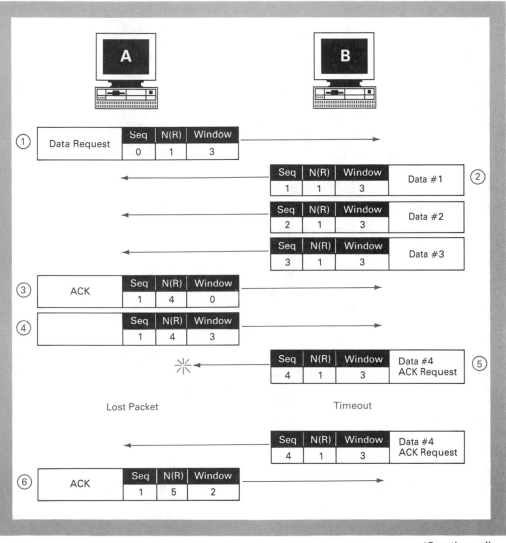

(Continued)

BOX 21.1 *(Continued)*

1. A data request is sent whose sequence number is 0. Station A expects that the next message it receives will have an N(R) value 1. The window size is set to 3 so that station B can send three messages before receiving an acknowledgment.

2. Station B begins sending back data. It sends three messages, with sequence numbers 1, 2, and 3. Since the message count has reached the window size, station B waits for an acknowledgment.

3. Station A sends an acknowledgment in the form of a system packet. The N(R) value of 4 acknowledges all messages through sequence number 3. The window size is set to 0, which prevents station B from sending any more messages.

4. Station A sends another system packet, setting the window size to 3. Station B can now resume sending.

5. Station B sends a message with a request for an acknowledgment. However, this packet is lost, and no acknowledgment is sent. Eventually, station B times out and retransmits message 4.

6. This time the message 4 is received, and station A sends an acknowledgment. The window size value of 2 indicates that station B can send two more packets before receiving another acknowledgment.

cial system packets can be sent to change the window size in response to changing congestion conditions on the network. Box 21.1 shows an example of a message flow using the SPP protocols.

PACKET EXCHANGE PROTOCOL

The XNS *Packet Exchange Protocol* (PEP) supports the sending of one request packet and the receiving of one reply packet. If the reply packet is not received, the request packet is retransmitted. However, sequence numbers are not used. This protocol is used as part of the name service, which we describe later.

MINDS PROGRAMMING INTERFACE

3Com supports a programming interface that operates at the level of the MS-DOS Internal Network Drive Scheme (MINDS) protocol. The various MINDS services are constructed in modules that can be treated as serial devices. These services can then be invoked using either the standard DOS interface to serial devices or a more streamlined interface that bypasses

DOS. When an application program uses this interface, a bind process takes place when the program starts. The bind identifies all the MINDS modules that are needed by the application and makes sure they are available.

REDIRECTOR/SMB PROTOCOL   At the level of the application layer, 3Com provides compatibility with the IBM PC LAN Program, allowing programs that use IBM's Redirector/SMB interface to run also on 3+ networks. 3Com uses the Microsoft Redirector, which is compatible with the redirector used by IBM. The Redirector intercepts DOS function calls that represent I/O requests that need to be redirected to a server and generates SMB control blocks. 3+Share provides the function needed to process Redirector output, including 2AH and 2FH interrupts, and to direct SMBs to the server. 3+Share on the server provides the functions needed to

BOX 21.2   FSP transactions

Core Transactions

tree connect	tree disconnect
create directory	delete directory
create spool file	open file spool byte block
close spool file	create file
close file	return print queue
flush file	negotiate protocol
read from file	write to file
delete file	create temporary file
rename file	make new file
get file attributes	seek set file attributes
get disk attributes	lock byte range
unlock byte range	check directory path
search directory	process exit

3Com Extensions

share object	unshare object
modify object	get info about shared object
add a user	delete a user
force off a user	get networked disks
get tree connects of a session	get names and session IDs of connected users
close a session	force shutdown service

process the SMB requests and create appropriately formatted output to be sent back to the Redirector and to the application program.

3Com supports all the DOS function calls associated with DOS file-sharing and record-locking facilities, as well as the standard server functions. The approach used is to support a core set of the SMB formats, known as the *file/print server protocol* (FSP). In addition, 3Com provides a set of extensions to FSP, using a method defined by Microsoft for adding extensions. The core FSP transactions and the extensions are shown in Box 21.2. The core set supports DOS 3.1 applications. The extensions are used to provide additional services, such as sharing, unsharing, and modifying resources and adding new users to a server.

In order to support the Redirector/SMB protocol, an emulation of the NETBIOS interface is provided. This interface accepts packets from the Redirector and also 2AH and 2FH interrupts and transmits packets across the network. 3Com emulates the NETBIOS function calls necessary to support the sending of SMB packets to the server. 3Com has also integrated the NETBIOS interface with its MINDS protocols so that NETBIOS-based applications are able to communicate across interconnected networks.

Figure 21.2 illustrates the basic 3+ architecture. The Redirector and NET-

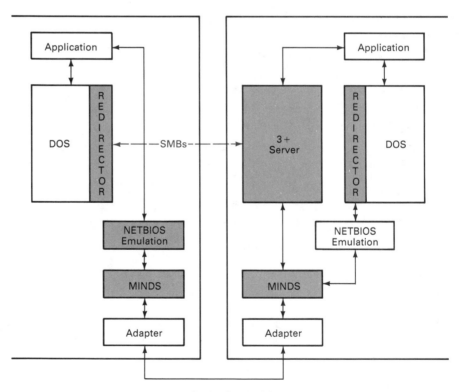

Figure 21.2   3+ architecture

BIOS emulation functions process the interrupts associated with the networking DOS function calls. The Redirector and server portion of the 3+ network operating system communicate using the SMB protocols. The MINDS protocols provide reliable data transfer and routing services needed to deliver SMB requests and responses across the network.

NAME SERVICE

The name service provides another protocol that operates at the level of the application layer. This service is modeled on the XNS service known as the *clearinghouse*. The name service uses the XNS Courier protocol to define the call and response format used to request and return name information from the central name directory. If the amount of information being returned requires more than one packet to send, the Sequenced Packet Protocol is used. If the response can be sent in a single packet, the simpler Packet Exchange Protocol is used.

SUMMARY

The 3+Share network operating system provides file sharing, printer sharing, and a directory-based name service. 3+Mail provides a messaging service. Connectivity products include 3+Route, which allows 3+ networks to be interconnected using remote communication facilities; 3+Remote, which allows a personal computer to access a 3+ network using remote communication facilities; 3+NetConnect, which allows 3+ networks to be interconnected using a direct connection; and 3+3270, which allows 3+ network stations to access an SNA host as a 3270 terminal.

3+Share supports the use of Ethernet, CSMA/CD, or token ring as the access control method. The Microcom Network Protocol is used to provide reliable communication over asynchronous lines. An implementation of the XNS transport and network layer protocols, known as MS-DOS Internal Network Drive Scheme (MINDS), is used to provide routing and data transfer. Routing is based on an address structure that contains a network number and on the use of distributed routing tables. Stations known as routers use their routing tables to determine the next network and the station address to use for a message. The Sequenced Packet Protocol (SPP) uses sequence numbers and acknowledgments to provide reliable data transfer and flow control. The Packet Exchange Protocol (PEP) uses acknowledgments to provide reliable data transfer for a single packet. At the application level, 3+Share uses the Microsoft Redirector and emulates IBM's SMB protocols and the NETBIOS interface. A name service is also provided at the application level.

22 NOVELLE: ADVANCED NETWARE

Novelle, Inc., offers a network operating system known as *Advanced NetWare* that can be used with a number of LAN architectures. It can be used with CSMA/CD networks, like AT&T's STARLAN and the IBM PC Network. It can also be used with token ring architectures, including the IBM Token Ring Network and Proteon's ProNET. And it supports a number of proprietary architectures, including Novelle's own S-Net and the Nestar Plan 2000.

The basic Advanced NetWare operating system product includes a number of functions, including file sharing, printer sharing, electronic mail, remote access, and the interconnection of Advanced NetWare–compatible LANs. Additional products provide communication between network stations and asynchronous devices, and a gateway to an SNA network.

FILE SHARING   Users can be granted access to a directory or subdirectory. When access is granted, the user's particular access rights are also specified. Possible access rights include *read, write, open, create, delete, parental* (can control subdirectories), *search,* and *modify* (can change file attributes). The user can define the access characteristics of a particular file by using file attributes. A file can be *read-only* or *read/write*, and *sharable* or *nonsharable*. Applications running on Advanced NetWare are able to employ standard DOS facilities for specifying file access modes and sharing modes and for using record locking. Advanced NetWare also provides a special implementation of record locking known as a shared physical lock, or read-only lock. With this facility, any string of bytes on disk can be locked. Users are allowed to access the bytes, but only for reading; none of the users are allowed to update these bytes on the disk.

PRINTER SHARING   Printer sharing allows print jobs to be spooled to queues that are managed by server printers. Queue management facilities include canceling print jobs, reordering queues, holding and releasing jobs, redirecting a queue to a different printer, spooling jobs and printing jobs from the spool, and using preprinted forms for printing.

ELECTRONIC MAIL   Advanced NetWare includes an electronic mail facility that allows various types of documents, including letters, files, and memos, to be composed, filed, and sent to individual users and groups of users. Messages can be sent in a way that will cause a message to be displayed on the receiving user's display screen, notifying the user that a message is waiting.

REMOTE ACCESS   The *remote access* facility allows a personal computer to access a LAN using standard telephone lines. The remote personal computer then acts as another station on the network and has access to the full facilities of the network. The Advanced NetWare operating system provides the support for remote access on the network side. The remote personal computer uses another program, called *NetWare Remote,* to provide the facilities on its side.

LAN-TO-LAN CONNECTION   Advanced NetWare includes the ability to interconnect NetWare-compatible LANs. The networks can be of different types; for example, an Ethernet network can be connected to a token ring network. Also, the connection can be made directly, if the networks are physically contiguous, or through telephone lines, if the networks are remote from one another. A server containing multiple network adapter cards acts as a bridge between the networks. A single server can be used to connect up to four networks. A separate product called *NetWare Bridge* allows an ordinary network station, rather than a server, to be used as the bridge. Any of the LAN products that support Advanced NetWare can be interconnected through the NetWare Bridge facility.

ASYNCHRONOUS COMMUNICATION   A separate product, the *Asynchronous Communications Server* (ACS), provides stations on a LAN with the ability to communicate with asynchronous devices. Communication takes place through a dedicated communication server, which can support up to 12 asynchronous serial ports. Using ACS, a network station can communicate with a remote host, a public telecommunications service such as The Source, MCI Mail, or Dow Jones, or a remote asynchronous device such a terminal or personal computer.

SNA GATEWAY

Another package, the *NetWare SNA Gateway,* allows LAN stations to communicate with a remote SNA host using an SDLC connection. A nondedicated network station, which emulates a 3274 controller, is used as the gateway. The network station that implements the gateway emulates a 3278 display or a 3287 printer. The NetWare SNA Gateway supports file transfers between the host and a network station and also printing on any network printer.

NAMING AND USER ACCESS

A user's access to various network resources is based on that user's profile. When a person is established as an authorized user on the network by the network administrator, a profile is created for that user. The profile specifies all the resources, such as servers, printers, directories, and files, that the user is allowed to access. For directories, the type of access that the user is allowed is also specified in the profile. Thus different users can have different access rights to a given directory. Group names can also be defined and given profiles. Users that are members of the group then have the access rights specified in the group profile as well as their own individual access rights. When a user logs on to the network, the stored profile information determines the resources to which the user has access.

Users and network resources, including servers, printers, directories, and files, are assigned unique names. Resources and users are defined as belonging to a particular server. A combination of the server name and the resource or user name is then used to identify uniquely the user or resource being accessed. If a user has access to more than one server, the user name must be defined for each.

UTILITY PROGRAMS AND COMMANDS

A number of utility programs and commands are provided as part of the Advanced NetWare operating system. Box 22.1 lists the utility programs. Some of the commands provided by the operating system relate to server and monitor functions; these are shown in Box 22.2. Other commands support the user directly; these are shown in Box 22.3.

BOX 22.1   Advanced NetWare utility programs

Utility	Function
CPMOFF	Disables the automatic system OPEN of closed files
CPMON	Enables the automatic system OPEN of closed files
EOJOFF	Disables the shell mode in which an end-of-job indication is sent by the shell to the network operating system each time a new command is requested by the command interpreter
EOJON	Enables the shell mode in which an end-of-job indication is sent by the shell to the network operating system each time a new command is requested by the command interpreter
GROUP	Assigns several users the same network identity (as one group)
HIDEFILE	Marks a specified file as hidden so that it will not show in a directory search and cannot be deleted or copied over
MAKEUSER	Adds users to the network and grants them all rights to all directories
PASSFIX	Repairs the password files if they have been damaged
PASSWORD	Creates and edits user definitions, creates directories, and assigns network rights to users, to groups, and in directories
SHOWFILE	Makes visible a file hidden by HIDEFILE

BOX 22.2   Advanced NetWare monitor and server commands

Command	Function
ATTACH	Connects multiple servers
BROADCAST	Broadcasts a message to all network stations
CHANGE QUEUE	Rearranges print queue
CLEAR MESSAGE	Clears message line
CLEAR STATION	Effective cold boot for specified station
CONSOLE	Switches a file server or station from local DOS mode into console mode
DISABLE LOGIN	Disables login of additional network stations
DISMOUNT	Dismounts removable volumes
DOS	Switches a file server or station from console mode into local DOS mode
DOWN	Writes cache buffers to disk in preparation for a network shutdown
ENABLE LOGIN	Enables login of network stations

312

BOX 22.2 *(Continued)*

FORM CHECK	Prints a row of 80 asterisks without a line feed at current form position for the specified printer number
FORM SET	Issues a form feed to specified printer
KILL PRINTER	Stops specified printer
KILL QUEUE	Removes specified job from print queue of specified printer
MONITOR	Displays system monitor screen for specified station
MOUNT	Mounts removable volumes
OFF	Turns off monitor display and clears screen
QUEUE	Displays job list for specified printer
REROUTE PRINTER	Reroutes job list of first specified printer to newly specified printer
REWIND PRINTER	Stops specified printer, backs up the specified number of pages in the printing file, and resumes printing from that point
SET TIME	Sets the system date and time
START PRINTER	Resumes transmission to specified printer
STOP PRINTER	Stops transmission to specified printer
TIME	Displays system time and date

BOX 22.3 Advanced NetWare user commands

Command	Function
CASTOFF	Disables message interrupts from other network stations and the system console
CASTON	Enables a station to receive messages from other users
CHKVOL	Displays disk allocation statistics for a specified volume
ENDSPOOL	Terminates LST: device capture mode. Places the captured file in the spool queue
ERASEDIR	Removes an empty subdirectory
FLAG	Displays or modifies a file's sharable read/write status
FLAGDIR	Displays or modifies the access attributes of a (sub)directory
GRANT	Grants trustee privileges for a particular directory to a user or user group

(Continued)

BOX 22.3 *(Continued)*

LARCHIVE	Archives network files to local disks
LISTDIR	Lists subdirectories directly beneath the specified path
LOGIN	Identifies and logs a user onto the network and initializes the user's environment
LOGOUT	Logs a user out of the network system
LRESTORE	Restores files that were stored on local disks by means of the LARCHIVE command
MAKEDIR	Makes a new subdirectory
MAP	Assigns or maps a network drive to a directory path
NARCHIVE	Archives network files to system disks
NCOPY	Provides a fast way to copy files within network directories
NETXXX.COM	NetWare station interface shell
NPRINT	Queues files for printing by the network
NRESTORE	Restores files for printing by the network
PURGE	Permanently erases files that have been marked for deletion by a previous erase
Q(ueue)	Displays network print spooler information including a list of files in the queue; allows for deletion of unwanted entries
RENDIR	Renames a subdirectory
REVOKE	Revokes trustee privileges for a particular directory from a user or group
RIGHTS	Describes a user's rights in a particular directory
SALVAGE	Recovers files after they have been erased
SEND	Sends messages directly to other network users or to the system console
SETLOGIN	Edits script that is used by the LOGIN command to set up the user's customized network environment automatically at login time
SETPASS	Changes a password
SHOWDIR	Shows the directory tree structure of the specified volume, drive, or path
SPOOL	Reroutes LST: device to the network print spooler
SYSTIME	Displays the current network system time and date and synchronizes the network station clock with the system clock
TARCHIVE	Archives network files to tape cartridge
TLIST	Displays user and group trustees and their privileges for specified subdirectory
TRESTORE	Restores files that were stored on a tape cartridge by means of the TARCHIVE command
UDIR	Performs a global file search
USERLIST	Displays a list of users who are currently logged onto the network
WHOAMI	Displays the user information for the requesting station

IBM COMPATIBILITY Advanced NetWare provides compatibility with the IBM PC LAN Program at the program interface level. Advanced NetWare supports the DOS function calls associated with networking by emulating the functions provided by the IBM Redirector and the SMB protocols. It also provides complete IBM NETBIOS emulation. This allows software packages and programs that have been written or adapted to run using the IBM interfaces to run using the Advanced NetWare operating system as well.

ADVANCED NETWARE SYSTEM ARCHITECTURE Figure 22.1 shows the system architecture used by Advanced NetWare. The shell performs the basic functions required to emulate the Redirector and the SMB protocols. There are some differences between the ways the Advanced NetWare shell and the Redirector operate. With the Redirector, all interrupts are first processed by DOS. DOS passes 21H interrupts to the Redirector, which then formats SMBs and passes them to NETBIOS for transmission across the network. With Advanced NetWare, all interrupts are captured by the shell. Those that do not relate to networking are then passed to DOS. Those related to networking are formatted using the *Network File Service Protocol* (NFSP) and passed to the *Internet Packet Exchange* (IPX) protocol for transmission across the network. (These protocols are discussed later.) Interrupts normally passed straight to NETBIOS (interrupts 2AH and 2FH) are processed by the Advanced NetWare NETBIOS emulation function and are also transmitted across the network using IPX.

On the server side, NFSP requests are received and processed by the server function. One difference here is that the Advanced NetWare server function interfaces directly with the hardware in the server machine, rather than going through DOS. Replies are formatted in accord with NFSP, and responses are returned to the requesting network station.

REDIRECTOR/SMB EMULATION Advanced NetWare emulates all DOS function calls associated with networking, with the exception of certain 2FH interrupts that are specific to the use of the SMB protocol. It supports a number of additional function calls. These calls provide functions such as the shared physical (read-only) lock, deadlock prevention by locking a group of records at one time, the processing of orphan locks, and a semaphore system that can be used for synchronization processing. The additional calls, which are all part of interrupt 21H, are shown in Box 22.4.

In addition to emulating the Redirector and the SMB protocols, Advanced

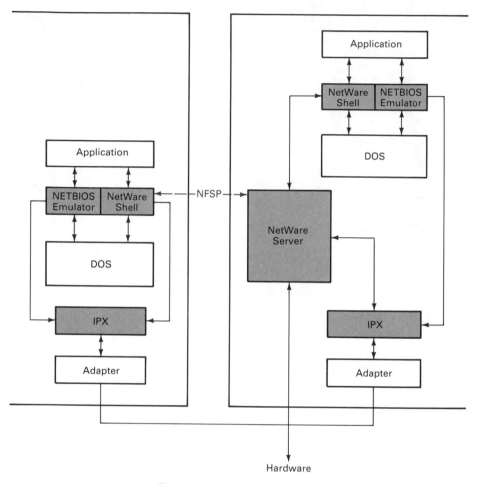

Figure 22.1   NetWare architecture

BOX 22.4   Extended function calls

Extended Open File	Release Record String
Release Physical Record	Release Record String Set
Clear Physical Record	Clear Record String
FCB Lock Physical Record	Clear Record String Set
FCB Release Physical Record	End of Job
FCB Clear Physical Record	System Logout
Lock Physical Record	Allocate Resource

BOX 22.4   *(Continued)*

Release Physical Record Set	Deallocate Resource
Clear Physical Record Set	Get Volume Statistics
Open a Semaphore	Return No. of Local Disks
Examine a Semaphore	Get Station Number
Wait Semaphore	Set Error Mode
Signal a Semaphore	Set Broadcast Mode
Close a Semaphore	Modify LST: Device
Get and Set Lock Mode Spec.	Print Spooling Request
Begin Transaction Update	System Pipe Request Spec.
End Transaction Update	Directory Request Spec.
Transaction Backout	Login Request Spec.
Begin Transaction	Set File Attribute
End Transaction	Update File Size
Log Personal File	Network File to File Copy
Lock File Set	Return Data Time String
Release File	Set Close Mode
Release File Set	Set Shell Base Status
Clear File	Return Shell Version
Clear File Set	Log File ASCIIZ String
Log Record String	Release File ASCIIZ
Lock Record String Set	Clear File ASCIIZ String

NetWare allows both the Advanced NetWare shell and the Microsoft Redirector to coexist in the same network station. This lets the network station communicate both with Advanced NetWare servers using the shell and with other types of servers using the Redirector.

ADVANCED NETWARE FILE SERVER PROTOCOL   The *NetWare File Server Protocol* (NFSP) is responsible for packetizing requests and data for transmission over the network to and from a server. NFSP provides all the functions that are part of the SMB protocols, including connection control, file and directory access, printer sharing, and messaging. NFSP also provides a number of additional functions related to application software copy protection, communication, user maintenance, and data access synchronization. Box 22.5 lists the various functions that are provided as part of NFSP.

BOX 22.5 Advanced NetWare File Service protocol functions

Service Connection Maintenance

Create Service Connection
Destroy Service Connection
Check Server Version
Negotiate Buffer Size
Identify Client (Login)
Release Client (Logout)
End of Task
Check Connection
Request Being Processed

File Maintenance

Open a File
Close a File
Read from a File
Write to a File
Give File Access to a Task
Commit a File
Create a File
Create a New File
Create a Temporary File
Rename a File
Erase a File
Search for a File
Get a File's Attributes
Set a File's Attributes
Get a File's Current Size
Get a File's Status Info
Set a File's Status Info
Copy from One File to Another
Recover an Erased File
Commit All Erased Files

Data Access Synchronization

Log/Lock a File Byte Range
Lock All Logged Byte Ranges
Release a File Byte Range
Release All Byte Ranges

Directory Maintenance

Create a Directory
Destroy a Directory
Rename a Directory
Search for Subdirectories
Get Directory's Status Info
Set Directory's Status Info
Get Client's Access Privileges
Modify Directory's Max Access
Get a Directory's Trustee List
Add a Trustee to a Directory
Remove Trustee from a Directory
Create a Permanent Dir Handle
Destroy a Directory Handle
Reset Handle to New Path
Get Handle's Current Path

User Maintenance

Create a New User
Delete a User
Change a User Name
Map User Name to Trustee Name
Map Trustee Number to User Name
Search the Bindery
Change a User's Security Level
Add a Property to a User
Remove a Property from a User
Change Prop. Security Status
Scan a User's Properties
Read a Property's Value
Write a Property's Value
Verify a User's Password
Change a User's Password
Add a User to a Group
Remove a User from a Group
Check User's Membership in Group
Get User's Trustee Dir. Paths
Get Client's Bind. Access Level
Clear a File Byte Range

BOX 22.5   *(Continued)*

Clear All Byte Ranges
Log/Lock a Complete File
Lock All Logged Files
Release a Complete File
Release All Files
Clear a Complete File
Clear All Files
Log/Lock a Synch. String
Lock All Synch. Strings
Release a Synch. String
Release All Synch. Strings
Clear a Synch. String
Clear All Synch. Strings
Open a Semaphore
Examine a Semaphore
Wait on a Semaphore
Signal a Semaphore
Close a Semaphore

File Server Statistics

Get Volume's Usage Statistics
Get Handle's Usage Statistics
Get Volume's Mount Number
Get Volume's Name
Get User's Volume Usage Stat.
Get Connection's User Status
Read Server's Time Clock

Communications

Open Communication Pipe
Close Communication Pipe
Check Communications Pipe Status
Send a Message
Retrieve a Message
Log a General Message
Check for a General Message
Disable General Messages
Enable General Messages
Map User to a Connection
Map Connection to an Address

Printing Services

Create a Print Catch File
Add Data to a Catch File
Close and Queue Catch File
Set Print Parameters
Queue on Existing File
Search a Spool Queue
Delete Job from Spool Queue
Report Current Printer Status

*Application Software Copy
Protection*

Flag File Execute Only
Load Execute-Only File
Get Server's Serial Number
Verify Software Serialization
Restrict Maximum Program Users

INTERNET PACKET EXCHANGE   The NETBIOS emulation functions of Advanced NetWare provide services at the level of the session, transport, and network layers. In addition, Advanced NetWare implements internetworking capabilities through the use of the *Internet Packet Exchange* (IPX) protocol. IPX is an implementation of the XNS *Internetwork Datagram Protocol*. This protocol provides best-effort delivery of packets, using underlying routing services. If guaranteed delivery is required with Advanced NetWare, using sequence numbers and acknowledgments, individual networks must implement these functions.

To handle routing, each network in a connected internet is defined and named. A central device on the network manages a list of the resources that are part of that network. Calls are then made to specific names. The network name identifies the particular network to which the call should be routed. The rest of the name then identifies the particular destination within that network.

SUMMARY

Advanced NetWare offers file sharing, printer sharing, electronic mail, remote access, interconnection of NetWare-compatible networks using either direct or remote communication facilities, access to local or remote asynchronous devices, and access to an SNA host as a 3270 terminal. A name service allows all users and network resources to be accessed on a name basis.

Advanced NetWare supports a wide range of access control methods, including standard methods such as Ethernet, CSMA/CD, and token ring, and various proprietary access control methods. Advanced NetWare acts as a shell and intercepts all DOS interrupts. Nonnetworking interrupts are passed to DOS. Networking interrupts are processed by Advanced NetWare, emulating the Redirector and SMB protocols. This emulation is provided through the NetWare File Server Protocol, which packetizes requests and data for transmission to and from the server. The Internet Packet Exchange Protocol is used to provide datagram service for data transfer and a routing service. To handle routing, each network is assigned a name, and that name determines the route to be used.

23 APPLE COMPUTER: APPLETALK

The increasing popularity of Apple Computer's Macintosh in the business environment has led to increased use of Apple's networking protocol, *AppleTalk*. One reason for AppleTalk's popularity is, like the Macintosh itself, its ease of use. The AppleTalk protocols have been implemented and included in the Macintosh hardware and operating system software, so basic networking capability is included in every machine. The protocols are also built into other devices, such as Apple's laser printers, so Macintosh networks with shared printer capability can be built simply by plugging the devices together with the appropriate cables. Software is also available from Apple that allows a Macintosh computer to function as a file server on an AppleTalk network.

The basic AppleTalk network provides simple device-to-device communication and printer sharing. Network installation and reconfiguration are both easy and inexpensive. No special software, hardware, or administration is required. However, the basic AppleTalk network provides only a limited range of functions. There are also physical limits, with a maximum of 32 devices on a network, a total cable length of 300 m, and a data rate of 230 kbps.

However, many third-party developers have used AppleTalk as a development platform and provide products that extend the capabilities of AppleTalk-based networks. For example, it is possible to construct AppleTalk networks that include non-Apple devices, including IBM-compatible personal computers, DEC VAX machines, computers from Hewlett-Packard, and various UNIX computers. Some AppleTalk networks have been constructed without a single Apple device! Third-party products also extend the range of AppleTalk functions, providing such facilities as file sharing, electronic mail, communication servers, and printer spooling. Gateways provide dial-up access to AppleTalk networks and interconnection with Ethernet networks. Networks can be constructed that support larger numbers of devices, extend over longer distances, and operate at higher speeds. The wide range of capabilities available through these additional products has contributed to AppleTalk's popularity.

BASIC APPLETALK CHARACTERISTICS   The AppleTalk network uses a bus or tree topology, with shielded twisted-pair wire most frequently used as the transmission medium. Optical fiber and standard telephone wire is used with some AppleTalk implementations. The medium access protocol is carrier sense multiple access with collision avoidance (CSMA/ CA). The maximum number of devices on a single network is 32; however, interconnected networks can be constructed using bridges and routers. The maximum total cable length for an individual network is 300 m, and the data rate is 230.4 kbps (compared to rates in the range of 1–10 Mbps typical of other LAN architectures.)

The protocols defined by AppleTalk reflect the general layered architecture used for the OSI reference model and other network architectures. However, the protocols are not based on specific published standards, such as those in IEEE Project 802.

PHYSICAL SPECIFICATIONS   At the physical layer level, AppleTalk specifies electrical and mechanical characteristics for the network. These include the functions of bit encoding/decoding, signal transmission/reception, and carrier sense. The encoding method specified is known as FM-0. With FM-0, there is always a transition at the beginning of a bit cell. For a 0 bit, there is also a transition in the middle of the cell; for a 1 bit, there is no transition in the middle. Signal transmission is differential balanced-voltage, based on the EIA RS-422 signaling standard. Carrier sense provides an indication to higher layers of whether or not a transmission is in progress on the transmission medium.

APPLETALK LINK ACCESS PROTOCOL   At the level of the data link layer, AppleTalk specifies a protocol called *AppleTalk Link Access Protocol* (ALAP). This protocol provides for the transmission and reception of frames by devices on the network. It includes specifications for medium access management, addressing, data encapsulation/ decapsulation, and frame transmission dialogs.

Medium Access Management

As mentioned earlier, the medium access management method employed in AppleTalk is a form of carrier sense multiple access with collision avoidance

(CSMA/CA). When a node has a frame to send, it uses carrier sense to determine if the transmission medium is free. If it is, the node waits an additional time based on a pseudorandom number that it generates. If the medium is still free, the station transmits the frame. Since the amount of time the node waits is generated randomly, it is possible that two stations will transmit at the same time and that a collision will occur. Collisions cannot be detected directly. Instead, frame transmission dialogs are used to ensure that frames are sent without loss due to collision.

Addressing

Each node in the network has an 8-bit node identifier number, or node ID. Node IDs are not assigned externally or hard-coded in the devices. Instead, the node ID is assigned dynamically, at the time that a network station is powered on. When a node is activated, it attempts to determine its node ID by extracting it from some form of long-term memory (nonvolatile RAM or disk) or by generating a random number. It must then verify that this node ID is not already in use on the network. It does this by sending out a special frame to all nodes on the network, known as an ALAP inquiry control frame, and then waiting for an acknowledgment. If another node is using that node ID, it sends back an ALAP acknowledge control frame, indicating that the node ID is already in use. The new node then repeats the process, using another node ID value. If no acknowledgment is received, the node assumes that the node ID is unique.

Since there is no guarantee of frame delivery at this level, the node sends out the inquiry control frame repeatedly. Node IDs are divided into two classes: server node IDs (128 to 254) and user node IDs (1 to 127). Since servers are sometimes busy for extended periods of time and may be unable to reply to an inquiry frame, the inquiry frame must be rebroadcast for a longer period of time when the new node is a server node, using a server node ID.

Data Encapsulation/Decapsulation

Data encapsulation/decapsulation involves adding header and trailer information to form a frame before transmission and then removing that information after reception. The ALAP frame format is shown in Box 23.1.

Prior to transmitting a frame, ALAP sends out a *frame preamble,* consisting of two or more *flag* bytes. A flag byte consists of the bit pattern 01111110. This preamble is used to identify the beginning of a frame. To ensure that no data is mistaken for a flag byte, a technique known as *bit stuffing* is used. With bit stuffing, whenever a sequence of five 1 bits occurs in data outside a flag byte, ALAP inserts a 0 bit. This ensures that a sequence of six 1 bits will occur only in a flag byte. On the receiving side, ALAP removes a 0 bit from a sequence of five 1 bits followed by a 0 bit, thus restoring the data to its original form. This provides data transparency, meaning that any bit configuration can be transmitted without problem.

BOX 23.1 ALAP frame format

Frame Preamble		Frame				Frame Check Sequence	Frame Postamble	
Flag	Flag	Dest. Address	Source Address	ALAP Type	Data	Frame Check Sequence	Flag	Abort
1 Byte	1 Byte	1 Byte	1 Byte	1 Byte	0-600 Bytes	2 Bytes	1 Byte	1 Byte

Destination Address. The *destination address* contains the node ID of the destination node. The address can be of an individual node or a broadcast address. A node ID of 255 is the broadcast address; it indicates that the frame should be received by all nodes on the network.

Source Address. The *source address* contains the node ID of the sending node.

ALAP Type. The *ALAP type* field identifies the type of frame being transmitted. ALAP inquiry and acknowledgment control frames are used to determine a node ID value. ALAP request-to-send and clear-to-send frames are used in frame transmission dialogs.

Data. The *data* field contains user data and can vary in size from 0 to 600 bytes.

Frame Check Sequence. The *frame check sequence* contains a cyclic redundancy check value calculated using the destination address, source address, ALAP type, and data fields. When the receiving node receives the frame, it recalculates the CRC value and compares it to the value in the frame. If the two are not equal, an error is assumed to have occurred, and the frame is discarded.

The ALAP frame itself consists of a 3-byte header, a variable-length data field, and a frame check sequence field. These fields are summarized in Box 23.1. A *frame postamble* follows the frame. This consists of a flag byte and an *abort* sequence. The abort sequence consists of seven or more 1 bits.

Frame Transmission Dialogs

Frame transmission dialogs are used to ensure that frames are transmitted without collision. Two types of dialogs are defined: directed and broadcast. These dialogs are based on certain intervals, known as the *minimum interdialog gap* (IDG, 400 μsec) and the *maximum interframe gap* (IFG, 200 μsec).

A directed transmission is used when a frame is being sent to a single destination address. The sending node waits until the carrier has been idle for the minimum IDG and then waits an additional random wait time. It then sends out a request-to-send frame to the intended destination. The destination node returns a clear-to-send frame to the sending node if it is able to receive the transmission. If the sending node receives a clear-to-send frame within the maximum IFG, it transmits the data frame. If the clear-to-send is not received within the maximum IFG, the sending node repeats the process.

If the sending node finds that the carrier is busy at any point during the wait time, it *defers,* or waits, until the carrier is idle before starting the process again. If the sending node does not receive a clear-to-send frame within the maximum IFG, it assumes that a collision has occurred. The method used to determine the random wait time is based on recent transmission history, in terms of the number of deferrals and presumed collisions that have occurred while attempting to send the current data frame. As the number of deferrals and collisions increases, the range from which the random number is chosen increases. Thus when transmission loads are heavier and there is higher contention for the transmission medium, the random wait time will be selected from a larger range, spreading out in time the nodes contending for transmission.

A broadcast dialog is used when a frame is being sent to the broadcast address and is intended to be received by all nodes on the network. With a broadcast dialog, the sending node waits the minimum IDG and a random wait time and then sends out a request-to-send frame with a destination node ID of 255. It waits the maximum IFG time. If no transmission is sensed during that time, it transmits the data frame. If a transmission is detected during the maximum IFG time, the sending node repeats the process.

With either form of dialog, if the sending node is unable to transmit the data frame after 32 attempts, the station reports a failure condition to its higher-layer client.

DATAGRAM DELIVERY PROTOCOL

AppleTalk allows individual networks to be interconnected via bridges, or internet routers, forming what is called an *internet*. (AppleTalk uses the terms *bridge* and *internet router* interchangeably for a node that interconnects two networks. To be consistent with terminology used elsewhere in this book, we will use the term *router* in this context.) Internet connections can take the form of a device that belongs to two AppleTalk networks, a communication link between two devices on different networks, or even an intermediary backbone network to which two AppleTalk networks connect. These possibilities are illustrated in Fig. 23.1. The Datagram Delivery Protocol (DDP) operates at the network layer level to provide for the delivery of datagrams, either within a network or across the internet. Delivery is on a best-effort basis, with error recovery being left to higher layers.

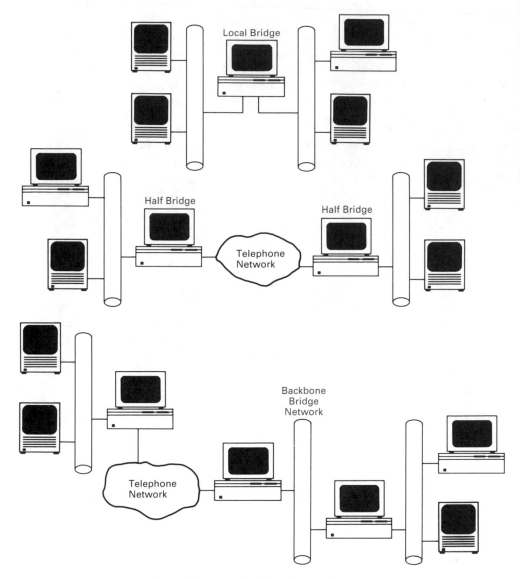

Figure 23.1   AppleTalk bridge configurations

Internet Addressing

AppleTalk allows multiple communicating processes within a single node. These processes are known as *socket clients*. A socket client employs a logical entity, called a *socket,* to send and receive datagrams on the internet. Each socket is identified by an 8-bit socket number. Each network in an internet has a 16-bit network number that uniquely identifies it. A complete *internet address*

BOX 23.2 DDP packet format

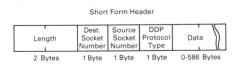

Short Form Header

Length	Dest. Socket Number	Source Socket Number	DDP Protocol Type	Data
2 Bytes	1 Byte	1 Byte	1 Byte	0-586 Bytes

Long Form Header

Hop Count/ Length	Checksum	Destination Network Number	Source Network Number	Dest. Node ID	Source Node ID	Dest. Socket Number	Source Socket Number	DDP Protocol Type	Data
2 Bytes	2 Bytes	2 Bytes	2 Bytes	1 Byte	1 Byte	1 Byte	1 Byte	1 Byte	0-586 Bytes

Hop Count. The *hop count* field occupies the first 6 bits of the first byte. This field is used with the long-form header to keep track of the number of routers that the packet has visited. If a router receives a packet with a hop count of 15, it does not forward the packet to another router but will deliver it if its destination is on the local network.

Length. The *length* field, which is 10 bits long, gives the length of the packet in bytes, including the packet header. When a packet is received, the actual received length is compared to this value, and the packet is rejected if they do not match.

Checksum. The *checksum* field in the long-form header is also used for the detection of errors. A value is calculated using the bytes in the packet that follow the checksum field. The destination node recalculates the value, compares it to the stored value, and rejects the packet if they do not agree. Use of a checksum is optional.

Network Numbers. The *destination network number* identifies the network in which the destination node is located. The *source network number* identifies the network in which the source node is located. They are included in the long-form header so the packet can be routed to its destination.

Node IDs. The *destination node ID* identifies the node to which the packet is being sent. The *source node ID* identifies the node sending the packet. These fields are not needed in the short-form header since they are present in the header that is added to the packet by ALAP.

Socket Numbers. The *destination socket number* identifies the socket within the destination node to which the packet is being sent. The *source socket number* identifies the socket within the source node from which the packet was sent.

DDP Protocol Type. The *DDP protocol type* field identifies whether a short-form or long-form header is being used.

Data. The *data* field contains the client data being sent in the packet. It is a variable-length field that can range from 0 to 256 bytes.

then consists of a network number, a node ID, and a socket number. It identifies both the node and the process within the node (socket) that is communicating.

Routing

A key function of the Datagram Delivery Protocol is routing datagrams, or packets, within the internet. If a datagram is being sent to a destination node on the same network as the source node, it is transmitted directly using ALAP. If the destination node is on another network, the source node sends it to any router node on the local network. The router then uses a stored routing table to determine the next destination for the datagram and sends it there. The next destination can be another router or, if the destination network has been reached, the final destination node. A separate protocol, the Routing Table Maintenance Protocol (RTMP), has been defined for constructing and maintaining routing tables. This protocol is described later in this chapter.

DDP Packet Format

The formats used for a datagram, or packet, as part of DDP are described in Box 23.2. A datagram consists of a DDP header followed by data. Two header formats are used: short and long. The short-form header is used when the source and destination nodes are both on the same network. The long-form header, which contains information needed for routing across the internet, is used when the source and destination nodes are on different networks.

ROUTING TABLE MAINTENANCE PROTOCOL   The *Routing Table Maintenance Protocol* (RTMP) provides for establishing and maintaining routing tables used by DDP as part of its routing function. Each router maintains a complete routing table. For each destination network number, the routing table indicates where the packet should next be transmitted and how many hops are left to reach the destination network. Routers periodically exchange their routing tables, allowing changes to be propagated throughout the internet.

Each router node is attached to a network or communication link through a port and can have any number of ports. The ports are numbered, and certain information is stored in the router about each port. For a port directly attached to an AppleTalk network, the router knows the number of that network and its node ID in that network. For a port connected to a backbone network, the router knows its node ID in that network. When a router is turned on, it builds an initial routing table, called the *routing seed*, from information it contains. For each directly connected AppleTalk network, the router records the port number, network number, and a number of hops of zero. As the router then receives routing table information from other routers, it adds to its routing table, until it has complete information on the internet. An example of this is shown in Fig.

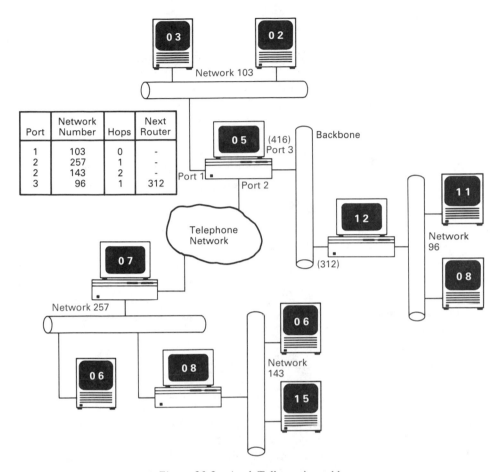

Port	Network Number	Hops	Next Router
1	103	0	-
2	257	1	-
2	143	2	-
3	96	1	312

Figure 23.2 AppleTalk routing table

23.2, which shows the routing table for node 05. The first entry in the table is its routing seed. The second and third entries are built when it receives routing information from node 07 in network 257. The last entry comes from node 12 in network 96 and reflects the node ID of node 12 as part of the backbone network (312). This form of the node ID reflects the addressing structure used in the backbone network, which may be different from the AppleTalk node ID.

RTMP also keeps track of how long it has been since a particular entry in the table has been confirmed by receipt of routing information from another router. If an entry is unconfirmed for longer than a certain period, it is presumed that the route no longer exists and the entry is removed.

With this approach to routing information, routes are discovered and maintained dynamically, with a minimum of information (network numbers and backbone node addresses) being predefined. This reduces the network administration requirements for building and reconfiguring even very complex internets.

NAME BINDING PROTOCOL

AppleTalk includes a name service, defined in its *Name Binding Protocol* (NBP). Names can be assigned to network-visible entities, such as socket clients and services available over the network. A particular entity is allowed to have several names, known as *aliases*. A name consists of three fields: object, type, and zone. The object field identifies the entity, the type field provides information about its attributes, and the zone field identifies a subset of the internet to which the entity belongs.

Each node maintains a *name table* that contains the name-to-internet-address mappings for all entities in that node. The *name directory* consists of all name tables in the internet. The NBP protocol provides for the following services:

- **Name Registration.** This allows an entity to add a name to the name table. Before a name is added, a check is made to ensure that the name is not already in use.

- **Name Deletion.** This allows an entity to remove its names from the name table.

- **Name Lookup.** This allows a user application to determine the internet address associated with a given name.

- **Name Confirmation.** This allows a user application to confirm that a particular internet address is still valid for a given name.

Zones

An internet can be divided into *zones*. Each zone contains a subset of the networks in the internet, and each network belongs to only one zone. When a name lookup is performed, it is done only within the zone specified as part of the name. This reduces the traffic generated when a lookup is performed.

The *Zone Information Protocol* (ZIP) defines how zone information is generated and managed. Each router maintains a *Zone Information Table* (ZIT) that contains network number and zone name information for each network in the internet. When a router is attached directly to an AppleTalk network, its port information also contains the zone name for that network. When a router is turned on, this information is stored in its ZIT. The router then checks its routing table to identify additional network numbers in the internet. For any additional network numbers, it sends out ZIP queries, asking for corresponding zone names. A router receiving a ZIP query responds with a ZIP reply for any zone names that it knows.

The ZIP process periodically checks the routing table to discover new network numbers for the ZIT. The ZIP process also identifies network numbers that no longer appear in the routing table and should be removed from the ZIT.

APPLETALK TRANSACTION PROTOCOL

At the transport level, AppleTalk includes the *AppleTalk Transaction Protocol* (ATP), which provides reliable, loss-free delivery of packets from a source socket to a destination socket. ATP is based on the idea of a *transaction,* which consists of a request and its corresponding response. The request must consist of a single packet, and the response can consist of from one to eight packets. Each request is assigned a 16-bit transaction ID. This transaction ID is also included in the response, allowing a response to be correlated with its corresponding request. If a response is not received within a specified time limit, the request is retransmitted. This mechanism is used to ensure that the request is received and processed.

Each request contains a bit map that indicates how many packets are expected in the response. If a partial response is received, the request is retrans-

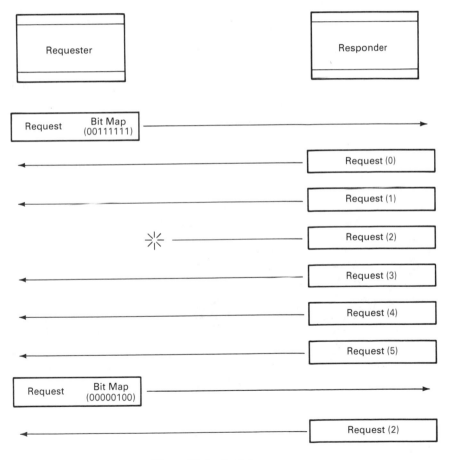

Figure 23.3 Partial response

mitted with an altered bit map so that only the missing response packets need to be sent again. This process is illustrated in Fig. 23.3. If a responder does not have enough data to make up the requested number of packets, the responder is able to send an end-of-message signal.

BOX 23.3   ATP packet format

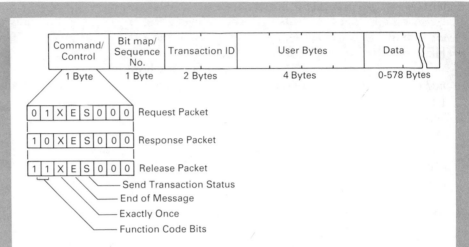

Command/Control. The *command/control* field is used for several purposes. The *function code* identifies the type of packet being sent as a transaction request, a transaction response, or a release packet, used with an exactly-one transaction to indicate that the results no longer need to be stored. The *exactly-once* bit is used to identify an exactly-once transaction. The *end-of-message* bit is used to indicate the end of the data being sent by the responder. The *send transaction status* bit is used with an exactly-once transaction when the responder has limited buffer space and needs to know as soon as possible which response packets no longer need to be stored.

Bit Map/Sequence Number. On a transaction request, this field contains the *bit map* indicating the number of packets expected in the response. On a transaction response, this field contains a *sequence number,* used to sequence the packets in the response.

Transaction ID. The *transaction ID* identifies a particular transaction and is used to correlate a response with its request.

User Bytes. The *user bytes* are not defined as part of the ATP protocol and are left for use by higher-level protocols.

Data. The *data* field contains client data and can vary in length from 0 to 578 bytes.

Two types of transaction are defined: *at-least-once transactions* and *exactly-once transactions*. With at-least-once transactions, if the request is retransmitted, the responder client reprocesses the request and sends another response. With an exactly-once transaction, the first time the request is processed, the results are saved. If the same request is retransmitted, the saved results are sent again as the response, and the request is not reprocessed.

The packet format used with ATP is shown in Box 23.3. An ATP packet consists of an ATP header followed by data.

OTHER PROTOCOLS

Additional AppleTalk protocols are under development, including a session-level protocol known as *AppleTalk Session Protocol* (ASP). This protocol provides for the establishment of a session between network entities and for the exchange of commands and replies using the session. Sequence numbers are used to ensure that commands are received in sequence and without duplication. Other protocols address print servers (*Printer Access Protocol,* or PAP) and provide a transmission test function (*Echo Protocol,* or EP).

SUMMARY

AppleTalk uses a bus or tree topology and operates at a data rate of 230.4 kbps. At the level of the data link layer, AppleTalk defines the AppleTalk Link Access Protocol. In ALAP, the medium access protocol is CSMA/CA. Each node is identified by its node ID, which is dynamically assigned when the node is turned on. AppleTalk's frame format uses a frame preamble, destination and source addresses, an ALAP type field, data, a frame check sequence, and a frame postamble. The beginning and end of a frame are identified by flag bytes. Bit stuffing is used to ensure that data is not mistaken for a flag byte. Frame transmission dialogs are used to ensure transmission of a data frame without collision.

At the level of the network layer, AppleTalk defines the Datagram Delivery Protocol. DDP provides for the delivery of packets across an internet based on an internet address consisting of a network number, node ID, and socket number. Routing is performed using information contained in routing tables. This information is constructed and maintained dynamically by the exchange of routing information between router nodes.

AppleTalk includes a name service. An AppleTalk name consists of an object, type, and zone. Each node maintains a name table containing the name-to-internet-address mappings for all names used in that node. Name registration, deletion, lookup, and confirmation services are provided. Name lookup is done on a zone basis, where a zone consists of a subset of the networks in the internet. Like routing information, zone information is constructed and maintained dynamically.

The AppleTalk Transaction Protocol provides for the loss-free delivery of packets between a requester and a responder. A transaction request consists of a single packet and a transaction response of from one to eight packets. Each transaction request is assigned a transaction ID, which is included in the transaction response. If a response is not received, the request is retransmitted. An at-least-once transaction is reprocessed if it is retransmitted. An exactly-once transaction is not reprocessed if it is retransmitted; the results of the processing are saved and sent again if the transaction is retransmitted.

24 AT&T: STARLAN

AT&T's STARLAN local area network is a CSMA/CD network; however, it operates at a transmission rate of 1 Mbps, rather than the 10 Mbps rate associated with Ethernet and other CSMA/CD physical transmission standards. The network is designed to use unshielded twisted-wire-pair cable, which means that already installed telephone wire can be used as the network transmission medium in many instances. Specifications for the 1-Mbps transmission using unshielded twisted-wire pairs are being standardized by the IEEE Project 802 committee. The goals of the STARLAN specification are listed in Box 24.1.

BOX 24.1 STARLAN goals

- Provide for low-cost networks, as relating to both equipment and cabling.
- Make it possible to use telephone-type building wiring—in particular, spare wiring when available.
- Provide for easy installation, reconfiguration, and service.
- Ensure interconnectability of independently developed stations and hubs.
- Ensure fairness.

STARLAN supports the use of both the MS-DOS and the UNIX operating systems on the network stations and servers that are part of the network. The services provided vary with the combination of server and network station.

- **DOS Server/DOS Station.** With this combination, a DOS-based server provides services to DOS-based network stations. Services include file sharing, with the file-locking and record-locking facilities associated with DOS 3.1 being supported. Printer sharing is also supported, with printer queue query and management. Electronic mail is available, and communication with asynchronous devices is supported. Resources are accessed on the basis of names. Both a full-screen menu interface and a command-line interface are available to the end user.

- **UNIX Server/UNIX Station.** With this combination, a UNIX-based server can provide services to both UNIX stations and DOS stations. When a UNIX network station is used, printer sharing with queue query and management is supported. File transfer is supported, but not remote file access or sharing of file access among multiple users. Peer-to-peer communication and electronic mail are available, along with communication with asynchronous devices. Resources are accessed on the basis of names. With UNIX network stations, a full-screen menu interface is available.

- **UNIX Server/DOS Station.** When a DOS network station is used with a UNIX server, the network station is able to store files on the UNIX server and share the use of server peripherals, such as printers. Resources are accessed on the basis of names.

STARLAN PROTOCOLS AND INTERFACES

Figure 24.1 illustrates the approach STARLAN has taken in implementing the architecture of the OSI model. At the lower layers, STARLAN includes logical link control functions and uses protocols from

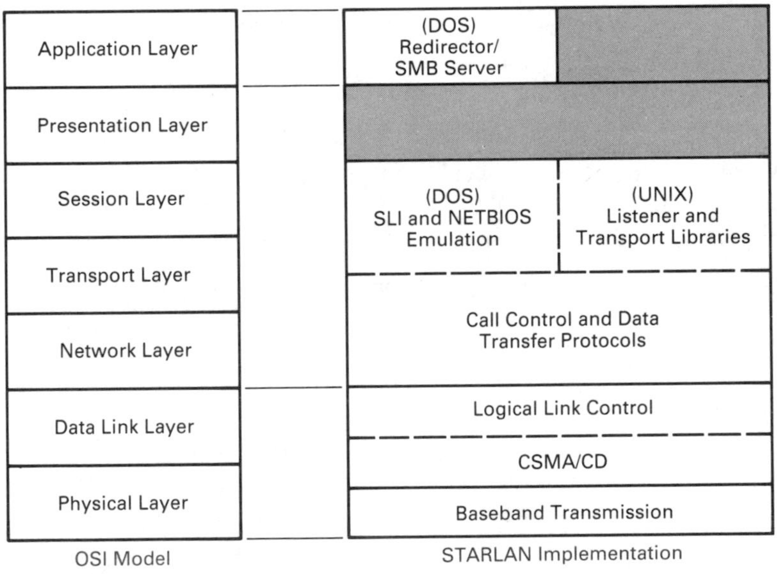

OSI Model	STARLAN Implementation
Application Layer	(DOS) Redirector/ SMB Server
Presentation Layer	
Session Layer	(DOS) SLI and NETBIOS Emulation / (UNIX) Listener and Transport Libraries
Transport Layer	Call Control and Data Transfer Protocols
Network Layer	
Data Link Layer	Logical Link Control / CSMA/CD
Physical Layer	Baseband Transmission

Figure 24.1 STARLAN protocols and interfaces

the IEEE 802.3 CSMA/CD standard for media access control. Physical transmission uses baseband techniques. At the transport and network levels, STARLAN uses its own protocols.

　　Session and transport layer interfaces are provided to the STARLAN protocols, with different interfaces used for DOS and UNIX. In the DOS environment, the NETBIOS emulation function provides support for the NETBIOS interface and for interrupts 2AH and 2FH. In the UNIX environment, support for

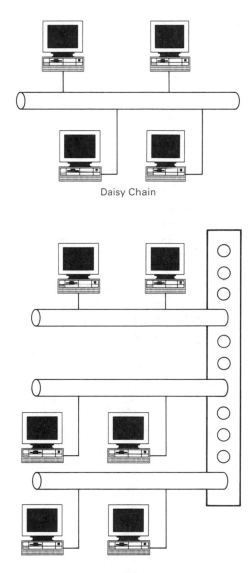

Daisy Chain

Star

Figure 24.2　STARLAN configurations

the listener library provides a session-level interface, and support for the transport library provides a transport-level interface.

At the level of the application layer, the MS-DOS Redirector and Server Message Block (SMB) server provide support for the interrupt 21H interface. The Redirector and SMB server, along with the NETBIOS emulation function, combine to provide compatibility for applications written to run with the IBM PC LAN Program.

NETWORK TOPOLOGY

Networks can be constructed, typically using ordinary telephone wiring, in either a daisy chain or star configuration, as shown in Fig. 24.2. With a daisy chain, up to ten stations can be attached to a single length of cable, which can be up to 400 ft in length. With the star configuration, a network extension unit is used to connect daisy chain segments in a star form. Up to 11 daisy chains can be attached to one network extension unit, and up to 12 network extension units can be interconnected.

THE LLC AND MAC SUBLAYERS

At the LLC sublayer, STARLAN implements Type 1 operation, or connectionless service. Figure 24.3 shows the data unit format used by STARLAN LLC. The destination service access point (SAP) and source SAP identify the processes in the sending and receiving stations that are involved in this transmission. The control byte identifies the type of the data unit. For Type 1 operation, possible data unit types are unnumbered information (UI), exchange identification (XID), and test (TEST).

With connectionless service, no sequence checking is performed, no acknowledgments are sent, and no flow control is provided. User information is sent using UI data units. The XID command can be used to exchange information about the types of services a particular LLC entity supports. The TEST command can be used to elicit a test response from the destination LLC that tests the transmission path between the stations.

At the MAC sublayer, STARLAN uses a variation of the IEEE 802.3 CSMA/CD access control method to control access to the transmission medium. The frame format for the MAC sublayer is shown in Box 24.2.

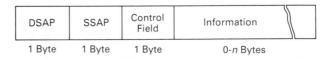

DSAP	SSAP	Control Field	Information
1 Byte	1 Byte	1 Byte	0-n Bytes

Figure 24.3   LLC packet format. DSAP = Destination Service Access Point; SSAP = Source Service Access Point.

BOX 24.2   STARLAN transmission frame

Preamble	Start Frame Delimiter	Destination Address	Source Address	Length	Logical Link Control Information	Pad Bytes	Frame Check Sequence
7 Bytes	1 Byte	6 Bytes	6 Bytes	2 Bytes	0-*n* Bytes	0-*p* Bytes	4 Bytes

- **Preamble.** The *preamble* contains a bit pattern of alternating 0 and 1 values, used to achieve synchronization.

- **Start Frame Delimiter.** The *start frame delimiter*, a bit pattern of 1101 0101, identifies the beginning of the frame.

- **Address Fields.** The *destination address* identifies the station the frame is being sent to, the *source address* the station it is sent from. The destination address can be an individual address, a group address, or the broadcast address.

- **Length Field.** The *length* field contains the length of the LLC information field.

- **LLC Information Field.** The *LLC information* field contains the LLC packet passed from the LLC sublayer for transmission.

- **Pad Field.** STARLAN specifies maximum and minimum frames sizes of 1518 and 64 bytes (called *octets* in STARLAN terminology), respectively. If a MAC frame is smaller than 64 bytes, padding bytes are added in the *pad* field to bring the size up to 64 bytes. The length field is used on the receiving side to identify and remove the padding bytes.

- **Frame Check Sequence.** The *frame check sequence* contains a CRC value calculated from the information in the frame. On the receiving side, the CRC value is recalculated, based on the data received. If the CRC values do not match, the frame is discarded as an error.

NETWORK AND TRANSPORT PROTOCOLS

The network and transport layer protocols used by STARLAN are incorporated in two components called *call control* and *data transfer*. The protocols used by these components provide for both connection-based (virtual circuit) and connectionless (datagram) data transfer. The protocols also provide a name service.

NAME SERVICE

At the program and menu interface levels to STARLAN, devices and resources such as a file or printer are identified using logical names. One of the functions of the transport and network protocols is to translate a network name into a network address. This is done using a broadcast technique. Each station can store a minimum of 16 logical names in a name table. These names can be either individual names, which are unique, or group names, where the same name appears in more than one name table.

One of the services provided by the call control component is the determination of the network address or addresses associated with a given name. This is done by sending out a broadcast message that contains the name in question. Every station that has that name in its name table responds by returning a message that contains the network address of that station. That address (or those addresses, for a group name) is used as the MAC destination address when messages are transmitted to that name.

DATAGRAM AND VIRTUAL CIRCUIT SERVICES

Datagram service involve basic message transmission services with no sequence checking, acknowledgments, retransmission, or flow control. Virtual circuit service provides full-duplex reliable data transfer, with sequence checking, acknowledgments, retransmission, flow control, and segmentation and reassembly. Both types of service are implemented using protocols of the call control and data transfer components.

CALL CONTROL COMPONENT

Call control is responsible for initiating and terminating network connections and for supporting the name service. Call control uses the packet types shown in Box 24.3 to perform the following functions:

- Determine the network address or addresses that correspond to a network name.
- Register a name with the network, ensure that a MAC address is unique, and, for an individual name, ensure that the name is unique.
- Establish and terminate virtual circuit connections.
- Add a device to the network.

DATA TRANSFER COMPONENT

Data transfer is responsible for the actual sending and receiving of data, either as a datagram or over a virtual circuit. The packet types associated with data transfer are shown in Box 24.4. The first three types are used with virtual circuit service and indicate to the receiver whether user data, control information, or both is contained in the packet. A datagram packet is used to send information using the datagram service.

BOX 24.3 Call control packets

Packet	Function
Call Inquiry Command	Request physical address associated with a logical name or name listening entity
Call Inquiry Response	Return requested physical address if name matches local name for which calls or datagrams are being accepted
Address Inquiry Command	Ensure that a name or MAC address is unique on the network, or post a group name
Address Inquiry Response	Indicate that a name or MAC address has been previously registered with the network
Call Request	Request the establishment of a virtual circuit connection
Call Confirm	Acknowledge establishment of a virtual circuit
Call Pending	Increase the retransmission timeout value associated with the request for a call setup attempt
Call Disconnect	Disconnect a virtual circuit, or respond negatively to a call request
Keepalive	Ensure that a virtual circuit connection is not in a hung state
Join	Announce the presence of a machine joining the network

BOX 24.4 Data transfer packets

Packet	Function
Control Only	Packet contains only control information.
Mixed data	Packet contains control information and user data.
Data Only	Packet contains only a block of user data.
Datagram	Packet contains a block of user data sent using the datagram service.

Figure 24.4   Sequenced block format

With the virtual circuit service, two modes of operation can be used: *character* mode and *block* mode. With character mode, user data and control information are intermixed in the data stream. With character mode, flow control is provided, but not error detection or correction. With block mode, user data is sent in contiguous groups of bytes known as sequenced blocks. Control information is sent between blocks. Sequence checking, acknowledgments, and retransmission are provided, along with flow control. The format of sequenced blocks is shown in Fig. 24.4. Each block of user data is followed by a trailer. The trailer begins with a byte that identifies the beginning of the trailer. The length field specifies the length of the user data, not including the trailer. The last field contains a sequence number that is used both for error detection and correction and for flow control.

FLOW CONTROL

Flow control is provided for both character and block modes, and it operates in essentially the same manner for both modes. When a virtual circuit is established, information received from higher layers and information available about the transmitter and receiver are used to determine the maximum block size for data transmitted across the virtual circuit and the maximum number of blocks that can be transmitted before receiving an acknowledgment.

As data is transmitted, a count is kept of the characters sent. When the maximum block size is reached, a sequence number is sent. For block mode, the sequence number is contained in the trailer that marks the end of the block. For character mode, a specific control byte containing the sequence number is sent. The transmitter keeps track of the number of sequence numbers it has sent. When the count reaches the maximum number of blocks that are permitted to be outstanding, the transmitter stops sending until it receives an acknowledgment from the receiver. With both modes, the receiver sends back an acknowledgment packet for each sequence number it receives. For character mode, the acknowledgment is used only for flow control purposes. As acknowledgments are received, the transmitter sends additional blocks, until the maximum number of blocks outstanding is reached.

ERROR DETECTION AND CORRECTION

With block mode, the sequence number in the trailer is used for error detection and correction as well as flow control. The receiver keeps track of the sequence numbers received and checks for out-of-sequence, missing, or duplicate blocks. If the sequence number is correct, the receiver sends a positive acknowledgment. If the sequence number is not correct, the receiver sends a Frame Reject response, which contains the last correct sequence number it received. When the transmitter receives a Frame Reject, or if the transmitter times out having received no acknowledgment, it retransmits blocks starting from the block following the last one that was acknowledged as correctly received.

MS-DOS PROGRAM INTERFACE

STARLAN supports three levels of program interface for the MS-DOS environment. The highest level consists of the Redirector, SMB server, and Session Level Interface (SLI). Combined, these facilities provided compatibility for applications written to use the Redirector/SMB interface to the IBM PC LAN Program. These STARLAN facilities support the DOS functions calls for networking services associated with interrupts 21H, 2AH, and 2FH.

The SLI includes support for the use of interrupt 2AH to execute NETBIOS requests, as well as for the administrative services provided by interrupts 2AH and 2FH. STARLAN also emulates the NETBIOS interface, providing support for interrupt 5CH, which is used to execute NETBIOS functions directly. A few specific features are not included in the STARLAN DOS interfaces, among them IPL remote program node, unlink, two network access units in one network station, send and receive timeout values, direct I/O function, and setting and getting a post address.

UNIX PROGRAM INTERFACES

For the UNIX environment, STARLAN provides a session-level program interface through the *listener library,* a transport-level program interface through the *transport library,* and a set of routines, known as the *server program support features,* that aid in the development of server programs.

UNIX LISTENER LIBRARY

The listener library consists of a set of primitives that can be used to connect to and request a network service from a remote machine. Each network service is assigned a service code. The services available on a particular machine are associated with a listener, which is known by a name. To request a service, a connection is first established with the appropriate listener, based on its name. The service is then requested by specifying its service code. Box 24.5 lists the listener library primitives that are used to provide these services.

BOX 24.5   Listener library primitives and commands

Primitive	Function
nlsestablish	Establish a connection between a network application and a listener on a remote machine
nlsrequest	Issue a service request message that invokes a remote network service
nlsgetcall	Return data to the requesting client process from the server program
nlsname	Calculate the name that can be used to connect to a remote listener
nlsprovider	Return the path name of the transport provider (such as STARLAN)
nlsadmin	Invoke the listener and administer the listener and its configuration database

UNIX TRANSPORT LIBRARY

The transport library interface can be used to access reliable-mode and datagram-mode data transfer services directly. Reliable-mode service involves the establishment of a virtual circuit and provides for error detection and correction. Datagram-mode service does not detect or identify undelivered data.

To perform either mode of data transmission, the communication path between the user application program and the transport services provider must first be initialized and later be discontinued. A number of general status and management functions are also required. Box 24.6 lists the transport library primitives that provide initialization and management functions.

With reliable-mode service, an active network application establishes a connection with, and requests services from, a passive network application. Once the connection has been established, the two applications are able to transfer data back and forth. The primitives used to do this are shown in Box 24.7.

Datagram-mode service can be used when an application does not require guaranteed in-sequence delivery of data. Once basic initialization has been completed, data can be sent and received using the primitives shown in Box 24.8.

A network application can operate either synchronously or asynchronously. In synchronous mode, the application waits for data to arrive or for some an event to occur before continuing execution. In asynchronous mode, execution continues and the application program checks periodically to see if the data has arrived or the event has occurred. The primitives shown in Box 24.9 are used to detect the occurrence of events.

BOX 24.6 Transport library management primitives

Primitive	Function
t_open	Perform initialization and return a file descriptor that is the local identifier of the transport endpoint
t_bind	Activate an endpoint and provide a name for it that other network processes can use
t_optmgmt	Enable the user process to get or negotiate protocol options with the transport provider
t_unbind	Disable a transport endpoint
t_close	Inform the transport provider that the user process is finished and free any resources associated with that endpoint
t_getinfo	Return protocol-specific information associated with a transport endpoint
t_getstate	Return the current state of a transport endpoint
t_sync	Synchronize the data structures managed by the transport library with the transport provider
t_alloc	Allocate storage for a library data structure
t_free	Free storage for a library data structure
t_error	Print out a message describing the last error encountered
t_look	Return the current event associated with a transport endpoint

BOX 24.7 Transport library reliable-mode service primitives

Primitive	Function
t_connect	Request a connection with a transport endpoint
t_revconnect	Determine the status of a previously sent **t_connect** request
t_listen	Prepare network application to receive connect requests
t_accept	Accept a connect request
t_snd	Send data over a transport connection
t_rcv	Receive data over a transport connection
t_snddis	Initiate release of a connection
t_rcvdis	Identify the reason for a disconnection

**BOX 24.8   Transport library datagram-mode
service primitives**

Primitive	Function
t_sndudata	Send a data unit
t_rcvudata	Enable a network application to receive data units
t_rcvuderr	Enable a network application to retrieve error information for a previously sent data unit

BOX 24.9   Transport asynchronous events

Event	Meaning
T_LISTEN	Connect request has been received by a transport provider
T_CONNECT	Connect request has been issued by a transport provider
T_DATA	Data has been received by a transport provider
T_DISCONNECT	Disconnect indication has been received by a transport provider
T_ERROR	Fatal error has been generated by a transport provider, making the transport endpoint unavailable
T_UDERR	An error has been found in a previously sent data unit

UNIX SERVER PROGRAM SUPPORT FEATURES

In addition to the transport library primitives, STARLAN provides three features that aid in the development of server programs. The *poll* feature provides a polling mechanism that enables an application to monitor the occurrence of events on several file descriptors simultaneously. The *virtual circuit passing* feature allows a virtual circuit to be transferred from one process to another. The *name-to-network-address translation* feature provides the network address associated with a given network name. This service is useful since some primitives require the specification of a network address.

SUMMARY

STARLAN provides file sharing, printer sharing, and electronic mail facilities in the MS-DOS environment and file transfer, printer sharing, and electronic mail facilities in the UNIX environment. STARLAN implements a variation of the IEEE 802.3 CSMA/CD standard for media access control and uses physical transmission over unshielded, twisted-wire-pair cable at a data rate of 1 Mbps.

The call control and data transfer protocols are used at the network and transport layer levels. These protocols provide a name service, datagram service, and virtual circuit service. The name service allows network devices and resources to be identified by name. The datagram service uses no acknowledgments and does not provide reliable data transfer. Virtual circuit service provides full-duplex, reliable data transfer using sequence numbers and acknowledgments along with flow control.

STARLAN emulates the Redirector and SMB protocols and NETBIOS interface, providing compatibility with the IBM PC LAN Program. For the UNIX environment, STARLAN uses the listener library as a session-level interface and the transport library as a transport-level interface. The listener library provides a service request and response function. The transport library provides reliable-mode and datagram-mode data transfer services.

25 ALLEN-BRADLEY: VISTALAN/1

The various implementations that we have examined have all been based on either the CSMA/CD or the token ring media access control protocol. Token bus implementations are also available, although this architecture is not common in personal computer–based networks in the office environment; as might be expected from its inclusion in the MAP specification, it has been more often used as part of factory automation networks. One company that offers a token bus product is Allen-Bradley, with its VistaLAN/1 product family.

FUNCTIONAL CAPABILITIES   VistaLAN/1 uses broadband transmission, a bus or tree network topology, and token passing for media access control. Various types of devices can be attached to a VistaLAN/1 network, including mainframe computers, minicomputers, terminals, printers, and personal computers used to emulate terminals. Figure 25.1 shows a sample VistaLAN/1 network. Devices are attached to the network through a *network interface unit* (NIU). The NIU contains the logic necessary to implement the LAN functions.

VistaLAN/1 is primarily a *terminal server* network. Through the network, a given terminal can access different mainframes or minicomputers, and a given printer can be used to print data from different mainframes or minicomputers. Each NIU has two, four, or eight ports. These ports can be used to attach multiple terminals or printers to a single NIU or to provide a mainframe or minicomputer with ports through which it can access the network. To communicate, a session or virtual circuit is established between two ports. These ports can be in different NIUs or in the same NIU. A given NIU can establish up to 12 concurrent sessions and can switch between them to transmit or receive data.

A session can be established directly between the two communicating par-

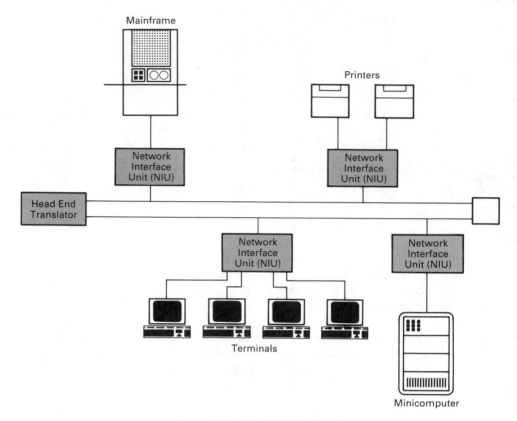

Figure 25.1   VistaLAN/1 network

ties. For example, a terminal user can establish a session with a mainframe and then use the session to interact with a program running on the mainframe. A third party can also establish a session between two other parties. For example, a terminal user can establish a session between a computer and a printer so that the printer can be used to print data from the computer.

NETWORK NAMES AND ADDRESSES

A network address consists of an NIU number and a port number. When a session is established, the network address of the port with which the connection is to be made can be specified directly. There is also a facility that allows a table of network names and their corresponding addresses to be built. If such a table has been built, a name can be specified when a session is being established, and the table is used to translate the name into an address. On a given network, NIU addresses range from 1 to 255. Address 0 is reserved for a system broadcast function.

Certain ports can be specified as protected. When a session is established with a protected port, a user name and password must be specified. These are checked, and the session is not established unless they are entered correctly. If a bridge or gateway is used to interconnect VistaLAN/1 networks, an "internet" address must also be used. An internet address consists of two parts: The first part, consisting of three fields, identifies the network; the second part identifies the port within the network (NIU and port number.) Names in the name and address table can correspond to either a local network address or a full internet address.

MEDIA ACCESS CONTROL PROTOCOLS

A token passing protocol is used to determine when a given NIU is allowed to transmit. The protocol is based on a token passing scheme developed by Datapoint Corporation for its *Arcnet* LAN products. The token is transmitted from one NIU to the NIU that has the next sequentially higher address. When an NIU receives the token, if it has data to transmit, it is allowed to send it. When it finishes sending data or if it has no data to send, it transmits the token to the next NIU.

TOKEN RETRANSMISSION

During normal operation, each NIU knows the address of the next higher NIU in the network, and it sends the token directly to that NIU. When an NIU receives the token, it will transmit either a data packet or another token. In either case, there will be activity on the transmission medium. The NIU that has sent the token monitors the transmission medium. If it detects activity within a certain time period, it assumes that the token was successfully received. If there is no activity within this time period, it increments the address used previously and sends the token again. This continues until the token is sent to an address where it is successfully received. The sending NIU then continues to use this address in subsequent processing.

One condition that triggers this type of processing is an NIU's being turned off. When this happens, the preceding NIU will increment the address and retransmit the token until it reaches the next NIU in sequence. This process also takes place if a token is lost or not received successfully by the intended NIU. In this case, the NIU that failed to receive the token is eliminated from token processing. When this NIU fails to receive a token for a period of time, it triggers a process called reconfiguration by destroying with a noise burst the token being passed.

RECONFIGURATION TIMEOUT

All NIUs in the network monitor the transmission medium. If a period of time equal to the maximum delay between transmissions expires and no transmission is detected, the network goes through the process of reconfiguration. Each NIU waits a period of time based on its NIU address, with an NIU with a higher address waiting a shorter period of time. When the time period elapses, the NIU sends a token to the address that is its own address plus 1. If it detects no activity after waiting the appropriate period, it increments the address by 1 and sends the token again. This continues, with the address wrapping around to 1 if necessary, until the NIU detects activity after it has sent the token. Activity indicates that the token has been successfully received and recognized by another NIU. The original sending NIU then saves the address used when the token was successfully transmitted. Each NIU on the network follows this procedure, sending the token to each address in sequence until the token is successfully received. From that point on, NIUs transmit the token to the saved address.

Several conditions will trigger the reconfiguration process. When the network is initially turned on, the reconfiguration process prepares the network for operation. When a new NIU is turned on and wants to be added to the network, it transmits a reconfiguration burst. This transmission interferes with any other transmission on the network. The reconfiguration burst is long enough to ensure that it will interfere both with any data being transmitted and with the token following it. After the token is destroyed through this interference, a reconfiguration timeout occurs, and the reconfiguration process takes place. Since the token is sent to each possible address, the new NIU will be included in the network following the reconfiguration process.

Reconfiguration will also occur if the token is destroyed by noise on the network. The sending NIU interprets the noise as a transmission and does not attempt to retransmit the token. When no further transmission takes place, the NIUs begin the reconfiguration process. Reconfiguration processing is also used following a lost token. Here the sending NIU retransmits the token to successively higher addresses until it is successfully received and token passing continues. However, the NIU that was eliminated in the process will eventually time out and transmit a noise burst that destroys the token. Reconfiguration then follows.

ERROR PROCESSING

A 16-bit cyclic redundancy check (CRC) error-checking code is appended to each data packet transmitted on the network. Logical link control protocols in the NIU recalculate the CRC value when a packet is received. If the CRC values do not agree, the packet is rejected and then retransmitted.

PHYSICAL SPECIFICATIONS

VistaLAN/1 uses broadband transmission with a single-cable configuration. Data is transmitted at one frequency. When the signal reaches the head end, the head-end translator translates the signal to a second frequency and retransmits the signal. The transmit and receive frequencies are each 6 MHz wide. The broadband cable used for VistaLAN/1 supports up to five different transmit and receive channel pairs coexisting on the same cable. Each NIU operates using only one channel pair. Up to 255 NIUs, supporting up to 2040 users, can communicate on a given channel pair. With the five possible channel pairs, this allows up to 10,200 users on the same broadband cable. Data is transmitted using continuous-phase frequency-shift keying, at a data rate of 2.5 Mbps.

SUMMARY

VistaLAN/1 uses broadband transmission, a bus or tree topology, and token passing for media access control. Devices are attached to the network via network interface units. Each NIU has two, four, or eight ports. Communication is based on a session, or virtual circuit, being established between two ports. An NIU can establish up to 12 concurrent sessions. When a session is established, either a name or an address must be specified. A network address consists of an NIU number and a port number. For interconnected networks, an internet address must be specified. An internet address consists of a three-field network identifier and a two-field network address.

Permission to transmit is based on a token that is passed from one NIU to the next in address sequence. If the NIU that sends the token does not detect another transmission in a specified period of time, it retransmits the token to successively higher addresses until the token is successfully received and a subsequent transmission is detected. If no transmission is detected for the maximum delay period, reconfiguration takes place. One NIU begins transmitting a token to successive addresses until the token is successfully received. Each NIU repeats the process until the token has traversed the entire network. Each NIU saves the address that resulted in successful transmission and uses that for future token transmission. This process is used when an NIU is turned on and when the token is destroyed by noise or lost. A CRC technique is used for error detection.

VistaLAN/1 uses broadband transmission, with different frequencies for transmission and reception. The head-end translator converts from the transmission frequency to the reception frequency and rebroadcasts the signal. Data is transmitted using continuous-phase frequency-shift keying at a data rate of 2.5 Mbps.

INDEX

A

Access control method. *See* Media access
    control sublayer
Access mode, 261
Access rights:
    IBM PC LAN Program, 257
    3 + Share, 298
Acknowledged connectionless service, 145
Active monitor, 116
    IBM Token Ring Newtork, 213
Adaptive source routing, 285
Addressing, 193
    AppleTalk, 323
    Ethernet, 292
    IBM Token Ring Network, 216
    MAP, 146, 284
    TCP/IP, 280–81
    TOP, 146
    VistaLAN/1, 350–51
Advanced NetWare:
    asynchronous communication of, 310–11
    electronic mail facility of, 310
    file server procotol, 317–19
    file sharing of, 309
    IBM compatibility of, 315
    internet packet exchange, 319–20
    LAN-to-LAN connection of, 310
    naming and user access of, 311
    printer sharing of, 310
    Redirector/SMB emulation of, 315–17
    remote access of, 310
    SNA gateway of, 311
    system architecture of, 315
    utility programs and commands of,
        311–14
Advanced Program-to-Program
    Communication. *See* APPC/PC
Allen Bradley, 349
American National Standards Institute
    (ANSI), 127
Amplifiers, analog transmission, 22
Amplitude, electromagnetic waves, 20–21
Analog channel, digital transmission over,
    25–26
APPC/PC, 205–7, 245–46
    change of direction, 251
    control verbs of, 251–52
    conversations, 248–50
    interface, 252
    and LU 6.2, 248
    network protocols of, 252–53
    and PU 2.1, 246–48
    synchronization, 249
AppleTalk:
    bridge configurations of, 326
    characteristics of, 321–22
    datagram delivery protocol of, 325–28
    link access procotol of, 322–25
    name binding protocol of, 330
    physical specifications of, 322
    routing table maintenance protocol of,
        328–29
    transaction protocol of, 331–33
    zones of, 330

AppleTalk Link Access Protocol (ALAP),
    322–23
AppleTalk Session Protocol (ASP), 333
AppleTalk Transaction Protocol (ATP),
    331–33
Application layer, 191
    MAP, 149
    OSI, 54
    TOP, 149
Asynchronous Communications Server
    (ACS), Advanced NetWare, 310–11
Asynchronous transmission, 29
AT&T, 335
Attachment unit interface (AUI), 90, 92–94,
    294
Attenuation, 22

B

Backbone local networks, 128, 176–80
Backend local networks, 127
Back off delay, collision handling, 293
    CSMA/CD, 88–89
    IBM PC Network, 225
Bandwidth, 21
Baseband collision detection, 86–87
Baseband medium attachment unit, 94–95
Baseband transmission, 10, 19–20
    direction of transmission, 23–25
Basic conversation, LU 6.2, 248
Baud, 21
Beacon process, 132
Binary exponential backoff method, 88–89,
    225, 293
Bit duration, 26
Bit stuffing, 323
Bit time, 26
Bridges, 168–70
    IBM Token Ring Network, 198, 216–17
Broadband collision detection, 87–88
Broadband media access unit, 95
Broadband transmission, 10, 20–25, 111
    direction of transmission, 23–25
    frequency-division multiplexing, 22–23
    measurements of channel capacity, 21–22
    modulation techniques, 21
    signal amplification, 22
Bus topology, 33
Busy token, 113
Bypass switch, token ring network, 117

C

Cabling systems, 14–18, 188
    IBM Token Ring Network, 209–10
Call control, STARLAN, 339, 340
Carrier sense multiple access with collision
    avoidance (CSMA/CA): 40, 42–43
    AppleTalk, 322–23
    Ethernet, 293
Carrier sense multiple access with collision
    detection (CSMA/CD), 37–38
    attachment unit interface, 92–94
    backoff after collision, 88–89
    baseband medium attachment unit, 94–95
    broadband medium access unit, 95
    collision detection of, 86–88
    functions of, 81–83
    MAC/PLS interface, 91–92
    media access management, 86
    operation of, 81
    physical layer standards of, 89–90
    physical signaling functions of, 90–91
    physical signaling interfaces, 91
    PLS/PMA interface, 92, 93
    transmission frame of, 84–86
Carrier sensing, 86
Catanet, TCP/IP, 280, 281
CCITT, 49
Centralized control techniques, 34, 36
    circuit switching, 44–45
    polling, 43–44
    time-division multiple access (TDMA), 45
Channel access, Ethernet, 290, 295
Checksums, 147
Circuit switching:
    LAN access control method, 10, 44–45
    telephone network, 153–54
Cladding, optical fiber, 13
Claim frames, 131
Claim token procedure, 104, 131
Clearinghouse, 307
Client layer, Ethernet, 289
Coaxial cable, 12–13
Codec, 155
Collision avoidance:
    AppleTalk, 323
    Ethernet, 289, 293
Collision detection:
    baseband, 86–87
    broadband, 87–88
    CSMA/CD, 86
    IBM PC Network, 224–26

Command control block (CCB), 219, 234
Commands:
   Advanced NetWare, 311–14
   IBM PC LAN Program, 257
   information transfer, 75–78
   LLC, 65–66
   NETBIOS, 245
   supervisory, 76, 78, 79
Common application service elements
   (CASE):
   MAP, 149
   TOP, 149
Common carriers, 49
Communication server, 191
Compatibility sharing mode, 261
Computer manufacturers, 49–50
Concentrators, 188
Confirm-level synchronization, 249
Connectionless service, 67, 236
   MAP, 145
   primitives for, 69
   protocols for, 73
   TOP, 145
Connection-oriented service, 67, 236
   primitives for, 70
   protocols for, 74–75
Connectivity, 190–91
   Digital Equipment Corporation, 180–82
   of IBM LAN products, 197–98
   protocols and interfaces of, 300–301
   of 3 + network, 300
   use of Ethernet and token ring, 301
Consultative Committee on International
   Telegraphy and Telephony. *See* CCITT
Contention, LAN access control method, 10
Control verbs, APPC, 251–52
Conversation, LU 6.2, 248, 249
Cooperative processing, 6
Core, optical fiber, 13
CSMA/CA. *See* Carrier sense multiple
   access with collision avoidance
CSMA/CD. *See* Carrier sense multiple
   access with collision detection

D

Data encapsulation, 81–83
   AppleTalk, 323–24
   Ethernet, 289, 292–93
Data encoding, 82, 83
   CSMA/CD, 83

   Ethernet, 290
   FDDI, 134–35
Data flow control layer, SNA, 55
Data formats, 51
Datagram service, 67
   AppleTalk, 325–28
   NETBIOS, 196, 244
   STARLAN, 340
   TCP, 279–80
Data link layer, 56
   OSI, 53
   SNA, 55
Data rate, 21
Data transfer:
   STARLAN, 339, 340–42
   TCP/IP, 279
Data unit, LLC, 65, 234
DECconnect Communication System, 16–18
DECnet:
   inter-LAN connectivity, 182
   intervendor connectivity, 180–82
   SNA gateway function of, 181
Delimiter bits, 29
Destination service access point (DSAP), 65
Dibits, 21
Differential Manchester encoding scheme,
   26, 28, 122, 221
Digital Equipment Corporation, 180–82
Digital PBXs, 155–57
Digital switching, 158
Digital transmission, over analog channel,
   25–26
Directory services:
   MAP, 150
   TOP, 150
Disk and directory sharing, IBM PC LAN
   Program, 257
Distributed network structures, 159–60
Distributed routing tables, MAP, 284
Distributed transmission control, 34, 36,
   40–43
   carrier sense multiple access with collision
   avoidance (CSMA/CA), 42–43
   token bus method, 41–42
   token ring method, 41
Dual-cable broadband, 25

E

Echo Protocol (EP), AppleTalk, 333
Electromagnetic waves, 20

Electronic mail, 190
  Advanced NetWare, 310
Encoding schemes:
  differential Manchester, 26, 28, 122, 221
  Manchester, 26, 27–28, 110, 122, 294–95
  RS-232-C, 27
  zero-complemented differential, 27
End user, 246
Error processing:
  MAP, 147
  STARLAN, 342–43
  TOP, 147
  VistaLAN/1, 352
Ethernet, 189
  channel access of, 295
  data encapsulation function of, 292–93
  data encoding function of, 294–95
  definitions related to, 287–88
  functional model of, 288–90
  goals of, 287, 288
  layer-to-layer services, 290
  link management, 293
  local area network requirements, 7
  network addresses of, 292
  physical model of, 293–94
  physical specifications of, 295–96
  and 3+ network, 301
  transmission frame format, 289, 290–92

F

Fault management:
  token bus network, 103–4
  token ring network, 103–4, 116–18
Fiber Distributed Data Interface (FDDI):
  access protocol of, 128, 129–30
  capacity allocation of, 128, 131
  data encoding of, 134–35
  fault management of, 131–32
  future of, 138–39
  LLC/MAC interface, 132, 134
  physical layer specifications of, 134
  physical specifications of, 135
  reliability of, 135–38
  transmission frame format of, 132, 133
Fiber-optic links, 13
File/print server protocol (FSP), 305, 306
File server support, 190
  IBM PC LAN Program, 255
File sharing:
  Advanced NetWare, 309

function calls, 260–61
3+Share, 298
File transfer, access, and management (FTAM):
  MAP, 149
  TOP, 149
Flow control, 79, 240
  MAP, 148
  NETBIOS, 243
  STARLAN, 342
  TCP/IP, 279
  TOP, 148
Forwarded name, IBM PC LAN Program, 256
Free token, 113
Frequency, electromagnetic waves, 20, 21
Frequency-division multiplexing, 22–23
Full duplex transmission, 241
Functional layers, 51
Function calls:
  common sharing situations and, 262
  file sharing, 260–61
  interrupt 21H, 260
  network control, 261
  record locking, 261–62
  unique file names, 262

G

Gateways, 175–76
  Advanced NetWare, 311
  Advanced Program-to-Program Communications/PC, 205–7
  IBM LAN Asynchronous Connection Server Program, 202–4
  IBM PC 3270 Emulation Program, 201–2
  IBM Series/1 PC Connect Program, 204–5
  IBM Token Ring/PC Network Interconnect Program, 199–201
  TCP/IP, 281

H

Half duplex transmission, 241
Hertz, 21
High-priority token hold time, 100
High-speed office networks, 128

I

IBM Cabling Systems, 14–16
IBM LAN Asynchronous Connection Server
    Program, 202–4
IBM local area network products, 195–97
    connectivity of, 197–98
IBM Local Area Network Support Program,
    196
IBM logical link control (LLC) interface,
    231–41
IBM PC LAN Program, 197
    compatibility of Advanced NetWare with,
        315
    as de facto standard, 264–67
    disk and directory sharing of, 257
    DOS function calls, 260–62
    functions of, 255–56
    interface with server message blocks
        (SMBs), 257–59, 262–64
    menu and command interface of, 257
    naming using, 256
    station configurations of, 256
    and 3 + network, 305
IBM PC Network, 189
    backoff after collision, 225
    baseband version of, 229
    broadband version of, 226–28
    collision detection of, 224–25
    media access management of, 223–24
    network interfaces, 223
    transmission frame format of, 224
IBM PC Network—Baseband, 196, 228
    network topology of, 229
    transmission characteristics of, 229
IBM PC Network—Broadband, 196, 226–27
    network topology of, 227
    transmission characteristics of, 228
IBM PC 3270 Emulation Program, 201–2
IBM Series/1 PC Connect Program, 204–5
IBM SNA, 54–55
    layers of, 54–55
IBM Token Ring Network, 189, 196, 198
    addressing, 216
    components of, 209–10
    direct interface with, 219–21
    error conditions of, 213
    media access control services of, 213–14
    media access management of, 211
    physical layer of, 221–22
    priority scheme of, 211–13
    routing, 216–17

    routing information, 218–19
    source routing, 217–18
    transmission frame format of, 214–16
IBM Token Ring Network Adapter Card,
    209
IBM Token Ring Network Multistation
    Access Unit, 209
IBM Token Ring/PC Network Interconnect
    Program, 199–201
IEEE, 49
    common implementations of, 188–89
    802.2, logical link control. *See* Logical
        link control sublayer
    802.3, carrier sense multiple access with
        collision detection. *See* CSMA/CD
    802.4, token bus. *See* Token bus
    802.5, token ring. *See* Token ring
    Project 802, 55–59
Information transfer command (I-format
    command), 75–78, 236
Institute of Electrical and Electronics
    Engineers. *See* IEEE
Interfaces:
    STARLAN, 336–38
    3 + network, 300–301
Inter-LAN networks, 176–80
Intermediate system, 170
International Standards Organization. *See*
    ISO
Internet addressing, 325-26, 328
Internet Packet Exchange (IPX), 315,
    319–20
Interrupt 21H function calls, 260
ISO, 49

J

Jam, collision handling, 293

L

Link management:
    Ethernet, 289, 293
Link stations, 232, 234
Local area networks:
    applications of, 5–7
    basic functions of, 187
    characteristics of, 10
    common implementations of IEEE

Local area networks *(cont.)*
  architectures, 188–89
  components of, 8–9
  defined, 4–5
  interconnected network configurations,
    163–67
  network operating systems, 189–91
  physical components of, 188
  relationship to higher layers, 191–93
  requirements of, 7–8
  standardization of, 193
  wiring for, 13–14
Locally administered addresses, 66
Logical link control (LLC) sublayer, 56, 57,
  232–36
  commands and responses of, 65–66
  data unit of, 65
  establishing and terminating connections,
    75
  flow control, 79
  information and transfer commands,
    75–78
  interface between media access control
    sublayer and, 71–72, 83–84, 106–7,
    120–21, 132, 134
  interface between network layer and,
    67–68
  peer-to-peer protocols of, 64, 72–75
  primitives for Type 1 operation, 69
  primitives for Type 2 operation, 70
  protocols for Type 1 operation, 73–74
  protocols for Type 2 operation, 74–75
  sending acknowledgments, 78–79
  service access point addresses of, 66
  service access points (SAP) of, 64–65
  service interface specifications of, 63–64
  service primitive parameters, 70–71
  service primitives of, 68–71
  STARLAN, 338
  station addresses of, 66–67
  supervisory commands of, 76, 78, 79
  unnumbered commands of, 73–74
Logical unit (LU), 246

M

Manchester encoding system, 26, 27–28,
  110, 122, 294–95
Manufacturing Automation Protocol (MAP),
  189
  access control methods of, 145

  addressing of, 284
  application layer of, 148–50
  layer protocols of, 141–44
  network layer functions of, 145–47, 283,
    284
  network structure of, 144
  physical and data link layers of, 145
  presentation layer of, 148
  routing of, 284–85
  session layer functions of, 148, 283
  transport layer of, 147–48, 283
Manufacturing message format standard
  (MMFS):
  MAP, 149–50
  TOP, 149–50
Mapped conversations, LU 6.2, 248
Maximum interframe gap, 324
Media access control (MAC) sublayer, 20,
  56, 58
  centralized control, 43–45
  distributed transmission control, 40–43
  IBM Token Ring Network, 213–14
  interface with logical link control
    sublayer, 71–72, 83–84, 106–7, 132,
    134
  interface with physical layer and, 91–92,
    108
  MAP, 145
  network topologies of, 31–33
  random transmission control, 37–40
  STARLAN, 337, 338
  TOP, 145
  transmission control of, 33–37
  VistaLAN/1, 351
Media access management, 83
  AppleTalk, 322–23
  CSMA/CD, 83, 86
  Ethernet, 293
  IBM PC Network, 233–24
  IBM Token Ring Network, 211
Medium attachment unit (MAU), 83, 90, 92,
  94–95, 294
Message control block (MCB), 242
Message server, IBM PC LAN Program,
  255
Messenger station, 256
Metropolitan area networks (MANs), 4
Microcom Network Protocol (MNP), and
  3+ network, 301–2
Microsoft Redirector:
  Advanced NetWare emulation of, 315–17
  IBM PC LAN Program compatibility
    with, 265, 266, 267

3+ network and, 305–7
Mid-split broadband, 23–24
Minimum interdialog gap, 324
Modems, 25
MS-DOS Internal Network Drive Scheme
    (MINDS), and 3+ network, 302,
    304–5
Multilevel duibinary AM/PSK, 111

N

Name Binding Protocol (NBP), AppleTalk,
    330
Name service, 190
    Advanced NetWare, 311
    AppleTalk, 330
    IBM PC LAN Program, 256
    NETBIOS, 242–43
    STARLAN, 339–40
    3+ network, 307
    3+ Share, 299
    VistaLAN/1, 350–51
Name-to-network-address translation,
    STARLAN, 346
NETBIOS, 199, 205, 241–42, 315
    datagram service of, 196, 244
    as a de facto standard, 245
    functions of, 242
    general commands of, 245
    name service of, 242–43
    routing of, 243
    session service, 196, 243–44
NetWare SNA Gateway, 311
Network adapter circuit card, 188
Network architectures:
    characteristics of, 50–52
    developers of, 48–50
    goals of, 47
    high-level objectives of, 50
    nature of, 48
Network control function calls, 261
Network File Service Protocol (NFSP), 315,
    317–19
Network interconnection:
    bridges, 168–70
    configurations of, 163–67
    gateways, 175–76
    repeaters, 167
    routers, 170–75
Network interface unit (NIU), VistaLAN/1,
    349

Network layer protocols:
    MAP, 145–47
    OSI, 53
    STARLAN, 339
    TOP, 145–47
Network management, 191
Network names, 192
    IBM PC LAN Program, 256
Network node, 51
Network-specific addressing, Ethernet, 292
Network topology, 10
    bus, 33
    ring, 33, 35, 36
    star, 31–33
Novelle, Inc. 309

O

Open Systems Interconnect. *See* OSI
    reference model
Optical fibers, 13
OSI reference model, 49, 52–54, 141, 142,
    166
    layers of, 53–54

P

Packet format:
    Ethernet, 289
    TCP/IP, 278–79
Packet switching, on PBX networks, 160–61
Passive monitors, token ring network, 116
Path control layer, SNA, 55
PBX, 33, 151–53
    digital, 155–57
    digital switching, 158–59
    distributed network structures, 159–60
    future of local area networks using, 161
    network reliability, 157–58
    networks using, 157
    packet switching on, 160–61
    switching techniques, 158
Phase, electromagnetic waves, 20, 21
Physical layer:
    FDDI, 134
    interface between media access control
        layer and, 91–92

Physical layer *(cont.)*
  interface between station management
    and, 109
  MAP, 145
  OSI, 53
  token ring network, 221–22
  SNA, 54
  TOP, 145
Physical-medium-dependent (PMD) sublayer,
  FDDI, 134
Physical transmission characteristics:
  baseband transmission, 19–20
  broadband transmission, 20–25
  cabling systems, 14–18
  coaxial cable, 12–13
  DECconnect Communication System,
    16–18
  digital transmission over an analog
    channel, 25–26
  encoding schemes, 26, 27–28
  fiber-optic links, 13
  IBM cabling system, 14–16
  synchronization, 26
  transmission medium, 11
  transmission techniques, 19–25
  twisted-wire pairs, 11–12
  wiring for local area networks, 13–14
Physical unit (PU), 245
Polling mechanism, 43–44
  STARLAN, 346
Port, TCP/IP, 278–79
Presentation layer, 191–92
  MAP, 148
  SNA, 55
  TOP, 148
Printer Access Protocol (PAP), AppleTalk,
  333
Printer sharing:
  Advanced NetWare, 310
  3 + Share, 299
Print server support, 190
  IBM PC LAN Program, 255
  token ring network, 118
Priority scheme:
  IBM Token Ring Network, 211–13
  token bus network, 100–101
Private branch exchanges. *See* PBX
Propagation time, 87
Protocols, 51
Protocol verbs, LU 6.2, 248
Pulse code modulation, 156, 157

R

Random control transmission control, 34
Random transmission control, 36
  carrier sense multiple access with collision
    detection (CSMA/CD), 37–38
  register insertion, 39–40
  slotted ring, 38–39
Read-only sharing mode, 261
Receiver station, 256
Record locking:
  Advanced NetWare, 309
  function calls, 261–62
Redirector station, 256
Register insertion, 39–40
Remote access, 191
  Advanced NetWare, 310
Repeaters, network interconnection, 9, 19,
  167
Reservation bits, 118
Resolve contention data unit, 102
Response window, 102
Restricted token, 131
Ring topology, 33, 35, 36
Router nodes, MAP, 284
Routers, network interconnection, 170–75
Routing, 193
  APPC/PC, 272–73
  IBM Token Ring Network, 216–29
  MAP, 146, 284–85
  NETBIOS, 243, 272
  stabilization issues related to, 285
  TOP, 146
  Transmission Control Protocol/Internet
    Protocol (TCP/IP), 278–82
  XNS Courier protocol, 273
  XNS Internet Routing Service, 277–78
  XNS Internet Transport Protocols, 273–77
Routing seed, AppleTalk, 328, 329
Routing Table Maintenance Protocol
  (RTMP), AppleTalk, 328–29
RS-232-C encoding, 27

S

Sequence numbers, 147, 148
Server message blocks (SMBs), 256, 262–64
  file access, 263–65
  print server and message, 265

session control, 263
Server station, 256
Service access point addresses, 66
Service access points (SAP), 64–65, 232, 234
Session layer, 192
    MAP, 148
    OSI, 53
    TOP, 148
Session service:
    NETBIOS, 196, 243–44
Set successor data unit, 102
Sharing mode, 261, 262
Shielded-twisted-wire-pair cable, 12
Simplex transmission, 241
Single-channel broadband, 23
Single-channel phase-coherent FSK, 110–11
Single-channel phase-continuous FSK, 110
Slotted ring, 38–39
Slot times, 88, 102, 225
Snowflake configuration, 32, 33, 153
Socket clients, 326
Solicit successor data unit, 101, 102
Source routing, 243
    IBM Token Ring Network, 217–18
Source service access point (SSAP), 65
Space-division switching, 158
Standards organizations, 49
Star configuration, 15, 16
STARLAN:
    call control component of, 340, 341
    datagram virtual circuit services of, 340
    data transfer component of, 340–42
    error detection and correction of, 342–43
    flow control of, 342
    goals of, 335
    logical link control and medium access control sublayers of, 338–39
    MS-DOS program interface of, 343
    network and transport layer protocols of, 339
    name service of, 339–40
    network topology of, 337, 338
    protocols and interfaces of, 336–38
    transmission frame format of, 339
    UNIX program interfaces, 343–46
Start bits, 29
Start-stop transmission, 29
Star topology, 31–33
Star wiring, token ring network, 117
Station addresses, 66–67

Stations, 9, 31
Stop bits, 29
Store-and-forward function, 168
Supermultiplexing, 161
Supervisory commands (S-format commands), 76, 78, 79, 238–39
Switching techniques, 158
Synchronous allocation (SA), 131
Systems Network Architecture. *See* IBM SNA

T

Tandem switching node, 159
Target token rotation time (TTRT), 100, 131
Technical and Office Protocols (TOP):
    access control methods of, 145
    application layer of, 148–50
    layer protocols of, 141–44
    network layer of, 145–47
    network structure of, 144
    physical and data link layers of, 145
    presentation layer of, 148
    session layer of, 148
    transport layer of, 147–48
Telephone network:
    data communication using, 155
    topology of, 153–54
3Com Corporation, 297
3+Mail, 297, 300
3+NetConnect, 297, 300
3+ network:
    connectivity products of, 300
    use of Ethernet and token ring, 301
    use of Microcom Network Protocol (MNP), 301–2
    use of Microsoft Redirector, 305–7
    use of MS-DOS Internal Network Drive Scheme (MINDS), 302, 304–5
    name service of, 307
    use of Packet Exchange Protocol (PEP), 304
    protocols and interfaces of, 300–301
    use of Sequenced Packet Protocol (SPP), 302–4
    support of internet datagram protocol (IDP), 302
3+Remote, 297, 300
3+Route, 297

3 + Share, 297, 298, 305
  file sharing of, 298
  name service of, 299
  printer sharing of, 299
3 + 3270, 297, 300
Time-division multiple access (TDMA), 45
Time-division multiplexing (TDM), 19–20, 23, 158
Time-multiplexed space-division switching, 159
Token, 128
Token bus, 37, 41–42
  fault management of, 103–4
  functions of, 97–98
  LLC/MAC interface service specification, 106–7
MAC/physical layer interface of, 108
  operation of, 97
  optional priority scheme, 100–101
  physical layer specification of, 108
  physical layerstation management interface, 109
  ring maintenance of, 101–3
  sending and receiving frames, 104–6
  service classes and access classes, 99–100
  station management/MAC interface, 107–8
  transmission types of, 109–11
Token handling, 98–99
Token passing, LAN access control method, 10, 40, 41
Token ring, 37, 41
  access protocol of, 113–16
  fault management of, 116–18
  optional priority scheme, 118
  physical layer of, 122
  service specifications of, 120–21
  3 + network and, 301
  transmission frame format of, 118–20
Transaction services layer, SNA, 55
Transceiver, 293
Transmission characteristics. See Physical transmission characteristics
Transmission control, 33–37
Transmission Control Protocol/Internet Protocol (TCP/IP):
  addressing of, 280–81
  flow control of, 279
  packet format of, 278–79
  reliable data transfer of, 279
  routing of, 281–82

Transmission Control Protocol/User Datagram Protocol, 279–80
Transmission frame format:
  AppleTalk, 323, 324
  CSMA/CD, 84–86
  Ethernet, 289, 290–92
  FDDI, 132, 133
  IBM Token Ring Network, 214–16
  STARLAN, 339
  token bus network, 104–6
  token ring network, 118–20
Transmission medium, 10
Transmission techniques, 10, 19–25
Transparent routing, 285
Transport layer:
  MAP, 147–48
  OSI, 53
  STARLAN, 339
  TOP, 147–48
Tree, bus topology, 33, 34
Tribit, 22
Twisted-wire pairs, transmission medium, 11–12
Type I operation, LLC, 67, 236
  MAP, 145
  primitives for, 69
  protocols for, 73
  TOP, 145
Type 2 operation, LLC, 67, 236
  primitives for, 70
  protocols for, 74–75

U

Universal addressing, 67
  Ethernet, 292
UNIX listener library, 343–44
UNIX transport library, 344–46
  asynchronous events of, 346
  datagram-mode service primitives of, 346
  management primitives of, 345
  reliable-mode service primitives of, 345
Unnumbered (U-format) frames, 240–41
User access, Advanced NetWare, 311
User names, IBM PC LAN Program, 256
Utility programs, Advanced NetWare, 311–14

V

Virtual channel, 25–26
Virtual circuit service, STARLAN, 340, 346
VistaLAN/1:
   error processing of, 352
   functional capabilities of, 349–50
   media access control protocols of, 351
   network names and addresses of, 350–51
   physical specifications of, 353
   reconfiguration timeout of, 352
   token retransmission of, 351

W

Wide area networks (WANS), 3, 5
Wiring closet, 15

X

XNS Courier protocol, 307
XNS Internet Datagram Protocol (IDP), 3 +
   network, 302
XNS Packet Exchange Protocol (PEP), 3 +
   network, 304
XNS Sequenced Packet Protocol (SPP), 3 +
   network, 302–4

Z

Zero-complemented different encoding, 27
Zone Information Protocol (ZIP), AppleTalk,
   330
Zone Information Table (ZIT), AppleTalk,
   330